LEADING INNOVATION

HOW TO JUMP START YOUR ORGANIZATION'S GROWTH ENGINE

JEFF DEGRAFF & SHAWN E. QUINN

McGraw·Hill

New York   Chicago   San Francisco   Lisbon   London   Madrid   Mexico City
Milan   New Delhi   San Juan   Seoul   Singapore   Sydney   Toronto

The McGraw·Hill Companies

1 2 3 4 5 6 7 8 9 10   DOC/DOC   0 9 8 7 6

ISBN-10: 0-07-147018-2
ISBN-13: 978-0-07-147018-6

McGraw-Hill books are available at special quantity discounts to use as premiums and sales promotions, or for use in corporate training programs. For more information, please write to the Director of Special Sales, Professional Publishing, McGraw-Hill, Two Penn Plaza, New York, NY 10121-2298. Or contact your local bookstore.

Contents

Acknowledgments

We would like to give special thanks to Robert Quinn and Kim Cameron, who have been our sponsors from the beginning of this project, and whose research is the foundation for this book. We also give special thanks to our wives Staney DeGraff and Lisa Quinn who have supported us daily on this journey. Lisa spent long hours helping with the writing and editing of this book. Thanks to John DeGraff who taught Jeff everything he knows about business, and so much more. We would also like to acknowledge the University of Michigan Ross School of Business, where we work, for its encouragement and belief that management theory should translate into practice.

Along the way, many people have jumped in to provide help. We would like to thank Riza Trinadad, Adrienne DeGraff, Katherine Cicchella, Ollie Thomas, Kristin Quinn, and Ian DeGraff who kept us organized and gave us much of our administrative support. Tom Jones, Kathy Nohr, Michael Thompson, Susan Lapine, Don Mroz, and Mark Jones all gave us regular feedback and asked us the right questions to help us focus the book in a way that is geared toward the reader.

We would like to thank Pete Bacevice who has spent countless hours tightening the book, making finishing touches, and providing insight. He worked with the publisher and developmental editor to move the book toward completion. His input and effort were vital in this process.

We would like to thank Lisa O'Connor, Roger Stewart, Dianne Wheeler, Maureen Walker, and Jeffrey Krames of McGraw-Hill as well as Katherine Wagner who served as an extremely valuable developmental editor.

Finally, we thank the many clients who have trusted us to come into their organizations and work on key strategic initiatives that allowed us to learn how to be most helpful to our clients in bringing about change, innovation, and growth to their organizations.

Preface

Why You Should Read This Book

This book is the story about how ordinary people put their creativity to work and make innovation happen.

Meet John, or Juan, or Juanita. They are not Steve Jobs, the CEO of Apple Computer and Pixar Animation Studios. They did not help create the personal computer revolution, the Silicon Valley boom, or the digital transformation of the movies and music business. John is not a cultural icon; instead, he works as middle manager in marketing where he is happy if the CEO knows his name. He has marketed everything from baby food to Internet start-ups and has played multiple roles from brand manager to entrepreneur. He has a lot of common sense and understands how to play the game—how to get results.

John used to read books about the impending revolution or his destiny to change the world, but his experience in his own life at work has taught him well that heroes of the imagination often turn out to be villains by the end of the film, and companies that have creatively transcended the petty concerns of management vanish into case-study mythology. John knows fashion talk and business school babble when he hears it. His life has been filled with tough choices. He knows how to manage differently in different situations; he knows where his skills are strong and where they are weak. John understands that everything he knows has come from his own experiences and experiments. Along the way, John has learned to be creative at work, and, in some meaningful way, he has made his job, his people, and his community better and new.

John knows he is not Steve Jobs. He knows that they are not equally creative. He learned it in fifth grade when he sat next to Mozart during his weekly piano lessons. He learned it again in ninth grade when he played on his junior high basketball team with Michael Jordan. He learned it yet again in college when Albert Einstein was his science lab partner. The difference in talent or good fortune didn't seem fair or democratic to John, but he knew it was real. So John learned to put his personal puzzle together and use what he had to the best of his abilities. He learned that what he lacked as a singularly extraordinary person could be offset by what he could achieve as an exceptionally whole person. He understood that creativity was as much about his own evolution as it was about any organizational revolution. John's genius was wrought in the fiery furnaces of failure, the redemptive journey of self-discovery, and the disciplined practice that brings mastery.

This book is for John, Juan, or Juanita, the real people who make innovation happen.

If you are a manager at any level or a person leading innovation in your organization, this book is for you. We often believe that innovation can happen only from the top down in an organization. We say, "If only my boss (or the CEO, president, etc.) would do things differently, everything would be fine." Our experience is that innovation happens when people decide to take action in whatever role they're in. In this book we lay out a process in which, although it's helpful to have the support of the senior leadership, innovation can be adjusted to meet the needs of any group, department, or business unit throughout the organization. In fact, within the process there are many stand-alone tools and methods that can be rearranged to meet your needs or that can be tied to ideas and tools you may already be using to lead innovation in your organization.

This book will show you how to be more innovative in your

- Leadership (leadership teams, development, and behavior)
- Strategic planning (e.g., identifying adjacencies and emerging opportunities)
- Organizational culture and competency development
- Performance management processes (e.g., metrics, resource allocation, and portfolio management)
- Innovation incubation processes (e.g., Stage-Gate development processes, communities of practice, and innovation networks)
- Human resource management and processes (e.g., hiring and staffing, team building, and organizational learning)

This book provides a unique, holistic approach to creating innovation at all levels of the organization. It focuses on systematically integrating business practices and connecting them to the value propositions they produce.

PART I

The Case for Innovation

The Innovation Genome

THE BOOM YEARS of the late 1990s have faded, the quick money deals have come and gone, and the disruptive technologies have disrupted us all. But the markets and shareholders remain demanding and influential. Productivity is no longer enough; companies must grow—whether it be in size, revenue, profit, or geographic locations.

An organization can grow in two ways. The first way is through acquisition—buying another company or product, or hiring away a competitor's best people. This is called *inorganic* growth because it is quick and requires little immediate nurturing to produce value. The problem with inorganic growth is that it isn't very sustainable or resilient. Think about all the mergers you've seen that have gone wrong.

Companies can also grow organically. This type of growth is fueled by innovation, which makes an organization better and new. To create organic growth, leaders need to understand how to build sustainable and resilient capabilities and culture, which in turn make innovation happen.

The Case for Innovation Everywhere, Every Day

Although there are only two ways for a company to grow, there are countless reasons why companies need to grow. The following scenarios are typical of the business challenges we see in our practice.

Case One: Barbarians at the Gate

A well-known life insurance company has been in business for over 100 years. It has solid earnings, good market share, and, most importantly, the trust of its policyholders. Its leaders have traditionally come up through the firm, so they understand what's required to run a reputable business. Recently, however, a law was passed that allowed large financial services conglomerates to start selling insurance at deep discount rates. Now this life insurance company needs to reinvent itself quickly at the grassroots level where policies are won and lost by the reputation and service provided by its agents. *This organization needs to make innovation happen now.*

Case Two: Grow or Die

A small software firm was started a few years ago by two entrepreneurial programmers who left a large company to develop their own ingenious product, which allows any desktop computer to communicate with any type of electronic device with a chip anywhere on the planet. Originally, the firm had seven people working in an old studio loft, but its initial product launch has been so successful that it has not been able to keep up with demand, even by doubling its staff size every six weeks. Recently, three of its top programmers were hired away at twice their salary by a large firm that intends to quickly develop a competing product, which it can make and distribute easily. *This organization needs to make innovation happen now.*

Case Three: The Good Samaritan in Need

A well-respected community-funded organization in a midsized Midwestern city provides food for people needing interim support. The large manufacturing company that employed a sizable segment of the population in that city and provided much of the support for the nonprofit organization has relocated. The city's unemployment has skyrocketed, and the tax base for funding has dwindled. The need for food for out-of-work families continues to rise. Federal, state, and local governments can't provide more funding in this time of need. This nonprofit organization can continue to operate the way it has been, but that will mean that it must turn away people in need. Or the organization can find other sources of support and operate in a different way in order to fill the demand for its services. *This organization needs to make innovation happen now.*

Case Four: Getting Better Every Day Every Way

A firm has been making brakes for three of the major automobile companies for over 75 years. It makes the best product in the business, but it is slightly more expensive than the other two major suppliers of brakes, and slightly slower than its competitors in introducing products to complement new car designs. One of the major automobile companies has notified this firm that it needs to reduce its costs by 5 percent each year, starting next year, and that its new products must be ready to ship at least six months earlier or it will lose the automaker's business. The firm knows that the other two automobile manufacturers will follow suit with demands for better pricing and speed. *This organization needs to make innovation happen now.*

Every day situations such as those above are taking place in businesses around the world—real people in real-world companies facing challenges that call for innovative solutions. The companies might be Fortune 500 concerns or start-ups just breaking into the industry. Regardless of the size or complexities of the organizations, these companies all have one thing in common: they need innovation to help them thrive in today's competitive world.

"And the survey says . . ."

Business leaders understand how innovation affects success. Surveys show that executives see change and innovation as necessary for organizational survival and growth. The annual Global Survey of Business Executives,[1] conducted by the consulting firm McKinsey and Company, gathered responses regarding risk and reward from over 9,000 executives worldwide. According to the latest survey released in spring 2005, the executives cited *ability to innovate* as the most important capability for business growth. In the same survey, the executives also cited *innovate in current products* and *develop new products* as the number one and number two most important actions companies will need to take to see their businesses grow in the coming years.

Don't be fooled into thinking that innovation is only for those in marketing or product development, because the truth is that innovation is everyone's job. Leading innovation goes beyond designing better products and services, or packaging or developing new delivery systems. If you have a stake in helping your company grow, you need to understand where innovation comes from and how to harness its power. Innovation cuts across company lines, affecting nearly every department or function. For this reason, leading innovation is vital for every employee to master—from the CEO to the department manager to the frontline worker. Although most business leaders acknowledge the need for innovation, they often are unsure of exactly what innovation is.

How to Know Innovation When You See It

What does innovation look like? That is, how do we know innovation when we see it? A quick look around reveals that innovation has many forms, including a better or new product, such as a car; a combination of products, such as a hybrid cell phone; a fashion, such as a designer dress; a business model, such as a short-distance airline; a marketing campaign, such as one for a mature product that makes it seem new; a service, such as a bank that offers customized products and services; an attribute, such as orange juice that helps clean your arteries; and a package, such as a paint can that never spills.

What do these forms of innovation have in common? *Nothing!* The type of design that makes for an aesthetically pleasing dress is quite different from that of a more efficient travel route for a low-cost airline. In addition, increasingly, innovation isn't restricted to any one type; it's often a combination of forms, which, when put together produce hybrid solutions. So, in order to recognize innovation, we will have to expand our definition to include all its various forms.

There are hundreds of competing definitions of innovation. Most of these are narrowly focused and somewhat restrictive because they associate innovativeness with a particular element or attribute. Words such as "technological" or "breakthrough" are common examples. But, as demonstrated above, innovation has a much wider role and application in the organization and therefore needs a more operational definition to identify how it works in practice.

The late Marshall McLuhan,[2] University of Toronto professor and cultural guru, suggested a functional definition for innovation that is easily recognizable by anyone in an organization:

Innovation . . .

- *Enhances something.* For example, Google enhanced searching the Internet by making the user interface simple and the behind-the-scenes search process more powerful. These enhancements consistently drew people away from Yahoo, Lycos, and other popular established search engines.
- *Eliminates or destroys something.* For example, in the 1980s, if you wanted to trade stocks, you called your broker, who in turn gave the information to a back-office computer system operator who executed the trade. Charles Schwab gave the client direct access to trading online. This cut out the need for a broker and changed the dynamics and pricing of an entire industry. Charles Schwab eliminated much of the need for a traditional brokerage house.
- *Returns us to something in our past.* For example, Amazon has one of the world's largest collections of books for purchase online at very competitive prices; yet people continue to shop at Barnes and Noble stores with all the limitations of a physical space. They browse books like they did as kids in the local library. They drink coffee like they did as college students in the local coffee shops. They sit in nice leather chairs and socialize like their parents did at any number of "neighborhood" establishments. The experience of Barnes and Noble reconnects the customers to their past.
- *Over time things become their opposite.* For example, e-mail was first introduced as a time-saving technology. It was going to make all our lives more efficient. Over time, more people began to use and abuse e-mail to the point that it now often confounds our workday and impedes our ability to be productive.

In addition to these functions, innovation has attributes and characteristics. For example, all types of innovation employ some form of useful novelty aimed at making things better or new. That is, useful innovation is intended to create some form of tangible or intangible value. An innovation is always specific to the situation and time in which it was given rise. Innovation has a transformative quality because it will both replace existing products and services, as well as replace ways of doing things, and, in turn it will be replaced by a subsequent innovation. Therefore, innovation is always involved in an endless cycle of emerging and dissolving.

How Creativity and Change Drive Innovation

Innovation is closely aligned with two other forms of transformation—creativity and change. Since these terms are often used interchangeably, it's useful to distinguish between them.

Creativity is the purposeful activity, or set of activities, that produces valuable products, services, processes, or ideas that are better and new. *Change* is the altered state of an individual or organization produced by both purposeful and unintentional transformational forces. *Innovation* is the intentional development of products, services, processes, or expressions, such as design and fashion, which results from organizational and individual creativity, as well as intentional and unintentional discovery.

To understand how these concepts work together, think about how an engine operates. Creativity is the spark that ignites the fuel. Change is the heat that the combustion produces. Innovation is the engine turning the heat into power and moving the vehicle up the road toward a specific destination.

Cracking the Innovation Genome

A *genome* is the ultimate map in that it contains the totality of an organism's genetic material called DNA. At its inception, a genome contains all the information it needs to grow into a mature organism. This map exists in every cell of the organism and provides specific instructions for each cell to integrate with other cells. It is both whole and complete in all its forms, and yet part of a larger system.

The term *Innovation Genome* is used here to describe how the entire system of organizational innovation functions at all levels: the individual, the organization, and the larger strategic environment where value is recognized by markets and consumers. One of the key pieces of the Innovation Genome is a map, which shows four different approaches to innovation. Once you understand how to read this map, you can unlock the hidden dynamics that determine how innovation works in everything from leadership behavior to macroeconomics.

A Brief History of How the Innovation Genome Was Discovered

The *Innovation Genome* is the result of over 20 years of applied research beginning with studies of organizational effectiveness and gradually relating them to studies of value creation and organizational creativity. (See Table 1.1 for a summary.)

In the mid-1970s, Professors Robert Quinn and John Rohrbaugh at the State University of New York—Albany's Rockefeller College of Public Affairs and Policy were conducting research to identify what leadership behaviors lead to high-performing managerial decision making. From their research, Quinn and Rohrbaugh discovered two major dimensions of underlying organizational effectiveness.[3]

The first dimension, *organizational focus*, produces a positive form of tension between the *internal emphasis* on the welfare and development of the organization's people and the *external focus* on the organization's ability to succeed in the competitive marketplace.

The second dimension, *organizational preference for structure*, produces a positive form of tension between the *stability and control* to maintain harmony within the organization and *flexibility and change* so that the organization can adapt to shifting external market conditions. Quinn and Rohrbaugh's research on these dimensions led them to create a model known as the Competing Values Framework, or CVF, because it showed the relationship of these positive tensions.

Since its inception, the CVF has been used by thousands of corporations, not-for-profit organizations, and government agencies around the world to transform company processes. It's helped companies of all sizes and types because, in part, the CVF is adaptable to just about any business operation.

By the mid-1980s Quinn had partnered with Kim Cameron at the University of Michigan Business School on a comprehensive research project to determine how these four leadership profiles supported or hindered high-performing organizational culture and competency development. In the mid-1990s, Quinn and Cameron were joined by Anjan Thakor and Jeff DeGraff, also of the University of Michigan Business School, to develop a unified theory of value creation, which they called *Wholonics*.[4]

Table I.I   Summary of the History of the Innovation Genome

Evolution of the Innovation Genome	Researchers	Timeline	Activities and Results
Competing Values Framework	Quinn and Rohrbaugh	1970s and early 1980s	Studies conducted to identify the leadership behaviors that lead to high-performing managerial decision making
Wholonics evolves from CVF	Quinn and Cameron	Mid-1980s	CVF research evolved into a project to determine how the model's four leadership profiles supported or hindered high-performing organizational culture and competency development
Wholonics evolves from CVF	Quinn, Cameron, Thakor, and DeGraff	Mid-1990s	Multiyear study of Fortune 2000 companies based on CVF principles to determine predictability of financial market-to-book variances that drive stock prices, which resulted in a unified theory of value creation
CVF and creativity	DeGraff and Lawrence	2001	Further organizational analysis extended the CVF to the subject of organizational creativity that produces value for companies
Innovation Genome evolves from CVF	DeGraff and Quinn (Shawn)	2005	Based on the practice of applying the CVF to organizational creativity, the Innovation Genome emerges as a model for leading innovation and growth

In 2001, DeGraff and Katherine Lawrence extended the CVF to the subject of organizational creativity that produces value.[5] In analyzing hundreds of cases containing a wide array of approaches to creativity, they observed the emergence of *secondary dynamics* of organizational creativity: The *speed* (how fast) and *magnitude* (how much) of the creative practices largely determine which quadrants produce successful results in specific situations and which do not. The book *Creativity at Work*, which was written by DeGraff and Lawrence, provides an in-depth analysis of their research.

Since 2001, Jeff DeGraff and Shawn Quinn have taken the CVF one step further and developed it as a model for understanding the different types of innovation that exist in organizations. When using the CVF as a model for innovation, they refer to it as the "Innovation Genome."

How the Innovation Genome Works

The Innovation Genome is represented as a four-quadrant model as shown in Figure 1.1. Each quadrant represents characteristics and practices that produce different forms of value. These quadrants operate essentially the same way for individuals, organizations, and markets. The strengths, weaknesses, and interactions of these four quadrants determine an organization's ability to produce specific forms of innovation in specific situations.

The categories that comprise the quadrants are Collaborate, Create, Compete, and Control. These quadrants are recognizable by the key measures, workplace environments, organizational practices, and leadership behaviors that are typically associated with each of the four types as best practices. There also are certain tools associated with these quadrants, which are part of a company's "innovation playbook."

It's useful to think of these quadrants as being right-handed or left-handed, because most individuals use both hands but usually have a stronger, more dominant side. In the same way, organizations possess characteristics from all quadrants but are stronger in one more than the others. Sometimes, quadrants are oppositional in nature; that is, when we use one type of innovation practice, we destroy or weaken another type of innovation. For example, a firm may opt to focus on high-risk breakthrough experiments that focus on growth, at the expense of innovation of low-risk incremental processes that lead to greater efficiency. In general, the most effective organizations have some proficiency in all.

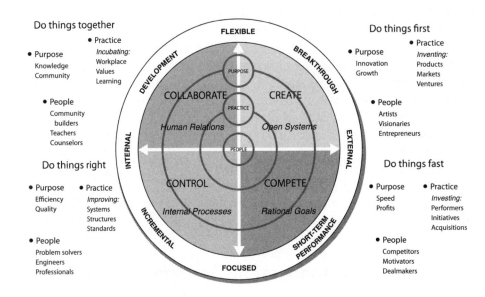

Figure 1.1   The Innovation Genome

The quadrants show organizational strengths, that is, those areas where there are the greatest competencies. While it's useful to manage with an eye on strengths, it's also important to work with people who have strengths from the other quadrants and thus create a well-rounded group. Leadership styles are only one part of the equation, however, as other factors, such as forces external to the organization, will also determine how successful you will be at changing existing processes.

The Collaborate Quadrant

Fellowship, learning, and value-based leadership are most commonly associated with the Collaborate quadrant. This approach to innovation is based on a human-relations view of organizations that emphasizes the need for individuals to unite in a positive way to build cooperative communities of practice. This profile connects individuals to a greater good or a high-principled mission. These organizations are often considered good companies to work for because of the emphasis on balance between job duties and personal life.

Empowering people to do what they believe to be right is essential for the Collaborate leader. Mutual trust and integrity are cornerstones of this culture, which creates highly committed individuals. Leaders develop their teams and team members through organizational learning practices, education, and coaching. This network also includes customers, who are treated as part of the family.

The Collaborate mode isn't focused on short-term gains. Instead, Collaborate individuals scan the horizon in search of long-term potential. Bloomsbury Publishing, a small independent publishing company, is an example of this type of thinking. Founder Nigel Newton, along with three editors, eschewed the idea of mass-marketed books. Instead the company publishes an eclectic mix of well-known and unknown writers. A number of Nobel, Pulitzer, and Booker prize–winning works have borne the Bloomsbury mark. The company has published books by authors such as Nobel Laureate Nadine Gordimer, Margaret Atwood, and John Irving. Ironically, one of the obscure authors Bloomsbury helped develop was JK Rowling, the author of *Harry Potter*, which became one of the best-selling books of all time.

What makes Bloomsbury tick? It strives to publish the best literature, not necessarily a best seller. Bloomsbury does what it thinks is right and not what investors tell it to do. The focus is on developing good writers into great writers. Authors are drawn to and remain with Bloomsbury because the publisher-writer relationship is cultivated, not exploited.

In many respects Bloomsbury reflects the practices that would be expected in a Collaborate environment. The workplace reflects employee values and supports collective learning. The company formed a guiding coalition to observe, advise, and teach apprentices. Mentors pass along their knowledge in a manner similar to the guild tradition.

The Collaborate Quadrant's Innovation Playbook

The Collaborate quadrant is based on a social approach. The leaders in this quadrant believe that an enterprise has as much purpose to build relationships, nurture community, and empower individuals as it does to produce goods and services. To accomplish this, the leaders must ensure that new ideas benefit the community and that communication systems and partnerships are sensitive to the needs, abilities, and ambitions of everyone in the organization.

Collaborate leadership fosters internal stability, security, and growth, even in the face of uncertainty. It assumes that the external environment is best managed through commitment and cooperation. It views customers as partners in an extended community. In a Collaborate environment, loyalty flows in all directions—up, down, and across the organization.

Collaborate leadership strives for a workplace with a strong sense of community and where individuals are encouraged to participate and contribute to the process. This environment can be especially beneficial when there are turbulent external forces that make long-term decision making and planning difficult, because the group's shared values, beliefs, and goals provide much needed direction. Collaborate workplaces often are quite informal, and there are few levels of management.

The Collaborate organization places an emphasis on a learning, nurturing environment. For this reason, these companies often include practices such as personal and professional training, customer-relationship management, team-building activities, and mentoring and coaching. (See Table 1.2.)

Collaborate Case Examples

Linux: Innovation Networks and Alliances

Linux, a simplified software kernel that can run outside any operating system, started as a hobby of a University of Helsinki student named Linus Torvalds. The Linux system is linked to a not-for-profit network, which has formed a community with shared goals and values. The network includes software developers and distributors who create new applications for open-source operating systems that compete with for-profit systems, such as Unix and Windows.

eBay: Searching for and Reapplying Innovative Practices

Pierre Omidyar started eBay, an online auction site, in 1995. It offers a wide array of goods for sale, ranging from rare collectibles to garage sale castoffs. Both hobbyists and multinationals, such as IBM, sell their wares in this online market. eBay serves as a virtual bazaar that brings together buyers and sellers from around the world. eBay provides a platform that can be used by sellers across most merchandise categories and real-world locations. Over the years, sellers have formed an online retail community in which they share information and learn from one another.

Singapore Air: Innovation as Customer Service and Experience

In 1965, Singapore separated from Malaysia and became an independent republic. The government formed Singapore Airlines in 1972 as part of a greater plan for the development of an economic engine and a national identity. The airline believes that if it does a good job, passengers will have a more favorable impression of Singapore. Consequently, the airline focuses on world-class customer service. It has pioneered in-flight services such as free drinks and complementary headphones. Singapore Air routinely appears at the top of most international customer satisfaction surveys. This applies not just to the airline industry, which typically shows poor numbers, but to all industries. It is one of the world's most successful airlines, as well as a profitable one.

The Create Quadrant

Big changes, radical experiments, and speculating on new and emerging markets are all hallmarks of the Create quadrant. The start-up firm, the maverick leader, and the iconoclast rebel-entrepreneur all fit here. It's the lottery quadrant—a high-risk affair that has big failures for most and big payoffs for a few. Create leaders are big thinkers, artists, and risk takers. They love an impossible challenge and have dozens of solutions to any problem.

Organizations in the Create quadrant excel at brainstorming, creating elaborate strategic plans, starting spinout ventures under the radar, and assembling a diverse array of characters that would rival any carnival. The Create organization attracts those who are willing to let go of perfection in order to create something new. Breakthrough products, services, ideas, and people are found in this fluid and ever-shifting environment.

The research and development (R&D) department is typically a Create environment. Unlike other areas that require consistency and uniformity, such as production and warehouse operations, R&D thrives on experimentation and speculation. For this reason, employees

Table 1.2   Collaborate Quadrant Characteristics

Situation: External conditions such as market forces and trends. When . . .	• A community united by shared beliefs defines the organization, such as environmental concerns. • Competency is closely linked to unique individual abilities, such as an entertainer. • Lifestyle identification determines the product or service, such as motorcycles.
Purposes: Outcomes, or the value the organization intends to create	• *Community:* Establishing and maintaining shared values and culture. Common ways of achieving this are networking, empowerment, and team building. • *Knowledge:* Developing understanding and skills. Common ways of achieving this are training, organizational learning, and human resource management.
Practices: Culture, competency, and processes of the organization mission and vision statements	• Knowledge management. • Learning organization. • Collaborative communities of practice. • Culture development and transformation. • Customer relationship management. • Competency development. • Team building. • Mentoring and coaching. • Training.
People: Individuals in the organization, at all levels	• See potential. • Build commitment and trust. • Are sensitive and caring. • Are patient listeners. • Encourage participation.

	• Respect differences.
	• Empower people.
Preferred *environments*	• Family atmosphere.
	• Collaborative workplace.
	• Shared values and vision.
	• Integrated personal goals.
	• Informal atmosphere.
	• Teaching and coaching.
Preferred *questions*	• *Interest:* Do we care about this idea?
	• *Knowledge:* What are we learning from this idea?
	• *Beliefs:* Does this idea fit with our values?
Preferred *communication*	• Talk about personal experiences.
	• Storytelling.
	• Smiles.
	• Expressing emotions.
	• Putting the person at ease.
	• Thinking out loud.
	• Using nonverbal communication.
	• Acknowledging the role of intuition.
	• Recognizing important spiritual symbols.
Example *organizations*	• Bloomsbury Publishing
	• McKinsey and Company
	• Harley Davidson
	• eBay
	• WL Gore and Associates
	• The Body Shop
	• Not-for-profits
	• Universities

in the R&D department need to be comfortable in an environment that calls for jumping tracks if a particular process isn't producing the desired results.

Companies employ the Create quadrant to drive innovative ideas. The companies strive to develop products, services, and methods that will serve their internal and external customers in the future. To achieve these aims, leaders often take on bold initiatives that rely on revolutionary technologies and methodologies. However, in a true Create environment, plans must also be flexible to allow the organization to quickly adapt to emerging trends.

Eureka! is Roger Newton's business. As a top researcher at Parke-Davis and Warner-Lambert, Newton was a key member of the team that developed *Lipitor®* (atorvastatin calcium), the world's top-selling cholesterol-lowering medication, and one of the most profitable products ever created. For most researchers, the development of the greatest blockbuster drug in history would have been enough, but ever the visionary, Newton saw new possibilities for reducing the risk of heart disease and acted on them.

Newton and a few key partners started a new firm, Esperion Therapeutics, to develop a synthetic version of good cholesterol that would reduce the plaque in the arteries of the heart. The company's approach to drug development, and the medication itself, was radically different from conventional drug-discovery methods that require thousands of experiments with minor variations to develop a highly effective drug molecule.

Instead, Newton focused on making sense of seemingly disparate data. For example, he found a statistical anomaly in some medical records from an Italian village in which residents had an unusually low rate of heart disease. Upon closer examination, these residents appeared to have a strain of ultraeffective good cholesterol (HDL) that offset the negative effects of the bad (LDL) cholesterol. Newton and his team believed they could create a synthetic version of this good cholesterol and use it to treat patients at risk for problems from bad cholesterol.

Even with Newton's winning record, few experts expected the new venture to succeed. With fewer than 70 employees and less than a quarter of the funding that the major pharmaceutical firms were spending to discover medications to treat the same disease, Newton hit it big again. His bold departure from the norm paid off. In 2003 Pfizer purchased Esperion Therapeutics for $1.3 billion in cash. In this case lightning struck twice for a visionary who seemed to know when and where the lightning bolts were going to hit before anyone else did.

The Create Quadrant's Innovation Playbook

The Create quadrant is the environment that keeps regenerating itself. In this environment, one idea leads to another and to another and so on. In a sense, the Create quadrant is about producing many radically different ideas instead of one big one.

The Create approach to innovation is highly responsive to turbulent and fast-changing conditions, which is why it's commonly found in high-tech and biotech companies. When the future is unclear or rapidly changing, the ability to launch a wide array of experiments and speculate on new markets provides a strategic advantage.

Create leaders judge their success on the innovativeness and future readiness of their products, services, and ideas. They keep an eye on future trends, judging which way they think the wind will blow and then applying their imaginations to the difficult task of making the wind blow in the desired direction.

Individuals who work in a Create organization are usually involved in all aspects of the enterprise. Power and responsibility flow from individual to individual or from team to team according to their capability and the project at hand. The glue that holds Create organizations together is a shared pursuit of a grand vision, seemingly impossible goals, radical innovation, and a culture of risk taking.

There are a number of common practices in a Create organization, including strategic forecasting, strong emphasis on new product development, growth and market disruption strategies, and product spin-offs. (See Table 1.3.)

Create Case Examples

Apple: Innovation as Design and Fashion[6]

Apple Computer, a San Jose–based company, was hailed as a success when it first introduced the personal computer in the late 1970s, but less than 20 years later, in 1997, Apple was faltering with few new products and an ever-shrinking share of the personal computer market. The board brought back founding father Steve Jobs as CEO with a mandate to reinvigorate the company. Jobs responded to the challenge with a number of products, starting with the iMac, a colorful desktop computer and an attention-getting marketing campaign called *Think Different*. Apple then introduced the iPod, a digital MP3 audio player and managed to hit a home run with development of iTunes, a pay-for-music download service, which allowed iPod owners to download songs for a fee from the Internet.

Celera: Creating a New Approach to a Difficult Challenge

In 1990, the United States' National Institutes of Health (NIH) and various international groups launched the Human Genome Project (HGP), a major effort to unravel the complex code of human genes. The project was projected to take 15 years to complete. Eight years after the project began, Craig Venter, a former NIH employee, formed Celera, a biotech firm, and announced that his company was going to sequence the human genome by 2001, four years ahead of the HGP's target date. Celera relied on a radical technique called shotgunning, first developed by Nobel laureate Hamilton Smith, that utilizes an army of gene-sequencing machines and advanced software. Celera managed to provide the first blueprints of the human genome within his proposed timeframe of four years. Although the company may not be a household name, it has helped pioneer fields such as genomics, the discovering and understanding of genetic blueprints; and bioinformatics, the collecting, mapping, visualizing, and modeling of genetic information.

IBM: Innovation as Market Making[7]

In January 1993, International Business Machines (IBM), considered a computer powerhouse, announced that it had suffered a $5 billion loss the previous year. The company then set on a course that led to one of the most legendary turn-around efforts in corporate history. Realizing that it couldn't compete on costs against rivals like Dell, IBM sold its desktop and laptop divisions. Next it unveiled a new generation of powerful technology that helped differentiate it from other computer manufacturers. Most importantly, it moved toward selling consulting services, focusing on creating complete solutions for clients. For example, it worked with the Mayo Clinic to develop technology for gene mapping, as well as an extensive system that supports patient care. IBM no longer waits for a client to call; instead it approaches clients directly and offers solutions to their problems.

The Compete Quadrant

The Compete quadrant is a survival-of-the-fittest approach to innovation where the strong eat the weak and sprint past the slow to new markets and riches. This is a quadrant in which high achievers thrive. They believe that business is a zero-sum game—everyone is either a winner or a loser.

High-achieving competitors thrive in the Compete quadrant. They are most comfortable in a results-oriented environment. They enjoy challenges and the hard work needed to win. Compete leaders motivate their employees by articulating clear objectives, which often are in the form of strategic moves to beat the competition.

Like the Create quadrant, the Compete environment maintains an outward focus on meeting customer demand. Where the two differ is in how they manage risk. A Create company takes risk in stride; a Compete company hedges against it. An example of this hedging is Procter and Gamble, the world leader in consumer products. With more than 300 brands and thousands of products, P&G is able to customize its products to individual markets. In some cases, its own brands rival each other, thus ensuring that the company garners a larger share of the overall market.

What is P&G's road map to success? It has developed a system to pick winners. Through exhaustive market research, P&G is able to identify those proposed products that will most likely do well in the marketplace. As a result, it is able to achieve greater returns with less risk. Existing products that are performing poorly are quickly yanked from the market. In addition, brands receive regular upgrades, so they stay vital instead of dying.

P&G exhibits various Compete characteristics, such as taking hard-nosed and decisive business action, putting money and talent in the best possible places, and focusing on short-term measurable results. P&G also makes deals whenever necessary in order to draw on other resources, whether they be products or services, partners or customers.

The Compete Quadrant's Innovation Playbook

The Compete quadrant is based on a business or profit-centric approach to innovation. In most cases, Compete companies are publicly traded business and therefore must demonstrate short-term profitability for shareholders. Firms in the pharmaceutical, consumer electronics, and financial services arenas are typically Compete organizations.

Compete leaders believe that the world is competitive and that customers are self-interested and choosy. Compete companies judge their success by their market share, revenue, brand equity, and profitability. Compete leadership focuses on external forces, including customers, competitors, business partners, suppliers, and licensees.

Table 1.3 Create Quadrant Characteristics

Situation: External conditions such as market forces and trends. When . . .	• Differentiation creates significantly higher margins, such as consumer electronics. • Start-ups compete through radical innovation with established firms. • An industry is situated around blockbuster invention, such as pharmaceuticals.
Purposes: Outcomes, or the value the organization intends to create	• *Innovation:* Making new and better products and services. Common ways of achieving this are creative problem solving, new-product development, and change management. • *Growth:* Prospecting for new and future market opportunities. Common ways of achieving this are strategic forecasting, trend analysis, and shared vision management.
Practices: Culture, competency, and processes of the organization mission and vision statements	• Creativity methods. • Strategic forecasting and scenario planning. • Corporate venturing. • Spin-offs. • Entrepreneuring. • Growth and market disruption strategies. • Change and innovation programs. • New-product development. • Radical experiments. • Borderless and virtual organizations.
People: Individuals in the organization, at all levels	• Are visionary dreamers. • Are clever. • Are optimistic. • Are enthusiastic. • Are quick on their feet. • Are expressive.

	• Are big-picture thinkers.
Preferred *environments*	• Stimulating projects. • Flexible hours. • Free from everyday constraints. • New initiatives. • Independent work streams. • Diverse workforce.
Preferred *questions*	• *Innovation:* Is this idea a breakthrough? • *Direction:* Does this idea move us toward the future? • *Emerging opportunity:* Will this idea allow us to experiment as we go along?
Preferred *communication*	• Be enthusiastic and energetic. • Look at the big picture. • Expect to be interrupted in midsentence. • Draw pictures and designs of concepts. • Use metaphors. • Look at the future. • Make ideas conceptually sound and clear. • Ask open-ended questions. • Explore how the pieces fit together.
Example *organizations*	• Pixar • Apple • Phillips • Google • Nokia • Versace • Biotechs • Start-ups

There are a number of practices that Compete organizations gravitate toward. Many of them are aggressive in nature and provide rewards to those who achieve or produce the most. These practices include mergers and acquisitions, performance management scorecards, pay-for-performance plans, and sales-channel management. (See Table 1.4.)

Compete Case Examples

Dell: Business Model Innovation[8]

Michael Dell founded his namesake computer company in 1984 while he was still a student at the University of Texas at Austin. His idea was simple: let customers design their computers. He advertised in the back of PC magazines and took orders by phone. By the early 1990s, Dell began selling over the Internet with a direct-to-consumer sales model. When Dell discovered that no one would service its computers, it established a worldwide, world-class customer support system. In addition, the company started selling peripherals and add-ons to the computers, such as software and printers. Eventually Dell expanded into other technologies, such as plasma televisions and MP3 players. Dell's success has rested in part on lowering the time and cost of making computers, which it was able to do through an innovative business model of just-in-time inventory and manufacturing practices.

Nike: Innovation through Marketing and Brand Management

In 1962, Phil Knight was a middle-distance runner at the University of Oregon under the direction of legendary track coach Bill Bowerman. Knight and Bowerman wanted to bring inexpensive Japanese shoes made of synthetic materials, such as nylon, to the U.S. market. In the early 1970s Knight sold his own brand of track shoes directly to the public under the brand name Nike. The brand's distinctive logo of a swoosh soon became synonymous with running shoes. Nike enjoyed a meteoric rise after it signed a rookie from the Chicago Bulls basketball team named Michael Jordan to endorse its basketball shoes. Nike soon expanded its product line to include cross-training shoes and apparel. It signed a new generation of superstar endorsers, such as golf great Tiger Woods. Its late 1980s *Just Do It* ad campaign was so successful that it became part of popular culture around the world.

Amazon: Innovation through Channel and Delivery

Founded during the height of the dot-com boom of the mid-1990s, Amazon began as an online bookstore. Founder Jeff Bezos chose the name Amazon as a metaphor for the great river on which all forms of life and commerce travel. Bezos adopted an unusual slow-growth business model for his company. He began by focusing on the logistics of delivering books ordered online. He did this by establishing a series of procurement and distribution warehouses around the United States and the world. The company also experimented with various marketing techniques, including Amazon associates, selling used books, and offering free shipping. He also expanded the items sold on Amazon to include music CDs, software, electronics, jewelry, toys, apparel, and even automobiles. In an era when Internet sales were just in their infancy, Amazon became associated with safe and secure transactions and a guarantee that products will be delivered as promised.

The Control Quadrant

The Control quadrant takes a systematic view of innovation. Through the discipline of applying multistep processes, such as continuous improvement, that are known to work with little risk, the slogan for this quadrant could well be, "Getting better every day in every way." This approach has a safety-net feature to it, and for this reason it's particularly useful for large complex organizations that need to create products and services that must have a hit at the first at-bat.

Control quadrant leaders are methodical, pragmatic, and precise. They excel in a workplace that has clearly delineated roles and responsibilities, systems and processes, and policies and procedures that ensure things are done correctly. They are clear-thinking realists.

The end result of the creative process in the Control quadrant is not so much an entirely new product but instead an existing product with minor variations.

The Control quadrant is often overlooked as a form of creativity because, quite frankly, implementing incremental changes in systems, structures, and standards just doesn't *look* creative. But think back to Aesop's fable, *The Tortoise and the Hare*. What lesson were we supposed to learn? Slow and steady wins the race.

In the real world, many industry giants are like the tortoise and use a safe, predictable method to win the race. One such company is Toyota,

Table 1.4   Compete Quadrant Characteristics

Situation: External conditions such as market forces and trends. When . . .

- A community is united by shared beliefs. Shareholder demands are the primary driver, such as financial institutions.
- Aggressive competition changes the market dynamics through mergers and acquisitions.
- Investors demand quick financial results.

Purposes: Outcomes, or the value the organization intends to create

- *Speed:* Moving quickly to capture an opportunity. Common ways of achieving this are mergers and acquisitions, branding, and customer service.
- *Profits:* Maximizing shareholder earnings. Common ways of achieving this are using goals and metrics, strategic resource allocation, and portfolio management.

Practices: Culture, competency, and processes of the organization mission and vision statements

- Economic value-added management.
- Mergers and acquisitions.
- Real options analysis.
- Time to market reduction.
- Performance management scorecards.
- Profit insight processes.
- Pay-for-performance plans.
- Branding.
- Sales channel management.
- Portfolio management.

People: Individuals in the organization, at all levels

- Are goal and action-oriented.
- Are impatient.
- Are assertive.
- Are driven.
- Are decisive.
- Are challenging.

	• Are competitive.
Preferred *environments*	• Competitive.
	• High pressure.
	• Fast moving and high energy.
	• Image-enhancing deal making.
	• With quantifiable results.
	• Winning and losing.
Preferred *questions*	• *Cash value:* Is the payoff for this idea big enough?
	• *Immediacy:* Can we get this idea done quickly?
	• *Leverage:* Can this idea be used to create value in other areas?
Preferred *communication*	• Get to the point and summarize.
	• Be logical and analytical.
	• Critically confront the downside.
	• Use quantifiable facts to illustrate points.
	• Be very matter-of-fact.
	• Don't get emotional.
	• Show personal ownership.
	• Demonstrate a bias toward action.
Example *organizations*	• Unilever
	• Microsoft
	• GE
	• Bloomberg
	• PepsiCo
	• Citicorp
	• Blue-chip companies
	• Conglomerates

the Japanese automobile manufacturer. The company has introduced or perfected many of the industry's foremost system and process tools for design and development.

Toyota is known for its leading methods such as continuous improvement, which are its never-ending efforts to boost quality and performance; flexible platform systems, which use common components in as many products as possible to reduce costs; and just-in-time inventory, which eliminates waste by providing what is needed, when it's needed, and in the exact amount needed.

These methods have helped make Toyota Japan's number one automaker. It also helped the company when it wanted to break into the luxury car market and had to compete against long-established European carmakers. Toyota's entry, the Lexus, ranks at the top of customer surveys, such as those conducted by JD Power. This reputation for consistent quality is helping to make the Lexus the world's most wide-selling brand of luxury car.

Toyota thrives in the Control quadrant. It breaks processes down to the most elemental level in order to understand how something works and how it can be made better. In true Control quadrant fashion, Toyota endlessly repeats a cycle of testing and improving its products.

The Control Quadrant's Innovation Playbook

The Control quadrant is based on a technological or engineering approach to innovation. Control leadership focuses inward and requires discipline. It is concerned with improving quality while at the same time cutting costs. This leadership style results in extensive processes, systems, and technology.

Control leadership is especially valuable in industries that require standardized procedures, rule reinforcement, and consistent products, such as medicine and transportation. Control measures serve to eliminate errors and increase the likelihood of expected outcomes. In today's manufacturing setting, Control-focused activities include business-process improvement, total-quality management, simulations, and contingency planning. (See Table 1.5.)

Control Case Examples

Samsung: Product Innovation[9]

In the 1970s, the South Korean conglomerate ("chaebol") Samsung quietly entered the electronics market. While Samsung products sold well in East

Asian markets, sales lagged in the U.S. and European markets, where they were viewed as inexpensive alternatives to better-recognized brands. This perception hurt the company, and, by the mid-1990s, with the onset of the Asian currency crisis, Samsung found itself deep in debt and facing bankruptcy. In the mid-1990s, Samsung Chairman Kun-hee Lee developed a global design initiative, which had company employees ranging from designers to engineers participate in design classes. As part of this effort, Samsung focused on creating the most advanced liquid crystal displays (LCDs) in the world. The LCDs it produced eventually became part of state-of-the-art computer monitors, large-screen plasma televisions, and the miniature screens found on cellular phones and PDAs. Through its emphasis on quality design, Samsung replaced its down-market image with that of a technology leader.

Wal-Mart: Process Innovation[10]

Historically, manufacturers provided retailers with the specifications and benefits of its products. In turn, the retailer would suggest to the customer what to buy. Not anymore. Wal-Mart, the retail giant, reversed that flow by using an enterprise system to track customer buying patterns and inform manufacturers of features that customers want. In the Wal-Mart world, the customer sets the targets for price, features, colors, and other attributes of the product. Wal-Mart continuously reviews all aspects of its business—from supply chain operations to service—for opportunities to cut costs and improve sales. In this way, it has managed to become the low-price leader.

Nokia: Platform Innovation

Nokia, named after a river in Finland, is a major manufacturer of cellular phones. But the company wasn't always a high-tech firm. In the late 1970s, Nokia broke free from its beginnings as a paper manufacturing and rubber processing business when it acquired communication technologies such as Private Mobile Radio. While global competitors like Motorola dominated the early cellular phone market with a "low band" or analog technology, Nokia worked the political venues in Europe for the adoption of a "digital" communication format called GSM. The GSM platform not only allowed for clearer and wider transmission, but it also enabled the sending and receiving of data, like on a computer network. By the early

Table 1.5 Control Quadrant Characteristics

Situation: External conditions such as market forces and trends. When . . .

- Scale and scope of organizational processes are very large and complex, such as automobile manufacturers.
- Government regulations and standards determine business practices, such as medicine.
- Failure is not an option, such as aerospace.

Purposes: Outcomes, or the value the organization intends to create

- *Efficiency:* Using resources in the best way possible. Common ways of achieving this are procedures, budgeting, and organizational design.
- *Quality:* Eliminating errors. Common ways of achieving this are process controls, systems, and technology.

Practices: Culture, competency, and processes of the organization mission and vision statements

- Business process improvement.
- Activity-based costing.
- Benchmarking.
- Lean manufacturing.
- Total quality management.
- Simulations.
- Contingency planning.
- Pervasive information systems.
- Reorganization.
- Supply chain management.

People: Individuals in the organization, at all levels

- Are pragmatic.
- Are organized and methodical.
- Are scientific or technical.
- Operate by the book.
- Are problem solvers.
- Are objective.

	• Are persistent.
Preferred *environments*	• Clear roles and responsibilities. • Stable project management. • Logical objectives. • Methodical processes. • Standards and regulations. • Ordered and structured work.
Preferred *questions*	• *Cost:* Can we afford this idea? • *Feasibility:* Can we really implement this idea? • *Standards:* Does this idea comply with critical standards?
Preferred *communication*	• Provide details. • Be neat and on time. • Follow the rules. • Explain in sequential order. • Conform to accepted esprit de corps. • Ask close-ended questions. • Provide detailed data. • Demonstrate how something works.
Example *organizations*	• Toyota • Shell Oil • Airbus • Wal-Mart • Siemens • LG • Government agencies • Medical centers

1990s, Nokia decided to focus its business on mobile phones using the digital standard. The company's technological design and platform helped it outpace competitors.

Building on the Innovation Genome

Recognizing what results your organization wants and the practices, competencies, and the leadership types associated with these outcomes is the first step toward crafting your own approach to making innovation work where you work. The Innovation Genome will give you insight into the best way to respond to challenges in multiple situations. The Genome will serve as a guide throughout the seven-step innovation process spelled out in the rest of this book, providing a way for you to gauge your company's progress and ensure that you get the outcomes you seek.

CHAPTER 2

The Creativize Method

Most managers labor under the delusion that they can't innovate where they work because they lack sufficient resources or support. They may also believe there is a gap between the competency required to innovate and the competencies they actually have in their workforce. Ironically, the major impediments to making innovation happen at work are not the absence of these institutional resources, but instead, their presence.

Consider for a moment that many of the most valuable biotech and dot-com start-ups of the last 10 years, like Google, were created in someone's garage without the benefit of extensive capital. Similarly, consider the "open source" approach to innovation many large firms are now taking to license new technologies and applications from emerging firms and federations of smaller firms so that they can bring these to market faster. What an organization lacks in terms of the scope and scale of its resources, it more than makes up for in its ability to maneuver in an agile way. In fact, the principal problem in most organizations isn't their lack of new technology or expertise, but rather their inability to get through their own systems, particularly those designed to aid innovation. Ironically, many firms are innovative and don't even know it. They have dozens of managers who routinely and successfully innovate by working the system to their advantage or flying under the radar. Because the institutionalized systems require people to avoid detection, these firms never harness their true potential.

Conversely, in firms, like WL Gore & Associates, where innovation is considered a democratic endeavor, something that everyone is expected to do, these same managers are considered travel guides to those yet uninitiated in the ways of innovation. They demonstrate ownership for all aspects of innovation. We refer to these informal innovation leaders as *Creativizers*, self-authorizing people who add creativity to ordinary business activities like hiring or budgeting. The *Creativize Method* spelled out in this chapter chronicles some of the key practices successful *Creativizers* use to make innovation happen where they work.

The word *Creativize* captures the essence of the transformation toward innovation. *Creativize* is a word that implies action, or a transformation toward an objective. Creativize starts with creativity—the fuel, or the raw material, of innovation. It is a capability that individuals and organizations must recognize and capture in all its forms. Once you or your organization have realized this capability, you will be set on a path toward systemizing a culture of innovation. As you become a Creativizer, you will develop the expertise necessary to put all these pieces together to lead an organization on a path toward innovation.

The *Creativize Method* takes the point of view that innovation isn't really anything special. It's part of most ordinary business activities. Indeed, every business already has some form of an innovation engine that drives its growth. If it didn't, it would quickly become insolvent. Once you know the Innovation Genome, recognizing the underlying innovation practices of any business process becomes relatively simple—planning, measuring performance, allocating resources, hiring and development, and so forth. It is through the day-to-day actions of leaders that innovations are conceived, developed, and implemented. Of course, creating a new space shuttle to go to Mars requires a greater effort and range of expertise than creating a new restaurant, but the innovation practices have more in common than you might suspect. So, we are going to deconstruct the most elaborate innovation practices with the Innovation Genome and then reconstruct them through the *Creativize Method* so that anyone, anywhere, anytime can make innovation happen.

The *DeGraff Hypothesis* states, "The amount of innovation a company produces is inversely related to the number of slick PowerPoint slides or elaborate process diagrams it makes about innovation." Instead, innovation takes root from experiments and experiences within the organization and emerges in ways that companies often don't suspect or plan for. The purpose of the seven steps is to show companies potential innovations that are emerging every day, right in front of them. Consider the case of Viagra, a drug that was originally intended to reduce blood pressure but was eventually discovered to have an "interesting" side effect.

The seven steps are intended to provide a structure for developing and recognizing innovation. But at the same time, they also allow for flexibility. You can start with step one and move forward from there, or you can refer to a specific section or tool if that's all you need at the time. In this way, you can customize the program to fit your organization's needs.

A Path to Innovation

The *Creativize Method* for leading innovation laid out in this book emerged from our observations of numerous companies that had successfully translated innovation into tangible forms of growth such as increases in revenue, market share, or new market penetration. Although these firms operated in different sectors and diverse geographies, we noticed that there were common patterns and similar paths that these companies took for integrating innovation into the organization's everyday business practices. We codified and refined our observations into seven steps, and associated tools, that could be replicated by leaders anywhere in their organization to create best practices for innovation every day, everywhere.

The strength of the seven steps is their ability to help an organization develop a sustainable and resilient culture for innovation and the corresponding capabilities. These steps are less about high-born strategies, and more about getting larger groups of people to execute the innovation playbook. While designing winning strategies and picking breakthrough innovations are important, ultimately they are dependent on a complex array of dynamic forces operating in a predictable way. Unfortunately, these forces typically function in a surprising and chaotic manner. In the end, *leading innovation* is really about *leading people*. It's about finding a way to engage people to draw innovation from themselves and bring it to life within their organization.

Once we identified the steps, we began to observe how they worked in a number of different settings. We soon realized that they were extremely versatile and applicable in multiple situations. For example, the steps have been used for a variety of situations such as identifying high-potential innovation leaders, launching a winning project, integrating best practices for innovation into existing organizational processes, and changing organizational culture and competency.

We also saw that these steps allow companies to pick and choose what they need for a given situation. While many firms choose to use individual steps, most run some combination. Few companies actually need to run all seven. Some companies have very strong strategies that allow for innovations to emerge, but they need to focus instead on the organizational aspects of getting the right teams assembled. Other companies are really good at assessing themselves and getting everyone on board to get things done, but they have a difficult time identifying winning projects.

Although the methods and tools in this book can be powerful mechanisms for innovation, they may not all be appropriate for your specific needs. For example, if you need to jumpstart a project (Step 6: Specialize), you may not need to develop an innovation strategy first (Step 2: Strategize). These steps are modular so you can pick and choose the steps that are right for your situation.

The Seven Steps

The seven steps are

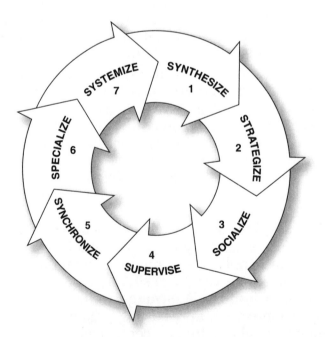

Figure 2.1

Synthesize: Assess and diagnose an organization's Purposes (outcomes), Practices (capabilities, organizational culture, and competencies), and People (individual employees who create capabilities, culture, and competencies).

Strategize: Create a vision for the future and a road map that leads to it.

Socialize: Establish a shared vision and shared values in the leadership team.

Supervise: Develop Facilitators to lead and sustain change and innovation.

Synchronize: Engage leaders throughout the organization to operationalize the vision.

Specialize: Jump-start change and innovation Action Teams.

Systemize: Review and revise projects, adjust organizational practices, and learn.

What Can Marina Do?

Marina is a brilliant marketer whose company needs to innovate—now!

Marina's story is one that captures all seven steps and shows how they might be employed in a single organization. Remember, all seven steps are seldom necessary in every organization, but the story of Marina will touch on many of the common situations that companies face every day and how those everyday companies can actually become innovative. Marina's story is based on real-life examples and is meant to drive home the point of how everyone can be a Creativizer and lead his or her company down a path to innovation and growth.

Marina was a brilliant marketer and was quickly promoted through the ranks of an esteemed consumer health-care products company to the top of all of its European operations. After five years of producing stellar growth, she was brought back to the United States as the chief operating officer to jump-start the company's fading sales. The company had some stellar competencies and people but was plagued by some prior organizational problems and an inability to come up with new products. She needed to introduce corporatewide innovation quickly.

Step One: Synthesize

Marina knew that there wasn't a consulting company that could resolve her dilemma. She needed to find her own solution. A friend recommended that she talk with Jeff who had worked with hundreds of leaders who were trying to make innovation happen in similar complex situations.

Jeff helped her assess and diagnose the organization. (See Table 2.1.) He helped her identify the three organizational key facets—Purposes, Practices, and People. *Purposes* are the outcomes the organization is trying to achieve. *Practices* are the capabilities, culture, and competencies of the organization. *People* are the individual employees who create the capabilities, culture, and competencies.

The biggest outcome the company was trying to achieve was growth-focused innovation at a time when it could not afford to see a downturn in its sales of current products or its productivity. The firm had world-class research and development (R&D), marketing, and strategy departments that were out of sync and had ceased collaborating effectively years earlier. The executive team she inherited was filled with outstanding leaders who were deeply devoted to the success of the company, but the firm had had three different CEOs in the past five years and was paralyzed by political infighting and a risk-adverse culture. Marina found herself at the helm of an organization without a robust pipeline of innovative new products and without the time and resources needed to create one quickly. As is often the case, this organization, so badly in need of growth, anointed a "miracle worker" to make innovation happen exactly when it found itself in a crisis without sufficient resources to support it.

Table 2.1 Step One: Synthesize

Objectives	Participants	Actions
Assess and diagnose.	Entire organization or individual units	• Interview key leaders and stakeholders. • Administer, collect, and analyze data. • Interpret the assessment.

Step Two: Strategize

Marina had long been frustrated with the firm's lack of rigor and honesty in developing its strategic plans. A typical strategy retreat started off with wishful thinking by senior leaders and support staff and was quickly followed by a stream of practical considerations voiced by operating leaders, leaving little room for great ambition. In addition, these strategies confused the staff and team members and left shareholders guessing as to the viability of the financial targets.

Determined to make the strategic planning process relevant and clear, Marina enlisted the help of Susan, the vice president of strategy, to organize a different kind of strategy stretch. (See Table 2.2.) First, Susan suggested that the process involve people outside the firm. Experts in given areas were invited to present their research on trends in markets, politics, and technologies. They were asked what was driving these trends and to predict, as much as that is possible, where they were going. Various leaders of the company at multiple levels were consulted to determine

Table 2.2 Step Two: Strategize

Objectives	Participants	Actions
Create a vision of the future and a road map that leads to it.	Leadership Team and other appropriate leaders and experts from within and outside the organization	• Identify the current strategic landscape competencies, opportunities, and threats to the organization. • Identify the forces driving the future of the organization, their impact and probability, and the competencies required to meet these future needs. • Integrate the road map to the future with current strategic and operating plans.

the relevancy, probability, and impact of these trends on the business. Scenarios were considered, and complex issues, such as timing markets, were discussed. Marina and the other leaders began to see how the future was unfolding right in front of them and how their existing strategy took little notice of it.

Teams were commissioned, numbers were crunched, and plans were aligned. But as the strategy became clear, Marina began to wonder about the ability of her organization to fully implement it. Did it have the resources, competencies, and culture to really make the strategy work? On a trip to London, Marina arranged to have lunch with Jon, someone she went to business school with who was now the head of Human Resources for an investment bank. She shared her concerns, and he told her about how his firm had also recently changed its strategy to be more aligned with emerging trends and how it quickly discovered it was completely unprepared to implement it. He lamented that the company had failed to consider how long it would take to develop new competencies and culture, and how much it would all really cost. He said that his company was now in the process of diagnosing its unique competencies and realigning its strategy to both capture emerging opportunities and play to its strengths, giving it a unique advantage over competitors.

Much to her surprise, when Marina returned to her office the next week to talk with Kent, her director of Human Resources, she learned that he had already performed an extensive diagnosis of the firm's culture and competencies but that no one had ever taken a serious interest in including these findings in the strategic planning process. Marina then asked Kent to join Susan and her, along with a small group of key operations leaders and outside experts, for a one-day strategy retreat to put all the pieces together. The group quickly determined that its level of ambition outpaced its abilities so members added joint ventures and even an acquisition to their plans until they could develop more potent and resilient capabilities in key areas. Marina was disappointed that her strategy wasn't as breakthrough as she had hoped for, but she was consoled by the knowledge that it was realistic and doable.

Once Marina had assessed the organization, she identified several key challenges she needed to address. First, she had to address leadership issues. The members of the executive team needed to learn to work more effectively with one another across organizational boundaries. They needed to create a compelling and shared vision of growth that they were committed to achieving and that was deeply understood by everyone at all locations and levels of the business.

Second, she needed to facilitate a pro-innovation culture in which risk-taking was supported and the competencies required to make innovation happen were developed. The company needed to stop planning and start experimenting with a wide array of breakthrough projects and ventures to see what really worked and what didn't. A small elite unit of highly practiced innovation facilitators was needed to lead these projects and ventures.

Third, she had to establish the processes that would support the culture of innovation. Organizational processes and systems were needed to identify, fund, manage, and harvest successful projects and ventures. The company needed to continue to refine its approach to innovation by establishing communities and networks of innovation practitioners and customers to integrate best practices into core business processes.

Marina could see rich pockets of innovation—an imaginative marketing campaign in Indonesia that tripled sales of a mature product, a novel delivery device designed in Finland that made vaccines painless, and an Internet portal that connected to a network of suppliers to rapidly reduce fulfillment time and inventory levels. There were promising signs of innovation everywhere, but she couldn't get through the obstacles that the organization itself presented. The underlying challenge wasn't the competition, the market, or intellectual property. It was finding a way to integrate innovation into the fabric of the firm without trying to re-create every aspect of the business.

Marina began to realize that searching, reapplying, and integrating innovation throughout the organization could be fully accomplished only by supporting innovation leaders who straddled disparate communities and transferred key ideas and practices through informal networks.

In order to help Marina manage an initiative of such great magnitude, Jeff codified the challenges into a series of steps. Some of these challenges were sequential in nature, so it made sense to perform these steps one after another. Others needed to be acted upon simultaneously. The handoffs between steps became an essential activity for getting the entire organization in sync in order to produce innovation. Selecting and developing ambidextrous leaders capable of managing between these steps and across boundaries became the most important factor to making innovation happen. Leading innovation was the key.

Step Three: Socialize

Over the next nine months, Marina and the other leaders on her team had to reconsider how their departments operated and reinvent their most cherished management practices to make room for innovation. The first step was to convene a series of off-site meetings to discuss the performance of the team itself and to get leaders to commit to making significant changes to their own departments and behaviors. Difficult issues were confronted such as who reports to whom and who has the power to move resources. Hard choices were made, and some team members opted to leave the firm in lieu of changing their role.

Slowly, the team began to jell and operate effectively across previously insurmountable departmental boundaries. Slowly the team members began to realize that the key barriers to innovation in their organization were not misaligned goals or wayward processes, but rather their own inability to come to a shared vision and common agreement on a course of action. (See Table 2.3.)

The team members began to develop a shared vision with a sense of destiny about how innovation needed to happen in the firm, but it was

Table 2.3 Step Three: Socialize

Objectives	Participants	Actions
Establish a shared vision and values in the Leadership Team.	Leadership Team	• Create a shared vision of the desired organization, and establish the shared values required to achieve it. • Leaders commit to changes in behavior required to achieve the shared vision and values. • Identify facilitators and a few strategic targets that will lead the organization to the shared vision and values.

only their vision. So Marina, along with the CEO's assistance, assembled the top leaders from all areas of the business for a mini summit to develop a comprehensive vision for growth that would be integrated into the strategy. Key strategic opportunities for growth were identified, and work streams were suggested. At the end of the mini summit, the company's top leaders now owned the vision.

Once the vision was clear, there was a general feeling of doubt that the firm had the required culture or competency to faithfully implement it. So the firm commissioned an organizational culture and competency assessment to diagnose (Step 1: Synthesize is still happening) its ability to achieve the vision. It wasn't surprising to most leaders that significant changes to the long-held beliefs and operation of the firm were required to implement the vision. Building a pro-innovation culture became the new priority.

However, changing the culture proved to be an arduous task because most leaders found it difficult to get a handle on what exactly was meant by the term "culture," and they were even more perplexed by how to measure it. They wondered if this focus on culture really meant that they were to be given some reprieve on hitting ambitious short-term revenue targets while they attempted to install an organizational esprit de corps that encouraged bold action and the assumption of greater risk. The process of translating the strategic vision into action became bogged down in myriad questions about how everything would work together. There was a general concern about whether the various units were aligned in purposeful action, and the reality of missing performance targets that drove bonuses heightened the resistance to the degree that the action stopped. In response, Marina's senior team went back to the drawing board and became mired in planning. Time and again it returned to the same vision, but found it almost impossible to get traction on it throughout the organization.

Marina called Jeff to get an outside view of the situation. He suggested that she show some proof of concept to reluctant leaders—a series of projects run like experiments to demonstrate what works and what doesn't. Marina was hesitant at first. This would require giving up some control on her part, and a willingness to assume some considerable risk of failure. After all, she had been brought to this senior executive position because the CEO believed that she could help revitalize the company, not make it worse.

Jeff told Marina his story about being an executive trying to lead innovation and how he was unable to change the firm he led until he changed himself first. Reluctantly, Marina agreed that she needed to change her approach and embarked on this new path to innovation that started where the first path left off. This path was untried and was built on the assumption that the leaders of the organization would learn as they went along and integrate their learning into their business practices.

Step Four: Supervise

Now the real task was to find the right highly practiced leaders who could make innovation happen and give these people a voice in identifying the right projects and the opportunity to lead them. (See Table 2.4.) Marina asked her innovation leadership team to nominate a dozen people who they believed were already key innovators in the firm. She compared the list of over 100 potential candidates and identified 15 people who were either on everyone's list or who were very strong candidates from one or two individual lists.

Next, Marina organized an off-site retreat with this small group of highly practiced innovators to lead these projects and ventures. Much to her surprise, they weren't sure they wanted to work together as a team.

Table 2.4 Step Four: Supervise

Objectives	Participants	Actions
Develop Facilitators to lead and sustain change and innovation.	Facilitators	• Train Facilitators in change and innovation methods and in facilitation tools and techniques. • Provide opportunities for Facilitators to help facilitate Action Teams. • Identify the development needs of Facilitators, coach them in improving their effectiveness, and review their progress.

These high-performing individuals had a history of being highly effective flying underneath the corporate radar and weren't sure that they wanted the increased visibility. They were also reluctant to be seen as collaborators with the very executives they had regarded as bureaucratic and clumsy. After all, these innovators had made a career of getting things done in spite of the senseless directives of senior management.

To make matters worse, they had differing points of view on how to advance innovation and strong opinions and egos that made it difficult to find a common approach. At first Marina thought that she had made a terrible mistake by turning to this group of talented but disjointed and opinionated dissenters. Yet, after two days with the group, she began to see that it was their self-authorizing behavior and ownership of their projects that had motivated each of them to navigate through the organization bureaucracy to drive innovation to success. Marina realized that she didn't need to motivate or guide this group; these people would motivate and guide her.

The group of innovators reviewed the strategic vision and opportunities that had been created by Marina's innovation team of senior executives. There was some debate over the viability of some opportunities and the addition of a few that may have been overlooked, but for the most part they agreed with the direction of the vision. Next, they identified a dozen highly diversified projects that could be quickly launched to demonstrate the viability of the vision. Each leader selected a project team of anywhere between six to a dozen team members to work on each project, some full time and others part time. Marina worked behind the scenes to gain the necessary buy-in from the executives to free up the team members required to work on the projects.

Finally, after weeks of staging, the Action Teams were jump-started. The Training Department was engaged to view how the projects were launched and to codify the various approaches into replicable methodologies. It continued its observation throughout the projects to see what practices really worked and which ones didn't.

Marina was overwhelmed at the speed with which the teams worked and how they moved around organizational boundaries and barriers. In less than 90 days, a host of winning products, services, and processes emerged from the teams. Some of these projects could be completed by the small teams working with the larger organization to integrate the product or practices into scalable initiatives, while others were essentially prototypes that needed to be reviewed by the capital committee for substantial investment.

In multiple cases, it was a side effect or an unintended result that showed the most promise. For example, one team was developing an improved adhesive bandage for everyday cuts and scrapes when it realized that it could incorporate some new material technology that made the bandage completely impervious to liquids and the adhesive stick resiliently to the skin like superglue. The team also was able to incorporate some pharmaceutical breakthroughs that kept the wound free from bacteria. They quickly realized that the applications of the improved bandage went far beyond the home and found uses for it in multiple surgical procedures in hospitals and for stabilizing wounded soldiers on the battlefield.

Step Five: Synchronize

Increasingly, Marina was asked by the team leaders to help secure resources for their projects and to assist with enrolling key stakeholders in the organization. She came to the revelation that her real role was to support those who were making innovation happen and find ways to transition their projects and best practices to the larger organization. (See Table 2.5.) Most importantly, these projects were building a pro-innovation community and culture. Ironically, innovation had gone from being a quick route out of the firm to the key passageway to the top. The new challenge Marina faced was how to engage more of the organization in this innovation community and how to spread the pro-innovation culture throughout it.

Now Marina was ready to revisit developing an integrated innovation process, but this time she was creating it based on what she knew worked in the firm and what didn't. Marina convened a three-day summit of the senior executive leadership team, the innovation leaders, and the Training Department who had been observing the Action Teams to craft an innovation process. There were numerous subgroups that focused on tough issues like divesting parts of the business in favor of investing more aggressively in emerging markets and technologies. The massive conference room looked like the trading floor of the New York Stock Exchange—chaotic, energetic, and purposeful. After several challenging meetings in which the conflicting approaches to innovation were confronted, the two groups developed a process for selecting, managing, and harvesting innovation that functioned at both a strategic level, capturing growth opportunities, and at a tactical level, effectively executing the plan. They gave their process a name, "The Innovation Way."

Table 2.5 Step Five: Synchronize

Objectives	Participants	Actions
Engage leaders throughout the organization to put the vision into operation.	Leadership Team, Action Teams, and other appropriate leaders and experts from throughout the organization. (This step requires the involvement of a large number of participants and needs to be held in a setting of significant size.)	• Convene a summit of the organization's leaders and break them into groups to execute a few strategic targets. • Determine what management practices need to be changed and how to change them; develop action plans. • Develop quick wins and integrate them into operating plans; get authorization to implement them immediately.

Step Six: Specialize

By this time, many parts of the company began to internalize the innovation culture and gradually incorporated new employee development programs around innovation practices. (See Table 2.6.) Human Resources began to identify the DNA of a growth leader, which it would use in hiring and staffing and succession planning. Training integrated these desired cultural elements into most of its programs and offerings. Operations leaders began working new performance measures that supported innovation into their yearly plans. The corporate training unit developed a series of workshops around The Innovation Way and several modules that could be incorporated into all course offerings. These workshops became compulsory and were even included in new employee orientation sessions. These workshops were used to identify potential new innovation leaders and to launch innovation projects throughout the firm.

Table 2.6 Step Six: Specialize

Objectives	Participants	Actions
Jump-start change and innovation Action Teams.	Action Teams and other appropriate leaders and experts from throughout the organization and other appropriate leaders and experts from within and outside the organization.	• Launch a wide array of Action Teams to work on quick-win projects and organizational practices. • Create ways to develop new competencies and expand market opportunities. • Learn what works and what doesn't, and make revisions.

Most of these projects were either incremental in scope or found little traction within the organization. But all the employees felt that they could participate in making innovation happen if they so chose. This engaged many of the disaffected in the organization and began to change the culture of the firm. Marina introduced a suggestion program for these initiatives and a greenhouse fund to provide resources for those projects that showed real promise of growth that could be leveraged throughout the firm.

Step Seven: Systemize

Many of the workshop participants created their own innovation communities and networks throughout the world. Once a year, these workshop groups, with clients and suppliers, assembled to share their triumphs and frustrations, to search and reapply their best practices, and to improve The Innovation Way. (See Table 2.7.) Marina helped make innovation happen by not playing the role of chief innovator, but rather by leading innovation. Within three years, the firm was back on a strong growth path, and Marina left to become CEO of another firm. But she

Table 2.7 Step Seven: Systemize

Objectives	Participants	Actions
Review and revise projects, adjust organizational practices, and learn.	Leadership Team, Action Teams, and other appropriate leaders and experts from throughout the organization	• Create processes for managing multiple projects: key measures, development process, resource allocation, and portfolio management. • Advance projects that demonstrate the ability to produce superior results, modify those with high potential, and stop all others. • Integrate the best practices of the Action Teams into the organization's practices.

moved on knowing that innovation was no longer an orphan; it was now owned by everyone.

Marina Learned as She Went through the Seven Steps

Marina worked through the seven steps of the *Creativize Method* with Jeff. But before she got started, Jeff told her how important it is at the end of each step to stop and think about what she did and where she was going next. This process helped Marina learn as she went along. Marina's story reminds all of us of the importance of learning in striving to be innovative.

At each of the seven steps, it's crucial that you have a way of learning as you progress and that you have a process for being aware of the options that you possess. This should be done regularly both individually and in a community for maximum effectiveness. Consider the key practices of the Innovation Genome (Table 2.8), particularly in regard to how these practices illuminate the approaches and effectiveness of individuals and teams trying to make innovation happen.

Table 2.8   Innovation Genome

Collaborate
- Values
- Hiring and staffing
- Work environment
- Informal networks
- Communication
- Training and development
- Mentoring and coaching
- Empowerment
- Work-life balance
- Resolving conflicts
- Teamwork

Create
- Experiments
- Speculating new markets
- Radical change
- Envisioning the future
- Entrepreneurship
- Spin-offs
- New products and services
- Destroying current practices
- Going around authority and boundaries
- Widening the type and array of projects
- Enlisting gurus with new and weird ideas

Control
- Large-scale operations
- Quality programs
- Continuous improvement processes
- Government regulations
- Policies and procedures
- Organizational structure
- Project management
- Information systems
- Technology

Compete
- Strategy
- Financial measures
- Acquisitions and mergers
- Eliminating unproductive initiatives
- Paying for performance
- Sales and marketing
- Portfolio management
- Resource allocation
- Rapid decision making
- Quick-strike Action Teams

The past, present, and future of an innovation project can be seen by looking through the lenses of the Innovation Genome at people and practices. At each stage of the innovation process, consider the following perspectives and ask the following questions:

Do: When looking forward at your project, community, charter, and goals, consider the Innovation Genome topics from the perspective of, "What do I need to do?" and, "How do I want to do it?"

Doing: When looking at your project while it is in progress, consider the Innovation Genome topics from the perspective of, "What's working and what isn't?" and, "Why?" and, "What changes should we make now?"

Done: When looking back at what has taken place on your project, consider the Innovation Genome topics from the perspective of, "What worked and what didn't? Why? What changes would we make if we ran this step or project again?" and, "What have we learned that can be applied to the current practices of the organization?"

Remember that innovation is typically a work in progress, as Marina's story is. Innovation always provides key insights into the past that will provide some wisdom about the future, but, more importantly, it allows us a wider range of courses to speculate and navigate. This 3-D (do, doing, done) view will help Integral Leaders like Marina not only integrate the four perspectives of the Innovation Genome but also their experiments and experiences into better and new innovation practices.

Throughout the book you will read the phrase, "What is working and what is not." This refers to your ability to learn from the 3-D perspective and to make necessary adjustments during your innovation journey. If you follow the process exactly how it is laid out in the book without adjusting as you experience, you will not likely be successful at leading innovation.

Conclusion

The story of Marina is the story of how the *Creativize Method* emerged in bits and pieces, and how it continues to do so with each firm that uses it. Marina learned the three most valuable lessons of leading innovation. First, innovation is about the future and things you don't know how to do now. So, excessive focus on strategic planning or developing a process for innovation upfront does little to really make innovation happen. You need the interesting experience or the meaningful experiment where you will learn what really works and what doesn't. You have to develop your approach in real time as you go along.

Second, leading innovation is more about enrolling the right people and selecting the right projects than it is about building the right process. Marina had a great vision but little of the necessary competency to pull it off. Rather than try to develop firmwide capabilities, she focused on building on the people she knew could lead innovation and let them select and run the projects. These people and projects carried the pro-innovation culture and imbued the firm with it. Marina discovered that her job wasn't to be the project leader of innovation, but rather to be the head developer of a pro-innovation culture and competencies.

Third, Marina learned that innovation isn't something separate from what leaders do day to day. It's an integral part of all business practices. It comes from Creativizing, adding creativity to, ordinary activities. The key is to select and develop leaders who are flexible and ambidextrous enough to make changes as they discover what works and what doesn't and to integrate these practices into the firm at large.

The *Creativize Method* is the result of dozens of stories like Marina's, each adding or connecting a piece to the innovation puzzle. The open-system approach is used in hundreds of firms worldwide, but it continues to be a work in progress as each use brings new customized versions. The *Creativize Method* can be used to lead innovation in any industry in any location at any level of the organization. It can be used by anyone to make innovation happen.

Enough talking already. Let's get to work. The next seven chapters will walk you through each step in the *Creativize Method* so that you can begin to gain experience and try your own experiments. (See Table 2.9.)

Table 2.9 The Creativize Method

Step and Objectives	Participants	Actions	Marina's Story
Synthesize Assess and diagnose	Entire organization or individual units	• Interview key leaders and stakeholders. • Administer, collect, and analyze data. • Interpret the assessment.	• Marina realized that her company needed growth-focused innovation at a time when sales were declining. • She saw that there were outstanding leaders who had endured numerous CEO transitions.
Strategize Create a vision of the future and a road map that leads to it.	Leadership Team and other appropriate leaders and experts from within and outside the organization	• Identify the current strategic landscape competencies, opportunities, and threats to the organization. • Identify the forces driving the future of the organization, their impact and probability, and the competencies required to meet these future needs.	• Marina worked with the vice president of strategy to get top-level support. • She worked with others to identify emerging trends, and she scanned the company to find pockets of innovation in an overseas unit.

Table 2.9 The Creativize Method (continued)

Step and Objectives	Participants	Actions	Marina's Story
Strategize (continued)		• Integrate the road map to the future into current strategic and operating plans.	• She worked with senior leaders to encourage a culture of innovation and risk taking.
Socialize Establish a shared vision and values in the Leadership Team.	Leadership Team	• Create a shared vision of the desired organization and establish the shared values required to achieve it. • Leaders commit to changes in behavior required to achieve the shared vision and values. • Identify facilitators and a few strategic targets that will lead the organization to the shared vision and values.	• Senior leaders in Marina's company were willing to work through a change process, but they were concerned with missing short-term targets. • Marina and the senior team worked and re-adjusted the strategy to keep it realistic. • Marina showed proof of concept that the changes were doable; the senior team was now on board.

Table 2.9 The Creativize Method (*continued*)

Step and Objectives	Participants	Actions	Marina's Story
Supervise Develop facilitators to lead and sustain change and innovation.	Facilitators	• Train facilitators in change and innovation methods and in facilitation tools and techniques. • Provide opportunities for facilitators to help facilitate Action Teams. • Identify the development needs of facilitators, coach them in improving their effectiveness, and review their progress.	• Marina started with a list of more than 100 potential people to facilitate project teams throughout the company. • She narrowed down the list to 15 of the best self-starters who knew how to get things done. • The facilitators selected and led projects that were innovative, aligned with the new strategy, and achievable.
Synchronize Engage leaders throughout the organization to put the vision into operation.	Leadership Team, Action Teams, and other appropriate leaders and experts from throughout the	• Convene a summit of the organization's leaders and break them into groups to execute a few	• Marina now had to help those facilitators who were making innovation happen. • Marina demonstrated that

Table 2.9 The Creativize Method (continued)

Step and Objectives	Participants	Actions	Marina's Story
Synchronize (continued)	organization. (This step requires the involvement of a large number of participants and needs to be held in a setting of significant size.)	strategic targets. • Determine what management practices need to be changed and how to change them; develop action plans. • Develop quick wins and integrate them into operating plans; get authorization to implement them immediately.	innovation was happening in her company. • Through a summit of company leaders, she coordinated the effort of taking innovation from small projects to a major company focus.
Specialize Jump-start change and innovation Action Teams.	Action Teams and other appropriate leaders and experts from throughout the organization and other appropriate leaders and experts from within and outside the organization	• Launch a wide array of Action Teams to work on quick-win projects and organizational practices. • Create ways to	• Marina led the process of integrating innovation practices into more Action Teams all over the company so that such projects would be more widespread and so that a companywide culture

Table 2.9 The Creativize Method (*continued*)

Step and Objectives	Participants	Actions	Marina's Story
Specialize (*continued*)		develop new competencies and expand market opportunities. • Learn what works and what doesn't, and make revisions.	of innovation would emerge.
Systemize Review and revise projects, adjust organizational practices, and learn.	Leadership Team, Action Teams, and other appropriate leaders and experts from throughout the organization	• Create processes for managing multiple projects: key measures, development process, resource allocation, and portfolio management. • Advance projects that demonstrate the ability to produce superior results, modify those with high	• The culture of innovation had taken hold in Marina's company. • Her role was defined not as chief innovator but as the leader in charge of making innovation happen. • Going forward, Marina's focus is on searching for and reapplying the best innovation practices; the company reviews and revises its direction.

Table 2.9 The Creativize Method (continued)

Step and Objectives	Participants	Actions	Marina's Story
Systemize (continued)		potential, and stop all others. • Integrate the best practices of the Action Teams into the organization's practices.	

PART 2

Implementing Innovation

Step 1:
SYNTHESIZE

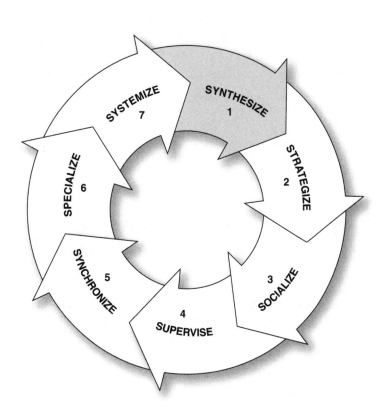

Synthesize Overview

- Objectives
  - Assess and diagnose an organization's Purposes (outcomes)
  - Practices (capabilities, organizational culture and competencies)
  - People (individual employees who create capabilities, culture, and competencies)

- Participants
  - Lead Facilitator
  - Entire organization or individual unit engaged in change and innovation effort

- Actions
  1. Lead Facilitator conducts interviews with key stakeholders.
  2. Lead Facilitator administers the *Change and Innovation Assessment*.
  3. Lead Facilitator collects and Synthesizes assessments.
  4. Lead Facilitator identifies themes and hot spots.

- Time
  - 30 minutes to take the *Change and Innovation Assessment*
  - 2 weeks to collect and process assessment results

This Chapter Will Help Me to Answer:

- What do we know about our organization, and how do we know it?
- What is the role of the senior Leadership Team in the assessment of the organization and the facilitation of change?
- Once we assess our organization, what will this enable us to do?

   This step is called the Synthesize step because it brings together a wide array of the information on the strengths and weaknesses of an organization and diagnoses its chances of achieving its desired goals.

Synthesize in Action—Allegro MicroSystems

Allegro MicroSystems, Inc., a leader in the development of integrated circuits and Hall-effect sensors for automotive, computer, communications, consumer, and industrial markets, was looking for a way to meet the performance expectations of its Japan-based parent company, Sanken Electric Company, Ltd.

Marybeth Perry, vice president of human resources for Allegro, saw improving the culture and competencies of the company as essential to achieving this goal.

To achieve this goal, Marybeth conducted a comprehensive assessment of the organization's current and desired culture. What she found was an organization with multiple personalities. There were significant differences in the assessment profiles between Sanken and Allegro, as well as differences among departments and manufacturing plants within Allegro. Through her interviews, Marybeth learned that Allegro was a collection of subcultures that added up to a dominant culture focused on manufacturing excellence. While this culture was essential to maintaining an incremental improvement focus, it didn't encourage the types of breakthrough innovation the company needed to grow. To foster the growth, Marybeth determined that the organization needed to tone down its Control culture and adopt more of a Create culture.

Marybeth wanted buy-in from the top level before embarking on the change initiative, so she enlisted CEO Dennis Fitzgerald as a sponsor. They held an informal off-site meeting with the executive team at which Marybeth presented the information she had gathered. She asked the executive team to help diagnose the situation. The team began with a discussion of how a new culture might be received by the parent company. The team agreed that Allegro needed a culture change, but only in specific areas. For example, the team wanted to keep the company's strong Control profile in its manufacturing plants, where quality and continuous improvements are essential. However, it also agreed that it would be beneficial to pursue a stronger Create culture in other departments, such as marketing and product development, where innovation was needed.

By letting the executive team interpret the data and create a shared vision of the preferred new culture, Marybeth gained their strong sense of ownership which was needed to make the changes a reality. It was no longer Marybeth's "culture project" but rather a path through which the executives could successfully support their strategy.

Now that she had buy-in from the top, she had the difficult task of making the new culture operational. The executives identified individuals from all levels at Allegro to form a team, which would be responsible for fostering culture change within the organization. These individuals participated in training sessions where they learned how to review culture assessments and how to pass their knowledge along. The team then held town hall meetings and encouraged the workforce to develop action plans that would help the company meet its goals.

By recognizing that Allegro had multiple cultures, Marybeth was able to initiate a change process that was sensitive to these internal differences. She used a number of methods to spark change in her organization. She engaged leaders at all levels, provided them with a shared language so that they were able to decide what type of culture they wanted to create, and encouraged them to develop their own paths to the new culture. Like most firms, Allegro is finding culture change to be challenging. Since it took decades to create the existing culture, it may take a few years to establish a new one.

One key lesson from this example is that *one size doesn't fit all*. By discovering a multifaceted culture within Allegro, Marybeth was able to initiate a change process that was sensitive to diverse perspectives. It will be easier to instill the value of innovation into the mission of the organization now that the organizational change is aligned with Allegro's multifaceted culture. Within this culture, she demonstrated another lesson by *developing a community of highly developed Creativizers* who demonstrated ownership in the company through their respective cultures. Through the different cultures, different groups within Allegro could foster creativity in order to lead to more breakthrough innovation, which would ultimately contribute to the value of the company's initial public offering of stock and would allow the company to grow.

Diagnosing the Organization's Situation

Before an innovation team can create a climate conducive to change, it needs to have a thorough understanding of the way an organization operates. To gain this understanding, the change team will need to gather as much information as it can about individual behavior, organizational practices, and organizational purposes.

One way to gather this information is to interview people who have relevant experience and expertise and who represent a broad range of

Table 3.1   How the Innovation Genome Relates to the Synthesize Step

Collaborate

Do things together.

- Gather the team to talk about needs.
- Ask questions that stimulate dialogue.
- Interview diverse groups.
- Encourage group ownership of the process.
- Strive for a shared interpretation of the situation.

Create

Do things first.

- Talk to individuals inside and outside the organization.
- Speculate on trends and emerging opportunities.
- Interview leaders from different fields.
- Consider a variety of options.

Control

Do things right.

- Talk to the boss.
- Review the plan, specifications, and data.
- Identify roles and responsibilities.
- Check facts.
- Identify areas that need improvement.

Compete

Do things fast.

- Start with the results in mind.
- Focus on a few key financial indicators.
- Talk to the key players.
- Compare findings against competitors.
- Identify performers and nonperformers.
- Look for quick wins.

roles, functions, departments, and levels. The interviewers want to find out what the individuals believe about the organization, such as its uses of power and influence, its processes for decision making, and its history and desired future. By the end of this task, the interviews will form a collective story about the organization.

Another information-gathering method is the *Change and Innovation Assessment*, presented in this chapter, which helps diagnose the relationships between the current state of the organization and its desired state, as well as where organizational levels, departments, and leaders are aligned or not aligned. This assessment uses the principles of the Innovation Genome to create a standard by which People (personal approach to work), Practices (culture, competencies, and methods), and Purposes (outcomes) can be compared, and by which corresponding actions can be taken to move the organizational culture toward a desired outcome.

An operating map can also be useful in the assessment process. The map provides a detailed representation of how an organization functions as a structural, technical, and systematic entity. The operating map is a more comprehensive version of a flowchart and gives a functional overview of how all the various groups within an organization operate as a single entity. To this end, it includes departments, processes, projects, boundaries, connections, interactions, and decisions. An operating map can be used in a number of the seven steps, including the Strategize and Synchronize steps, which come later in the process. How to create an effective operating map is detailed in the book *Policy Games for Strategic Management: Pathways into the Unknown* by Richard Duke and Jac Geurts.[1]

Once the information has been gathered, the innovation team will need to make a case for transformation that is clear and recognizable to the leaders, staff, and employees of the organization. Making this case is somewhat of an art because it requires constant interpretation, reshaping, and reinterpretation until a common understanding and point of view emerge.

Enlisting Sponsors and Key Stakeholders

The most important aspects of value creation in an organization, such as culture or competency development, seldom have an "owner" because they transcend the typical roles and responsibility of any particular function. For this reason, it's vital that change and innovation initiatives have a Sponsor who can passionately champion these causes beyond the traditional boundaries of the organization. Sponsors must possess a unique combination of power and influence, as well as a deep understanding of the company. They must understand where the company wants to go and what it will take to get it there. As such, the Sponsors often need to enlist a diverse community of activists and practitioners to their cause.

Finding the right person to be a Sponsor is vital to the success of the transformation process. The Sponsor has a number of responsibilities, including gaining the support of key stakeholders and making sure that there are appropriate levels of resources to get the job done. The Sponsor needs to encourage experimentation and to push to get results on key initiatives. The Sponsor is also responsible for communicating the findings and results to the rest of the organization.

It's important that the Sponsor be well connected at all levels of the organization and have the power and political capital to endure turbulent dynamics. The more strategic and pervasive the initiative, the more powerful and influential the Sponsor should be, and vice versa. Political capital is finite; don't waste it.

Creativizer Survival Skills

Once a change process is under way, the effectiveness of the transformation is inextricably bound up with the success or failure of the individuals initiating the change. If these individuals are compromised or ousted from the project, the initiative usually fails. In order to ensure the sustainability of the process, these individuals need to gain a set of skills that will keep them viable.

There are a number of ways that Creativizers can increase their effectiveness in this type of situation. At the top of the list is remembering that the Sponsor and other key stakeholders are the owners of the change. As such, the agents of change need to stay in touch with the Sponsor.

The Creativizer also needs to communicate with stakeholders, especially those who are resistant to the change, to establish a rapport. To accomplish this, it's important to appeal to the values of the stakeholders and use their language. It's also a good idea to focus most of the attention on stakeholders who have the ability to make change happen or the power to stop it. The Creativizer needs to understand why a stakeholder might be resistant to the change and identify remedies.

It's also important that initiatives be diversified to ensure small wins, which will demonstrate that the efforts were worth the trouble. It also can be beneficial for the Creativizer to pilot the change first to help reduce resistance.

One of the most important tasks in the process is selecting the right area to change. This point is crucial. As a general rule, one of the best areas for change is one in crisis. Just as people don't change simply because they've read a self-help book, organizations don't change because they have a change plan. People, and organizations, respond more readily to change when there is a crisis, such as severe financial problems. For example, if a company is on the verge of bankruptcy, the executives will most likely be willing to make changes because the pain of staying in the current situation outweighs the challenges of changing it. The crisis reverses the risk-reward ratio from what it would be if the organization were in a stable financial situation. A crisis, or "burning platform," forces people as well as organizations to confront the reality of their situation. This means that failure can be fertile ground for breakthrough change and innovation.

The same risk-reward ratio is reversed when an organization is significantly outperforming requirements, expectations, and competitors. Being on "a roll" means that the organization can take on a higher risk profile, similar to that of a venture capitalist who can make more speculative investments with higher rates of return than an ordinary investor. This makes high-performing areas ideal places to take on substantial transformational initiatives.

The objective of facilitating change and innovation is to direct and harness the natural dynamics that can naturally lead to the desired outcomes. The rule of thumb is that it is more favorable to launch a breakthrough transformational initiative where a part of an organization is in either a crisis or is significantly outperforming the norm. Conversely, more incremental initiatives are better suited for those parts of the organization that are currently operating effectively but still need to enhance their value.

Remember that the more significant the transformation, the more likely there will be greater resistance from key stakeholders. This means that maintaining a positive relationship with the initiatives' Sponsor and allowing enough time to develop buy-in from other key stakeholders is of paramount importance.

Creating a Diagnosis from the Assessments

Interpreting assessments is like reading a map. They are acts of translation. Assessments allow us to make sense of a complex array of activities and develop travel plans to desired destinations. The power of the *Change and Innovation Assessment* is that it provides a map for comparing the current and desired states for a variety of situations, such as individual and leadership preferences, organizational culture and competencies, and value propositions pursued.

The key to interpreting assessments is to describe what the visual image may mean in terms of tangible organizational practices. Like reading an X-ray, an assessment represents the actual condition of the organization. For example, a high score in the Compete quadrant may represent a strong pay-for-performance scheme that overshadows other key business practices. Ask members of the group being assessed for specific practices that confirm or refute the profile. The objective is to translate the graphic into meaningful examples the group recognizes. The preliminary diagnosis also includes seeing where there is alignment and where there is diversity or misalignment.

It is essential that the Leadership Team have a shared vision of the outcomes it seeks and has an understanding of how these outcomes will be pursued. Just because certain team members don't speak up doesn't necessarily mean that they are in agreement. Their silence could be a sign of resistance to the vision the team has created. If this happens, draw the individuals out through questions, and ask the other team members to address their concerns. It's important to validate their point of view to ensure that they establish personal ownership of the shared vision.

Conversely, different views of the desired outcome may create conflicts in the team. Look for areas of agreement so as to redirect the conflict into constructive solutions. The object is to build on commonalities, not to create a compromised view of the desired state.

Synthesize Phase 1: Conduct Interviews with Key Stakeholders

Before completing the *Change and Innovation Assessment*, the individuals who are serving as Lead Facilitators will want to conduct interviews with key stakeholders within the company. In doing so, the Lead Facilitators are trying to frame specifically what the challenges are within the company.

One of the most common challenges is solving or correcting a problem. That is, understanding what's not working. The interviewer is trying to develop a point of view about why something might be going on. The assessment itself may not tell the complete story about the inner workings of the organization.

The problem may be as small as a personality conflict or conflict over a specific project, or something much larger, such as a new competitor that has entered the market with a product the company doesn't offer or company supervision that is wrong in light of market shifts.

Another challenge is to understand what opportunities you think your company has that it's not taking advantage of. When dealing with an opportunity, a company needs to act quickly before the opportunity is no longer available. This can be done through things like solving a problem for a client and then selling the solution to other clients. What's important in the Synthesize step is being able to recognize where opportunities exist.

These two challenges are very different animals and require entirely different actions. The object of the interviews is to try to determine the company's needs and then to put the frame around the assessment. This helps to provide a specific idea of why something is happening.

The following are examples of the types of questions the interviewer will want to ask the stakeholders.

Current Client Situation

What's working in your organization? Not working? Why? Note that you don't need technical descriptions but rather examples, stories, benchmarks, and visions.

> What results do you seek? Why?
>
> What are the key opportunities and target areas for successful change at your organization?
>
> How do you currently plan to capture these opportunities?
>
> Discuss the next steps in the work streams, key players, current resources and those needed in the future, and the major obstacles to success.
>
> Who is doing what and when to make this happen?
>
> What specific behaviors and deliverables are you looking for from the innovation process to help you reach your desired results?

General Context Questions

The following are questions that help uncover the general context of the organization.

Example Business Situation Questions

Describe the general condition of your industry and sector. Has your firm had any recent crises or triumphs? Who are your main competitors? Who are your main clients? What are your main strengths? Weaknesses? What innovations are likely to drive this sector? What do shareholders look for from your firm? What do you see happening in the next three years?

Example Strategy Questions

Describe the strategy of the business. How is the strategy translated into implementation plans? What barriers exist, if any, to fully implement the strategy?

Example Vision Questions

What is your vision for your business unit? How was the vision developed? How do you communicate this vision? Do you think others in the company agree with this vision?

Example Value System Questions

What are the values of your business? Can you give some examples of how these values are demonstrated?

Example Culture Questions

Who defines or maintains the company's culture? What was the last major problem or conflict in the business and how was it resolved? How well do you think the business culture is aligned with the business strategy?

Example Organizational Structure Questions

Describe how your organizational structure is related to the execution of the business strategy. Have you made any structural changes recently? How did these changes come about? Describe the outcome of these structural changes.

Example Communications Questions

How do people find out what is happening in the business? Do you have an internal communications strategy? Is there any communications plan in effect for the efforts in which we are participating?

Example Decision-Making Questions

Tell me how you decide which projects are a priority. Does this work? Who directs this process? How do they direct it?

Example Rewards and Incentives Question

How are you rewarded for advancing business goals?

Example Organizational Capability Questions

How would you rate your capability relative to leading competitors? Do significant accomplishments result from heroic efforts of individuals, or are accomplishments largely the result of processes?

Example Key Skills Questions

Are organizational capabilities translated into defined individual competencies? Do defined individual competencies drive education, development, or staffing activities? Do you perceive any major skill gaps now or in the future? Do you acquire firms to get core competencies that you require?

Example Leadership Questions

What leadership qualities will this organization need in the future? What kinds of governance mechanisms will you need, that is, cross-functional steering committees, executives-management teams, and so on?

Example Morale Questions

What is the leading driver of morale in this organization? How would you characterize morale currently?

Example Tolerance for Change Questions

What particular challenges do you face in implementing change? Do you find employees flexible and willing to change? Why do you think this is the case?

Example Innovation Questions

Can you describe your vision for innovation? What will innovation produce, enhance, or make obsolete? What processes and practices do you have in place? Who are your innovation leaders? Where is innovation happening?

Synthesize Phase 2: Administer the *Change and Innovation Assessment*

Introduction

The primary purpose of the *Change and Innovation Assessment* is two-fold:

> *First*, it provides you with an accurate measure of the values and beliefs that drive you when you make leadership decisions and influence your team.

> *Second*, it shows you where to direct your action planning for the change and innovation you need to insure your team's future success and growth. It provides you with a template that you can use to plan and make decisions that will create value.

> *This approach focuses on outcomes!* It is effective because it focuses on the one thing that you must do to maintain your team's competitiveness—*create outcomes that meet future demands!*

Administer the *Change and Innovation Assessment*

Below (Table 3.2) is a timeline that lays out the steps to take in order to administer the assessment and get results in a timely manner. It is followed by the *Change and Innovation Assessment* and answer key.

Table 3.2   Assessment Timeline

Tasks	Date	Notes
Letter from change team to all assessment participants		
Web assessment addresses assigned and communicated (if online version)		
Assessments completed and collected		
Assessments aggregated and divided by groups		
Report presented to change group and distributed		
Analysis and diagnosis completed		

This assessment contains twenty-one questions (seven for each of the three sections) about you and your organization's current and desired future purposes, current and desired practices, and current and desired personal approach toward work. (See Tables 3.3–3.4.)

Your Team or Unit. While taking this section of the assessment think about the team (or organizational unit) that you lead or belong to right now.

Directions. The seven questions below ask about *how you define success for your team today and in the future.* What results or outcomes does your team need to achieve in the future to help the company realize its strategy? Under each question, *rank the four statements (recognizing they are all important) according to the order of importance your team puts on them currently and also in the order necessary for your unit to succeed* in the future. That is, which statement is most like your team's current desired outcomes and your needed future outcomes? Assign 1, 2, 3, or 4 to the statements A, B, C, and D depending on which one will have the 1st, 2nd, 3rd, or 4th priority for your team in the future. Assign 4 if the statement is most like your team's needed future and 1 if the statement is least like your team's needed future. *We have you rank the options because leadership is about making difficult decisions.*

Remember that for each of the seven questions, statements A, B, C, and D must be assigned a 1, 2, 3 or 4. No statement may be assigned the same number as another statement (forced rank).

Table 3.3   Example of Question 1 Filled Out

1	My organization defines success as:	Current	Desired
A	The development of people and teams	2	1
B	Having unique and the newest products and services	1	3
C	Market share and competitive leadership	4	4
D	Dependable and efficient operations	3	2

Table 3.4   Purpose Questions
Outcomes and value your organization intends to create

1	My organization defines success as:	Current	Desired
A	The development of people and teams		
B	Having unique and the newest products and services		
C	Market share and competitive leadership		
D	Dependable and efficient operations		

Table 3.4 Purpose Questions *(continued)*

2	My organization defines success as:	Current	Desired
A	A harmonious workplace		
B	Being an innovator		
C	Superior rates of return		
D	Being a low-cost operator		

3	Success in my organization is measured by:	Current	Desired
A	Improving employee satisfaction		
B	Increasing the number of products/services launched		
C	Increasing profits		
D	Reducing errors and the percentage of failures		

4	Success in my organization is measured by:	Current	Desired
A	Decreasing turnover of key personnel		
B	Expanding diversity of products/services pipelined		
C	Increasing the rate of return on investments		
D	Adhering to budget		

5	Success in my organization is measured by:	Current	Desired
A	Expanding workforce diversity		
B	Increasing new market growth		
C	Increasing cash on hand		
D	Achieving milestones		

Table 3.4   Purpose Questions (continued)

6	Success in my organization is measured by:	Current	Desired
A	Increasing the number of days for employee training		
B	Expanding percentage of sales from new products/services		
C	Reducing product/service time to market		
D	Increasing percent of on-time deliveries		

7	Success in my organization is measured by:	Current	Desired
A	Reducing grievances and complaints from employees		
B	Improving margins through innovations		
C	Increasing stock price		
D	Reducing redundancy and waste		

Table 3.5   Example of Score Totals

Current Scores		A	B	C	D
1	My organization defines success as	4	3	2	1
2	My organization defines success as	1	3	2	4
3	Success in my organization is measured by	4	1	3	2
4	Success in my organization is measured by	4	2	1	3
5	Success in my organization is measured by	2	3	4	1
6	Success in my organization is measured by	4	3	1	2
7	Success in my organization is measured by	3	1	2	4
	Total	22	16	15	17

Table 3.5   Example of Score Totals *(continued)*

Desired Scores		A	B	C	D
1	My organization defines success as	4	3	1	2
2	My organization defines success as	4	2	1	3
3	Success in my organization is measured by	2	4	3	1
4	Success in my organization is measured by	2	3	1	4
5	Success in my organization is measured by	3	1	2	4
6	Success in my organization is measured by	2	3	1	4
7	Success in my organization is measured by	1	3	2	4
	Total	18	19	11	22

Table 3.6   Purposes Answer Key

Current Scores		A	B	C	D
1	My organization defines success as				
2	My organization defines success as				
3	Success in my organization is measured by				
4	Success in my organization is measured by				
5	Success in my organization is measured by				
6	Success in my organization is measured by				
7	Success in my organization is measured by				
	Total				

Table 3.6   Purposes Answer Key *(continued)*

Desired Scores	A	B	C	D
1 My organization defines success as				
2 My organization defines success as				
3 Success in my organization is measured by				
4 Success in my organization is measured by				
5 Success in my organization is measured by				
6 Success in my organization is measured by				
7 Success in my organization is measured by				
Total				

Graphing Your Purposes Results

The Innovation Genome is used to help you create a visual picture of your Purposes results (Figs. 3.1 and 3.2). This visual picture allows you to better see and communicate the pattern of your Purposes to others. Start by plotting your Current scores using the key below. The highest score among A–D is given the value of 4; the next highest, a 3; and so on to 1. Use the example above as a guide. (See Tables 3.5–3.6.)

Column A represents the Collaborate Quadrant (upper left corner)

Column B represents the Compete Quadrant (lower right corner)

Column C represents the Control Quadrant (lower left corner)

Column D represents the Create Quadrant (upper right corner)

Once you have completed the Current scores, follow the same process for the Desired scores. (See Table 3.7 below.)

Table 3.7 Example of Score Totals

Column	Quadrant	Current Score	Rings	Desired	Rings
A	Collaborate	22	4	18	2
B	Create	16	2	19	3
C	Compete	15	1	11	1
D	Control	17	3	22	4

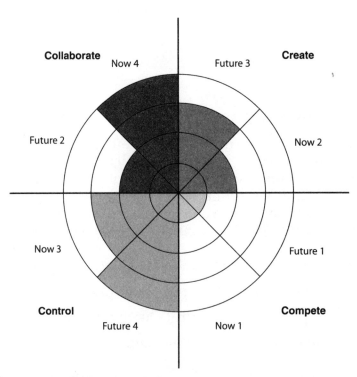

Figure 3.1 Example Assessment Profile

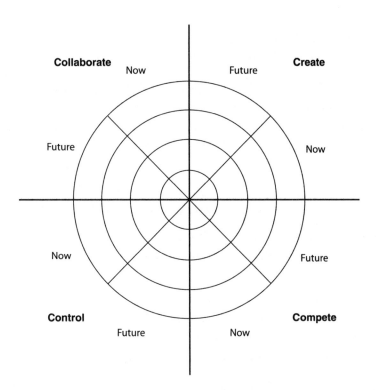

Figure 3.2

Tables 3.8–3.11 on the following pages walk you through the same process for the Practices and People questions.

Take the Test Online

The entire *Change and Innovation Assessment Test* is available online, and will automatically graph your test results for you. Take the test free at www.competingvalues.com.

Table 3.8   Practice Questions
Organizational culture, competency, and processes

- *Organizational competency* is the collective learning, ability, and skill of your organization to create value. Organizational competencies can reside in people, processes, and practices.
- *Organizational culture* is the shared beliefs, attitudes, rituals, and behaviors of an organization.

8	The mission of my organization is to:	Current	Desired
A	Encourage a cohesive community in the workplace and develop knowledge in the workforce.		
B	Stimulate innovative new products and services and growth in new markets and other emerging opportunities.		
C	Drive for increased speed and higher profits.		
D	Systematically produce efficiency and quality in its operations.		

9	My organization makes strategic plans by:	Current	Desired
A	Considering the collective competencies and culture of the firm.		
B	Speculating about emerging trends and prospects.		
C	Focusing on immediate and valuable market opportunities.		
D	Benchmarking internal processes and industry standards.		

10 The core processes of my organization are used to: Current Desired

A Build teams and facilitate learning and communication.

B Experiment with new ideas, methods, and technologies.

C Set and achieve financial goals.

D Implement systems and technology.

11 My organization makes decisions: Current Desired

A Through consensus building.

B Through brainstorming a range of possibilities.

C By simplifying complex issues and quantifying the results.

D By adhering to a clear set of rules and procedures.

12 My organization invests in: Current Desired

A High-potential people.

B New ideas.

C Winning projects and ventures.

D Systems and technology.

Table 3.8 Practice Questions (*continued*)

13 My organization improves performance by:	Current	Desired
A Maintaining an atmosphere of cooperation and community.		
B Giving freedom to individuals with unique vision and talent.		
C Paying a premium to individuals who achieve ambitious financial results.		
D Establishing a path for job planning, review, and promotion.		

14 My organization develops its people through:	Current	Desired
A Empowerment and mentoring.		
B Opportunities for new experiences and experiments.		
C Exposure to difficult challenges and obstacles.		
D Technical training and incremental increases in responsibility.		

Table 3.9   Practices Answer Key

Current Scores	A	B	C	D
8 The mission of my organization is to				
9 My organization makes strategic plans by				
10 The core processes of my organization are used to				
11 My organization makes decisions				
12 My organization invests in				
13 My organization improves performance by				
14 My organization develops its people through				
Total				

Desired Scores	A	B	C	D
8 The mission of my organization is to				
9 My organization makes strategic plans by				
10 The core processes of my organization are used to				
11 My organization makes decisions				
12 My organization invests in				
13 My organization improves performance by				
14 My organization develops its people through				
Total				

Graphing Your Practices Results

The Innovation Genome is used to help you create a visual picture of your Practices results (Fig. 3.3). This visual picture allows you to more effectively see and communicate the pattern of your Practices to others.

Start by plotting your Current scores using the key below. The highest score among A–D is given the value of 4; the next highest, a 3; and so on to 1. If the Collaborate Quadrant or A on the answer key received a value of 2, you would fill in the closest two cells in the Current Collaborate Quadrant to the center of the circle. Continue with all of the quadrants until you have filled in the cells for each of the four scores. Once you have completed the Current scores, follow the same process for the Desired scores.

Column A represents the Collaborate Quadrant (upper left corner)

Column B represents the Compete Quadrant (lower right corner)

Column C represents the Control Quadrant (lower left corner)

Column D represents the Create Quadrant (upper right corner)

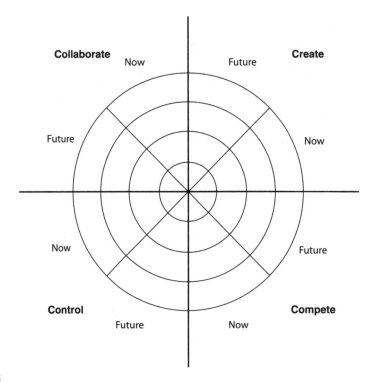

Figure 3.3

Table 3.10   People Questions
   You, individuals

15 My mission is to:	Current	Desired
A Encourage a cohesive community in the workplace and develop knowledge in the workforce.		
B Stimulate innovative new products and services and growth in new markets and other emerging opportunities.		
C Drive for increased speed and higher profits.		
D Systematically produce efficiency and quality in operations.		

16 I make strategic plans by:	Current	Desired
A Considering the collective competencies and culture of the firm.		
B Speculating about emerging trends and prospects.		
C Focusing on immediate and valuable market opportunities.		
D Benchmarking internal processes and industry standards.		

17 My core processes are used to:	Current	Desired
A Build teams and facilitate learning and communication.		
B Experiment with new ideas, methods, and technologies.		
C Set and achieve financial goals.		
D Implement systems and technology.		

Table 3.10 People Questions *(continued)*

18 I make decisions:	Current	Desired
A Through consensus-building.		
B Through brainstorming a range of possibilities.		
C By simplifying complex issues and quantifying the results.		
D By adhering to a clear set of rules and procedures.		

19 I invest in:	Current	Desired
A High-potential people.		
B New ideas.		
C Winning projects and ventures.		
D Systems and technology.		

20 I improve performance by:	Current	Desired
A Maintaining an atmosphere of cooperation and community.		
B Giving freedom to individuals with unique vision and talent.		
C Paying a premium to individuals who achieve ambitious financial results.		
D Establishing a path for job planning, review, and promotion.		

21 I develop people through:	Current	Desired
A Empowerment and mentoring.		
B Creating opportunities for new experiences and experiments.		
C Exposure to difficult challenges and obstacles.		
D Technical training and incremental increases in responsibility.		

Table 3.11 People Answer Key

Current Scores	A	B	C	D
15 My mission is to				
16 I make strategic plans by				
17 My core processes are used to				
18 I make decisions				
19 I invest in				
20 I improve performance by				
21 I develop people through				
Total				

Table 3.11   People Answer Key *(continued)*

Desired Scores	A	B	C	D
15 My mission is to				
16 I make strategic plans by				
17 My core processes are used to				
18 I make decisions				
19 I invest in				
20 I improve performance by				
21 I develop people through				
Total				

Graphing Your People (Individual) Results

The Innovation Genome is used to help you create a visual picture of your People results (Fig. 3.4). This visual picture allows you to better see and communicate the pattern of your leadership competencies to others.

Start by plotting your Current scores using the key below. The highest score among A–D is given the value of 4; the next highest, a 3; and so on to 1. If the Collaborate Quadrant or A on the answer key received a value of 2, you would fill in the closest two cells in the Current Collaborate Quadrant to the center of the circle. Continue with all the quadrants until you have filled in the cells for each of the four scores. Once you have completed the Current scores, follow the same process for the Desired scores.

Column A represents the Collaborate Quadrant (upper left corner)

Column B represents the Compete Quadrant (lower right corner)

Column C represents the Control Quadrant (lower left corner)

Column D represents the Create Quadrant (upper right corner)

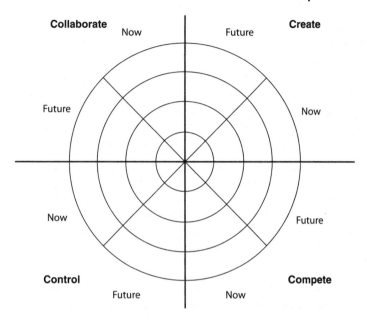

Figure 3.4

The profiles resulting from the assessments show the web of tensions among the four quadrants of the Innovation Genome—Collaborate, Create, Compete, and Control. For example, a company may be 80 percent Create and 20 percent Control. To be higher in one quadrant requires a lower score or percentage in another quadrant. In other words, to become stronger in one quadrant, a company must become weaker in another.

If the company is extreme in one quadrant, the desired change is often to become extreme in another quadrant because people often rebel against the existing way a company is run. To ensure that this doesn't happen, after all the data is Synthesized, it may be necessary to redraw lines so that the desired profile is less extreme.

One of the primary purposes of the *Change and Innovation Assessment* is to take a look at the alignment of the organization. What does the current profile of the organization look like? Where is the organization aligned? There are several different ways that an organization can look at alignment:

- *Business units or geographies:* A look at different units, such as marketing and finance, or at different geographic areas, such as Asia and North America.

- *Organizational levels:* A look at the alignment of leaders and staff within the organization.
- *Current and desired states:* Where are we today? Where do we want to be tomorrow?
- *Management capabilities, organizational culture and competencies, and performance outcomes:* A look at the People, Practices, and Purposes in the organization.
- *Difference between individual questions in the assessment:* A look at specific outcomes, practices, culture, and competencies.

When an assessment shows that a company is not aligned, there will need to be additional research to determine why. Generally there are three reasons why the company has this situation.

- *Divisions within companies are not equal.* For example, manufacturing's profile may look different from the general profile of the rest of the company. This is because manufacturing plays a different role. In this case, the company has a general culture with subcultures such as the manufacturing division. It is appropriate that different divisions have different cultures.
- *There is a pull or transition occurring within the company.* A company may be going through a transition, and it may be someone's job to pull the company in a new direction. The more misaligned a company is, the more conflict will occur. However, conflict can be productive in this case.
- *Skewed culture and competencies.* A company may have manufacturing pursuing innovation which is the wrong direction for manufacturing. This is when the alignment of the company becomes critical in proceeding with the change process.

Completing Your Profile

The company profile resulting from the assessment acts as a springboard for discussion within the organization. It presents important questions like: Who are we and where are we going? Answering these questions is important because what the profile does is tell the organization what it *is*. There are a few points to keep in mind while reviewing the organization's profile.

Balance is good because it allows an organization to be effective in all quadrants, and an organization is only as good as its weakest quadrant; however, balance can also mean "doing nothing really well." Sometimes it's better for the organization to pick its strengths. This implies trade-offs. To be stronger in one quadrant, an organization may have to give up something from another quadrant. It is important to remember that a company cannot be all things to all people. Strategy is about what you're not going to do, not what you are going to do.

Range is also important. It is extremely difficult to be proficient in all areas. High-performing states where the company is proficient in all areas are usually relatively short in duration and very difficult to achieve.

The assessment picture can be used to compare and contrast. The Creativizer should use it to try to tell a story about the organization. The job of the person interpreting the model is to see how things are. This person is not the expert but simply someone instigating a discussion. The discussion can't be abstract; it must lead people to telling tangible, tactical stories. To make this happen, the Creativizer should ask questions like:

- Where are there major differences in the profiles? Why?
  - Culture and competencies.
  - Outcomes, culture, competencies, and managerial capabilities.
  - Between your business unit and your operating unit.
  - Between your operating units.
  - Within your unit.
  - Other surveys.
- What are the strengths and weaknesses?
  - Your unit.
  - Yourself.
- Where are the biggest gaps between the current and desired profile? What pressing problems does this create for your business?

The stories that result from these questions being asked should address things like: why the organization is in its current state, why it's struggling to get to where it needs to be, and what the obstacles and pressing problems are in getting there.

People are often shocked, angry, or initially resistant to the outcome of the assessment. In reacting, it is important that people ask themselves, "Do I understand it?" "Is it true?" "Do I really want to work on it?"

Understanding how people may react to the data is just one of a number of points to keep in mind and deal with to ensure that a shared point of view is developed among a Leadership Team or other group. The first point is to avoid group-think and instead to redirect conflict into creative resolution. It's also a good idea to create and reinforce the current and desired state of the organization and to communicate the results.

The profile picture in and of itself does not mean anything. The key is in the interpretation of the picture. It must tell a story of the organization. It is important that people do not become obsessed with the picture but instead use it to look for trends, big gaps, and misalignments. Having something visual can help tremendously in this process, which is why the picture is necessary.

Synthesize Phase 3: Identify Themes and Hot Spots

Once the company has conducted interviews and looked at the profiles resulting from the assessments, the next task is to figure out if there are themes within the data. These themes help spotlight problems. For example, if a recurrent theme in the interviews is competition and if the Compete category is the company's strongest profile, it could be that the company has become so competitive that it has become an undesirable place to work. The hot spot would then be how to make the company a better place to work, or how to eliminate some of the extreme forms of competition.

Theme: "Are there any overarching things we're seeing?"

Hot Spot: "Can we identify something that's really a problem?"

The problem can be anything from very large and specific to something as small as one person. For example, the extreme competitiveness may be a cultural issue for the organization and will take a lot of effort to change. On the other hand, members of a team or group may find themselves behaving in such a competitive manner simply as a response to one argumentative member of the team. The second problem isn't necessarily easy to handle, but it's a much smaller problem than changing the culture of the organization.

The following will assist in identifying themes and hot spots.

Themes and Hot Spots

This is a summary of all the assessment and diagnostic work of the Synthesize step. It creates a picture of where the organization is now and where it needs to go.

- Where are we now and where do we need to go?
  - Compare and contrast current and desired Purposes, Practices, and People profiles with the interview results.
- Where are we aligned? Misaligned?
  - Which groups?
  - What does this mean?
- Interviews.
  - What's important?
  - What's working? What's not?
  - What do people think we need to do? Why?
- What do we need to do to get there? (point of view)
  - What does this mean?
  - What do we need to do?

Conclusion

1. What do we know about our organization, and how do we know it?

The purpose of the Synthesize step is to collect and process information from a variety of sources within the organization. Some of these sources are traditional interviews and discussions with stakeholders, while some are sophisticated tools such as the *Change and Innovation Assessment.* Organizational information can be very easy to find, while some can be latent or hidden within the organization.

2. What is the role of the senior leadership team in the assessment of the organization and the facilitation of change?

The senior Leadership Team is essential to this process. Its members' shared vision of the organization's future is critical to recruiting sponsors within the organization who will ultimately lead the various elements of the organizational change process.

3. Once we assess our organization, what will this enable us to do?

Now that the organization has assessed its current situation and has identified how it views creativity and innovation, it has a springboard from which to launch into the upcoming phases of the *Creativize Method*. Knowing where to start is the key to mapping out the rest of the organization's course.

The 3-D View

Remember from Chapter 2 that innovation is typically a work in progress. Innovation always provides key insights into the past that will in turn provide some wisdom about the future, but more importantly it allows us a wider range of courses to speculate and navigate. Once the Synthesize step is complete, it is important for the Creativizers and other appropriate people to ask in a separate meeting the Do, Doing, Done questions by thinking around the Innovation Genome. It is important that the meeting take place close enough to the Synthesize step so that everyone remembers the experience but enough removed so that people have had time to think about what really happened.

Do . . .
Looking forward to future projects, communities, charters, and goals that will flow from the Synthesize step, consider the questions in Table 3.12 from the four perspectives of the Innovation Genome.

Table 3.12

Collaborate View
- What do I need to do?
- How do I want to do it?

Create View
- What do I need to do?
- How do I want to do it?

Control View
- What do I need to do?
- How do I want to do it?

Compete View
- What do I need to do?
- How do I want to do it?

Doing . . .
Looking at any current work taking place around the *Creativize Method* at your organization, consider the questions in Table 3.13.

Table 3.13

Collaborate View
- What's working and what isn't? Why?
- What changes should we make?

Create View
- What's working and what isn't? Why?
- What changes should we make?

Control View
- What's working and what isn't? Why?
- What changes should we make?

Compete View
- What's working and what isn't? Why?
- What changes should we make?

Done . . .

Looking back at what has taken place with the Synthesize step and any projects that have been launched, consider the questions in Table 3.14.

Table 3.14

Collaborate View
- What worked and what didn't? Why?
- What changes would we make if we ran this step or project again?
- What have we learned that can be applied to the current practices of the organization?

Create View
- What worked and what didn't? Why?
- What changes would we make if we ran this step or project again?
- What have we learned that can be applied to the current practices of the organization?

Control View
- What worked and what didn't? Why?
- What changes would we make if we ran this step or project again?
- What have we learned that can be applied to the current practices of the organization?

Compete View
- What worked and what didn't? Why?
- What changes would we make if we ran this step or project again?
- What have we learned that can be applied to the current practices of the organization?

Step 2:
STRATEGIZE

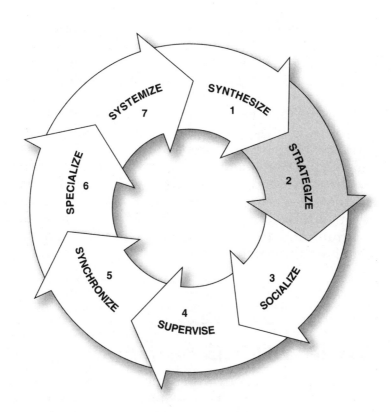

Strategize Overview

- Objective:
  - Create a vision of the future and a road map that leads to it.

- Participants
  - Leadership Team, Lead Facilitator, Sponsor, and other appropriate leaders and experts from within and outside of the organization.

- Actions
  1. Sponsor and Lead Facilitator select diverse and insightful individuals to join the Leadership Team as participants in this "Think Tank" process.
  2. Leadership Team, thinking creatively around the Innovation Genome, identifies competitors, customers, innovations, and driving forces that are currently creating opportunities and presenting threats to the organization.
  3. Leadership Team identifies current core competencies (i.e., unique strategic capabilities) of the organization and validates them.
  4. Leadership Team, thinking creatively around the Innovation Genome, identifies forces driving the future of the organization, their impact and probability.
  5. Leadership Team identifies desired core competencies and ways to stretch and leverage current ones, as well as develop new ones, to meet future needs.
  6. Leadership Team creates a brief but clear way to communicate the future and the path to it to be shared and discussed throughout the organization.

- Time
  - 2 days

This Chapter Will Help Me to Answer:

- How do we determine our firm's competitive advantage?
- Who develops the firm's strategy, and who owns it?
- How does innovation link to strategy?

Introduction

The purpose of the Strategize step is to assist an organization in "seeing the future first." In other words, it helps the company to focus on seeing where future value is going to be created, as well as where it is being created at this time. By Strategizing, we begin to understand where opportunities exist (opportunity space), and we create a shared vision or point of view of the future of the company, as well as focus in on in what direction the company desires to go and what core competencies it has or needs to develop to get there.

Upon completion of the Strategize step, a company should have a firm grasp on its vision, where it wants to go, and the tools and road map needed to set the plan in action.

Strategize in Action—Time Inc.

Time Inc.'s string of hits all started with *People* magazine in 1974, the first mass-market personality-driven news magazine marketed to women. *People* was radical for its time because it was a big departure from the more hard-news fare of the Time empire—*Time*, *Fortune*, and *Money* magazines. The *People* brand blazed a trail for new and innovative categories of magazines that built on its base of educated female readers. By the mid-1990s *InStyle* was introduced as a hybrid concept that combined women's interest in celebrities with home, fashion, and lifestyle. When it was first introduced, *InStyle* was criticized because it didn't appeal to a previously developed market, but in a few short years it not only found its audience but created an entirely new market segment along the way.

Time Inc. then assembled a small team to develop a suite of magazines to extend the *People* brand into adjacent categories. The team spent two years conducting consumer research, which led to five potential magazine concepts. Each of these concepts was tested with readers, and a unique new idea targeting educated women in the 25–54 age range emerged. This concept became *Real Simple* magazine, and its goal was to help its readers make life easier in an increasingly complex and demanding world.

Time Inc., started the development of *Real Simple* by establishing a team whose members talked to the readers of existing magazines and identified themes and trends. They looked at lists of best-selling books. They looked at other industries as well as the advertisers with whom they already had relationships. They talked with a diverse array of editors and advertisers. They conducted extensive marketing studies and consumer research. They spoke with thought leaders in the industry. These groups worked together and analyzed trends. One of the early revelations from all this work was that technology made peoples' lives busier rather than easier and that people had a desire to simplify their lives. They also realized that no other magazine was reaching readers with this lifestyle need. The *Real Simple* team began to piece together the shared vision of the magazine concept through a highly focused, yet emergent ad hoc, process. By the time it was through, the team had one of the best-researched concepts in Time Inc., but there was still left much to be developed.

As the consumer marketing director on the team, Steve Sachs began to learn that when the targeted population of women talked of simplifying their lives, one of their main goals was getting organized. In the end, it all came down to making sense of the plethora of data and insights gleaned from very diverse sources. The team stumbled upon this realization, which ultimately became the mission and concept of *Real Simple*. In strategizing, as with so many things, luck does indeed favor the prepared.

For all the work done on crafting a winning strategy, *Real Simple* wasn't an instant success when it hit the newsstands in March 2000 because, while the mission was a home run, the execution didn't get out of the infield. Readers found the magazine cold, impersonal, and impractical. It lacked humanity; there was no evidence of the real world, including children or pets, and readers could not relate to it. Everything from the art direction to the product advertisements said that the magazine was intended for a very select audience rather than the broader demographic that Time Inc., hoped for. After the third issue, a new editor from the *InStyle* launch team was brought on board to get the magazine on track. "It was like repairing a bicycle while riding it," Sachs noted. By the sixth issue, the magazine had successfully re-created itself, found its voice, and energized its readers; sales followed.

The iterative cycle of vision and execution continues at *Real Simple*. Since its initial mission was to help readers simplify their lives, members of the magazine staff started regularly asking focus groups, "What are the most common problems you confront on a daily basis?" They gave these group members digital cameras and asked them to chronicle these issues like anthropologists as they go about their normal routine. When they found something in their lives that they wanted to make easier, they were told to take a picture of it with the digital camera. This "problem detector" form of ethnographic consumer research led to 500–600 new ideas that were eventually pared down through quantitative analysis and have become a great resource for both the editorial and business sides of the brand.

The latest charge for Sachs and the team at *Real Simple* is to develop the *Real Simple* concept beyond a magazine. Ever since the magazine's launch, it was clear to Time Inc., that *Real Simple* is more than a magazine; it's a lifestyle. As a result, *Real Simple* has become a full-scale brand. Its Web site has evolved into an online solution space where readers can download tips, learn time-saving methods, utilize technology tools, and interact with a network of helpful experts and peers. In developing the site, the *Real Simple* team members began to think of themselves as a content company, rather than just a magazine. "Given all that digital media can do between the Internet and other mobile technologies, how can we solve our readers' problems?" the team inquired.

Real Simple has grown to include lines of cleaning tools and home organizing products available at Target, a weekly television show on PBS, and a syndicated newspaper column. Recently, *Real Simple* was launched in three overseas markets—Japan, South Africa, and Greece, where it quickly became one of the best-selling women's magazines. The *Real Simple* team is expanding as it works with retailers, media producers, and local publishers in the overseas markets to help them adapt the *Real Simple* concept to their local markets.

The creation of *Real Simple* plays on several key strategic strengths for leading innovation. First, the team members realized that in order to launch a new magazine, they had to start with the consumer. While some magazine publishers are strictly idea-driven, Time Inc., starts with the explicit goal of reinventing magazine categories and employs a rigorous process of consumer testing and product development much like you would expect to find in a packaged goods firm like Procter & Gamble. The team combined this customer-driven model with idea-driven creative people to arrive at a winning concept. Advertisers buy into their faith in Time Inc., and into its leaders, who have a track record of executing and leading innovative teams of people. This execution was critical immediately after the magazine was launched when management realized that the concept was not delivering on its promise. Managers' ability to assemble the right team while continuing to move forward was critical to the magazine's ultimate success. When developing the *Real Simple* Web site, Sachs and the team recognized the importance of asking, "What's working and what's not working, and how can we understand what's most important to our readers?" Finally, Time Inc., has learned from *Real Simple* how to search and reapply the best practices. The company gained better insight into how to research and launch a magazine, which helps it in its continuous goal of reinventing the marketplace.

There are two key lessons from this story. One is that *innovation only pays in the future*. Launching new magazines in a crowded magazine marketplace is risky business. Time Inc., diverted from some of its traditional readers and material to launch a string of successful new publications during the last decade that created entirely new categories and markets in which to grow the business. Future-focused innovative strategies like this one pay off in the long run when the team diligently works to create an authentic vision; this vision is updated in real time as new insights emerge and proof of concept has been made. This is then followed with superior execution.

The other lesson is to *diversify when you don't know your destination*. The development of *Real Simple* didn't follow a linear path to success. Instead it was an ambiguous path that grew from five separate concepts, any of which could have been launched. Sachs helped the *Real Simple* team diversify its approaches to gain real insight into the market and the consumer and then piece these approaches together to create a winning product, brand, and ultimately solution for busy, overextended women everywhere.

Table 4.1   How the Innovation Genome Relates to the Strategize Step

Collaborate *Do things together.* • Create high-performing culture and competencies.	**Create** *Do things first.* • See the future opportunities first.
Control *Do things right.* • Make plans operational.	**Compete** *Do things fast.* • Focus on overcoming competition.

Collecting and Making Sense of Data

Strategizing is all about creating a road map. Where are we now and where do we want to go? In the previous chapter, "Synthesize," a company begins to create the foundation for a road map using the Innovation Genome. In the Strategize step, a company introduces facts from its external and internal worlds in a way that provides those facts with a context or place with respect to such as competitors and emerging technology, while also drawing upon the information obtained from applying the Innovation Genome.

In order to create its road map, a company must first collect the necessary data and use those data in a way that makes sense. The following are three effective methods of doing this:

- *Deep Dive:* Identify a handful of experts who know about a subject, ask the experts some very specific and pointed questions about that subject, and have them brief you as to what works and what doesn't work. The product design firm IDEO takes this approach when launching a new project team.
- *Gaming Simulation Maps:* Represent ideas and their interrelationships as if they were elements of a game to be played. Have people go out and look at elements that affect strategy, and then create a comprehensive map (visual representation) showing how all these pieces fit together and how the data in the organization function. Urban Planning Professor Richard Duke[1] developed this power technique to make better decisions in complex situations, like when the United Nations has to distribute food to dozens of countries struck by famine.
- *Identify Contrarian Trends.*[2] By looking at trends and making stories out of them, Faith Popcorn, noted as an expert on trends, was able to predict how people were going to buy in the future. Look for countervailing or oppositional trends, things that don't really go together. For example, for many young people it is extremely difficult to get a job, and there is a lot of pressure in the market. However, young people actually take vacations and enjoy more free time than people who are deeply established in their jobs. Different lifestyle views have emerged in young people. They have different career hobbies; there are much more cohabitation and hybrid things that conventional thinking doesn't capture. If you're a marketing person, this is a new market, and you sell to it.

Levers—Points of Control

Levers are things that we control as opposed to things that drive us. When we create strategy, it is important to remember what we are in charge of, and what's in charge of us. In the words of Benjamin Franklin, "I have a sail and a rudder, but I'm not the ocean."

In looking at levers, there are things that we drive and things that drive us. Things that we drive include what we can control through our strategy or things that we can employ to our service such as:

- Leadership
- Organizational culture
- Hiring practices
- Training
- Performance metrics and rewards
- Resource allocation
- R&D
- Strategy

Things that drive us include things that are out of our control such as:

- Financial market demands
- Industry structure
- Market segments
- Customer preferences
- Emerging technology
- Competitor profiles
- Standards and regulations

The importance of levers is that they help leaders in an organization conduct an environmental scan of the environment both external to and internal to the organization. Certain parts of the external and internal environment can be controlled by the company, while others cannot. In working a strategy it is important to look at what's going on outside the organization, but it's also important to look at what's going on inside the organization. When creating a strategy, a team must be mindful of who on the "inside" is associated with what. Where will the company get traction on its strategy to make it run? Who does what? Who owns what?

Strategic Drivers and Sources of Competitive Advantage

Strategic drivers consist of things that push, things that pull, and things that clash. *Push* includes things like emerging technology. Companies have no choice but to adapt to technology because it's inevitable, and it's going to change industries and abilities. *Pull* refers to things we have to react to such as what consumers and clients want; it is demand and deliver. *Clash* includes things that make it necessary to respond to competitors. The key in Strategizing is not reacting to what people or companies are doing now, but anticipating what they're going to do. In strategy the world is dynamic; there are no fixed players. Strategists have to be able to think of a lot of moving parts and what's likely to be happening. As in football, it's not the last play that matters, but what the opposing team is going to do next.

Strategy depends on our strategic drivers and our sources of competitive advantage. Some examples of successful strategies include the following:

Consolidation: This strategy focuses product development on filling in the gaps. Think Pfizer: a big company that keeps adding to or developing what it has by buying or negotiating with smaller companies.

Bypassing: Think Charles Schwab: Charles Schwab got rid of the broker in the front room and moved the back office to the front. This cut out the need for a broker and changed the entire industry. Merrill Lynch, the brokerage firm Schwab ousted as industry leader never recovered because Schwab had bypassed it.

Big bet: Think New Line Cinema and *Lord of the Rings*: New Line laid out $3 million to make all three films in the *Lord of the Rings* trilogy at the same time. This had never been done before, but the films ended up being a huge success.

Expansion of a niche: Think Veggie Tales: Veggie Tales looked at the children's video and cartoon market, mixed it with Christian teachings, and added humor that both children and adults could enjoy. It found an area within the market that had not been previously tapped into.

Adjacencies and niches: This strategy employs value migration. Think GE Capital: GE Capital decided to compete in an area that was not its core area of expertise but an extension of its expertise, or one area over. It started out by financing industrial equipment, then medical equipment, then car fleets, and so on. It kept taking an ability that it already had and expanding it, until it was financing in multiple areas.

Teaming up: This strategy uses alliances. Think Yum! Brands: Taco Bell/KFC/Pizza Hut. These fast-food chains teamed up, combined, and were put in Target stores and gas stations everywhere.

Alternative delivery: This strategy uses pervasive turnkey systems. Think Amazon: Everybody thought Barnes & Noble would take over the book-selling industry, but Amazon used a warehouse, the Web, and UPS to become an enormously successful competitor.

Deep connections: This strategy uses emotional currency. Think Harley-Davidson: Harley-Davidson makes an extremely loud motorcycle (its sound is patented) which costs as much as a car; yet people line up, get on a list, and wait two years to get one. Harley has tapped into emotional currency: the loyalty, pride, and belief of its consumers.

End-to-end integration: Think Wal-Mart: Wal-Mart has an incredible integrated system for keeping track of inbound inventory and outbound purchasing. It uses the data to fine-tune where everything in Wal-Mart moves. The results are that the average price of goods at Wal-Mart is 13–25% less than at other stores.

Outsourcing the core: This strategy employs price performance leverage. Think University of Phoenix: By using practitioners instead of professors, the University of Phoenix has been able to expand rapidly and cover a broad area.

ASAP: This strategy taps into the power of now. Think Expedia: By using the Web to book cheap flights and travel, Expedia has nearly eliminated the need for travel agents.

Customization: The motto of this strategy could well be, "Let the user create it." Think Dell: Dell enables its consumers to get online and create a computer to fit their needs.

Mass market: This strategy sells premium products to the average consumer. Think Mercedes C-class: Mercedes took a high-end car and created a "c-class" for around $40,000, which was lower priced than its other models. It took something previously unavailable to the average consumer and made it more accessible.

Fix-it-for-me: This strategy solves customer problems. Think American Express Platinum card: Anywhere in the world its customers can call a number for help. Customer service can send personal items such as medication or glasses, or authorize an extra month in a hotel. These additional services are why people are willing to pay more for the card.

Customer obsession: Think Nordstrom's: Nordstrom is obsessed with its customers. The company is known for customer service such as sending cards to customers to find out how they liked the items they purchased at the store. It provides service beyond simply selling products and, in the process, creates loyalty in its shoppers.

Seeing the future first: This strategy creates a first-mover advantage. Think Pixar: When Steve Jobs left Apple, he created a company called NEXT which didn't take off, but it was good at creating graphics. Jobs still believed in the future of computer-generated graphics and purchased the computer graphics division of Lucasfilms from George Lucas, producer of the *Star Wars* movies. Jobs named the firm Pixar and made an alliance with Disney, and produced a string of hit films.

Platforms: This strategy creates standards, which in turn create variations. Think Microsoft Windows: Because there is a standard, it allows for millions of software variations.

Communities of practice: Think eBay: eBay has millions of users who relate to one another and deal with one another all the time. In this case, many conventional rules are out the window.

Core Competencies

When Strategizing, a company must look at its core competencies—in other words, its ability to make something of value. Core competencies are sometimes called *strategic abilities*. They are something that allows the firm to create a business or product, or allows the firm to keep competitors from creating a business or product. The following offers definitions that that determine what core competencies are and are not.

- Core competencies are the collective skills, knowledge, and processes of an organization.
- Core competencies can be contained in strategy, systems, technology, and human resources to create new products and services, markets, and value.
- Core competencies are valuable, rare, and difficult to imitate.
- Core competencies are not tangible assets, such as strong cash reserves.
- Core competencies may be fully realized, unexploited, or represent future value.

What drives a core competency? Core competencies have both external and internal drivers including:

- External drivers of core competencies:
  - Financial market demands
  - Industry structure
  - Market segments
  - Customer preferences
  - Emerging technology
  - Competitor profiles
  - Standards and regulations
  - Typical products used
  - Typical marketing strategies
- Internal drivers of core competencies:
  - Finance
  - Marketing
  - Production
  - Technology
  - Innovation
  - Capabilities (HRM, human resources management)
  - Leadership
  - Culture
  - Structure
  - Information systems
  - R&D

It is important to note that a company's core competencies come from a connection of both external and internal drivers. It is also important to note that core competencies are extremely difficult to achieve; attaining a core competency can be harder than building a business or entering a new market; they take both time and money. A core competency can be seen as *the* reason a company is valuable. A core competency is what is unique about the company. Most companies believe that they have anywhere from 7–10 core competencies, but taking these factors into consideration, in all probability the company actually has between 0 and 3 core competencies.

Here is one way in which Dell and IBM employed their core competencies to create value.

Dell innovates in a Control way, by producing relatively low-cost, back-office systems to produce machines; it lets its customer mass-customize the machines. Innovation happens in the logistics of the business. IBM innovated by spending an enormous amount of R&D money to create a high-end technology. As a result, the technology is not cheap, but it is highly differentiated. This is a good example of two different strategies succeeding and creating value in the same market.

A core competency helps companies enter new markets.[3] What kind of business can you be in? What kind of business do you have the capabilities for? As in the Time Inc., case, when Strategizing, they looked at other markets that their magazine development core competency could define.

Timing

Timing is extremely important to consider when Strategizing. The issue isn't what you're going to do, but when you're going to do it. Is there going to be a market for it, and who's going to be there when it happens?

Companies need to gauge the timing of any initiative because poor timing can have two different consequences—a company can bring a product to market too soon (the "it's ahead of its time" syndrome), or a company can bring a product to market too late (the "they're too far behind the game" syndrome).

General Motors designed an "ahead of its time" product in the early 1980s with negative consequences. In 1981, Cadillac introduced an engine that was designed to meet increasingly stringent fuel economy standards and the rising gas prices following the 1970s. The "V8-6-4" was a conventional V8 engine whose cylinders would disengage (either two or four at a time) during certain driving conditions in order to conserve fuel. While the idea was innovative, the engine suffered from numerous reliability problems, as many breakthrough new products do during their first year of introduction, and was discontinued on virtually all Cadillacs after only one model year. This decision was followed by a gradual decline in gas prices and a gradual increase in the size of cars throughout the 1980s and 1990s. GM was ahead of its time with "V8-6-4" engine.

Today, a similar design is available from Honda. Honda's version is a V6 that switches to three cylinders when the car is cruising. Honda's timing appears to be just right because it has a reputation in the auto industry for designing superior engines, and it would not have released an engine unless it met strict reliability standards. This engine is part of Honda's overall hybrid engine program, which is a concept gaining traction in the automobile market because of the growing need for more fuel efficient vehicles to meet today's rising fuel costs.

These two examples from Cadillac and Honda further show how timing and proper execution of an idea coincide to define a company's reputation in the marketplace. GM could not capitalize on an "ahead of its time" creative project at Cadillac, leaving it unable to lead the industry in hybrid engine design. On the other hand, Honda had better timing in coordinating its capabilities to develop a superior hybrid engine with the rising demands of consumers looking for a way to offset the rising costs of fuel. While GM and Honda may have led the way for hybrid engine development, it was Toyota who led the way in executing its development and marketing, and established itself as the market leader. Superior strategy and execution are required to create a new market.

Strategy and Operating Plans (Operating Rhythm)

Strategy does not sit alone. It is meant to initiate a sequence. For example, Strategy is at the top. With strategy, goals are created and operationalized into operating plans which lead to individual performance and management plans, incentives, bonuses, hiring, and succession practices.

At times this can be problematic because things are moving so fast that strategy cannot initiate the sequence. In this case, operating plans largely drive the strategy. Operating plans become compressed, and more and more strategy and operation plans are looking like one lump thing. This can lead to big gaps between what the vision is and what the pieces of operating rhythm are. It is extremely important when creating a strategy to distinguish between the strategy and the operating plan.

Workshop Preparations

The Strategize step is an optional step in the *Creativize Method* because many companies have already come up with a strategy. However, even if the organization has an existing strategy, the Strategize process may be valuable as a supplement to the company's strategy because it provides a method for checking the effectiveness of the strategy. It does this by determining whether the organization has the competencies and capabilities to make its strategy successful, whether its strategy will lead to the outcomes it is seeking, and whether it is recognizing and meeting external demands.

The Strategize process is often referred to as a "futuring" process or "strategic outlook" because it is meant to help the firm look at what is going to happen on two levels:

1. *Now versus the future:* How the company should Supervise based on this outlook, and how to develop competencies for the future.
2. *Internal trends versus external trends:* What's going on inside the firm as compared to what's going on outside the firm.

It is important to note that the future is about the unknown and as with anything unknown there is a lot of variability. Looking at the future is not a science but an art; it is not exacting, but a work in progress. In Strategizing we are looking for very large movements or big, bold brush strokes.

Because there are no data on the future, excessive planning in this activity is actually a form of resistance. The only way to find out about the future is through experimentation; the company must build the bridge as it crosses it.

There are three specific points to consider in carrying out the Strategize step:

1. *Who's on the team?* It's very important to consider who's at the workshop and how to best manage the varying relationships of those attending. In order to create the buy-in necessary to carry out the strategy, it is essential that every participant is involved in the Strategize process; however, it is also extremely important to have key leaders and decision makers present in order to ensure that the strategy aligns with the company's vision.

2. *Core competencies/strategic abilities:* In considering "now vs. future" or "inside vs. outside," the firm is going to have to consider opportunities that are arising in the world. These opportunities need to be contrasted with the real strategic ability that exists within the organization. This process is designed to identify strategic needs in a sequential order because to consider all key dynamics in parallel would be too complex and difficult to piece together. The goal of Strategizing is to get the "inside" and the "outside" to connect at a future point.

3. *Off-ramps and on-ramps:* Without the ability to integrate the strategy into organizational processes and experiments, the Strategize step can become virtually useless. Almost every organization has a futuring group, but often the problem is that the ideas from the futuring group are never implemented in operations. Strategizing requires mechanisms, off-ramps and on-ramps, to get the strategy off the futuring ramp and plugged into an operating plan, yearly planning cycles, or operating unit strategy.

Strategic Think Tank

Before coming together to Strategize. it is necessary to select the Think Tank, which is the group of people who will be involved in the workshop. The Think Tank should include three groups of people:

- *Internal owners:* The people responsible for running the business units or areas for which the group will be creating strategy.
- *Internal experts:* The people who know the most about what the company does.
- *External experts:* The people who are experts in the field or in the areas for which the group is interested in creating strategy.

The Think Tank should be made up of no more than 25 people. The job of the Think Tank is to "see the future first." This means that the Think Tank should be diverse in representing varying points of view relating to the task at hand; this is the basis for the Collaborate, Create, Compete, and Control categories (Table 4.2).

Table 4.2   Select Think Tank Team

	Internal Owners	Internal Experts	External Experts
Collaborate			
Create			
Compete			
Control			

Once the Think Tank is selected, the group will meet and begin to put together the pieces of the puzzle that will create the company's "story of destiny" (Figure 4.1). To do this, the group will look at four facets of the organization:

1. Current opportunity
2. Current competency
3. Future opportunity
4. Desired competency

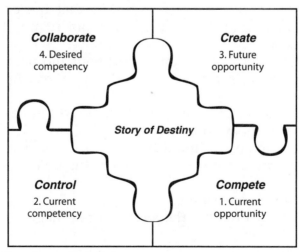

Figure 4.1   Put the pieces together

Before considering these four facets, you (and the group) must get into the right frame of mind:

- See the future as if you were watching a movie (this needs to be very real; you cannot build what you cannot imagine).
- Challenge market, customer, and organizational boundaries (break a lot of glass).
- Value people and ideas that are well outside your comfort zone.
- Escape assumptions about products, price, and performance.
- Tell a story with a sense of destiny that others will understand and tell to others.
- Provide a point of view that people can act on now.

Once the group is in the right frame of mind, it is time to start putting the pieces together.

Strategic Information "Sensemaking"

Strategy requires information to make it viable. Many aspects of the competitive environment and the internal workings of the organization inform the strategic process. The key is to connect these diverse and often disjointed views and to make sense of them as a collective picture. This picture provides the backdrop upon which strategic decisions are made.

One of the critical tasks of the Strategize step is to collect all the pertinent types of data, reports, and expertise that the organization has already created. These can include, but are not required or limited to, those listed in Table 4.3.

Prioritizing the information is most pertinent and useful for crafting a strategy. Try to limit this to fewer than 10 key sources of strategic information.

Identify the owners and experts for each of the sources of strategic information and ask them to produce an executive summary of their findings. These summaries should be no more than two or three pages in length. These summaries should spell out the following:

- Key facts, trends, and issues
- A point of view on what the sources of strategic information suggest about the strategy
- Decisions that need to be made
- Possible courses of action and a recommended one

Table 4.3   Strategic Information

Strategic Information on Current and Future Competencies	Strategic Information on Current and Future Opportunities
Values Scan: • Individual values • Organizational values • Organizational mission • Philosophy of operations • Organizational culture • Stakeholder analysis Operating Plans: • Annual report • P&L reports • Specialized business unit program plans • Performance audits • Gap analysis comparison and modification • Contingency plans • Vertical and horizontal fit • Implementation, review, and revision Ongoing Operating Processes: • Planning cycle and timing • Strategy roll-up and roll-down processes • Operating rhythm • Key indicators and performance management • Organizational development • Hiring and staffing • Training and development	Environmental Monitoring: • *The macro environment:* Social patterns, changes in consumer needs, technology, economic trends, and political factors such as governmental deregulation • *The industry environment:* The structure of the industry, how it is financed, the degree of governmental presence, typical products used, and typical marketing strategies • *The competitive environment:* General competitor profiles, market-segmentation patterns, segment competitor analysis, brand maps, research and development, etc. • *The internal organizational environment:* The structure of the organization, its history, and its distinctive strengths and weaknesses Driving Forces: • Market segments and needs • Sales channels • Products or services offered • Technology drivers • Development and distribution capability • Organizational competency and culture • Brand strength and position • Mergers and acquisitions agenda • Shareholder guidance targets

Distribute these executive summaries to all members of the Leadership Team involved in the Strategize step, and ask team members to call the appropriate owner or expert with questions or challenges *before* the Strategize summit workshop begins. This ensures that the Strategize step is focused on decision making and not the correctness of the information.

If key sources of strategic information have not been developed, it may be wise to do so concurrently with the Strategize step and make adjustments to the strategy as appropriate when the information is provided.

Give every owner or expert of a source of strategic information 15 to 20 minutes to present his or her findings to the Leadership Team. Give the rest of the team 15 to 20 minutes to ask questions, clarify the information, or provide insights. Direct the process toward making sense of how these sources of strategic information fit together and what decisions and actions they require. A few meetings may be necessary to work out an integrated view of the strategic context for the strategy.

The result of these meetings should be a report, diagram, or presentation that effectively spells out the facts, trends, and issues of the strategic context. This report, diagram, or presentation will serve as a key point of reference for each of the Strategize steps:

1. Current opportunities
2. Current competencies
3. Future opportunities
4. Desired competencies

Strategize Phase 1: Identify Current Opportunities

Before identifying current opportunities, review the data gathered regarding strategic information. The group as a whole should take some time to do a quick "current opportunities" scan. This information should be "admitted as evidence" but should not "lead the witness," meaning that although this information is important, it should not dictate the decisions or directions of the group.

In scanning current opportunities, the group should consider the following:

- Strategic plans
- Mission
- Business objectives
- Major projects and initiatives
- Business culture and values
- Key leaders and stakeholders
- Core organizational processes
- Current technology and methodologies
- Financials of competitors
- Publications and Web information on competitors
- Competitors' annual reports
- Consumer demand and customer segment reports
- Industry analysis

Once this information is briefly presented and discussed, the group will be divided into four groups and will look at each piece of the puzzle through different perspectives according to the group to which each member is assigned: Collaborate, Create, Compete, or Control. The four smaller groups will discuss current opportunities according to the four different points of view. Groups will accomplish this by looking at *value propositions, purposes* and the *culture and competencies* required to create them within each point of view. Then they will use the *Current Opportunities chart* (Tables 4.4–4.7) to look at the relative advantages and disadvantages the company has within the following three categories:

1. *Competitors:* What do competitors have? Competitors are constantly changing and moving. Groups need to look at current competitors as well as emerging competitors.
2. *Customers (pull):* What do customers want? This question is not and should not be based on marketing research because marketing research is based on false choices in that it's based on what's available today, not on what will be introduced tomorrow.
3. *Innovation (push):* How is innovation pushing the future? How is the future encroaching on our business?

Collaborate

Value creation:

- Community:
  - Establishing and maintaining shared values and culture. Common ways of achieving this are networking, empowerment and team building.
- Knowledge:
  - Developing understanding and skills. Common ways of achieving this are training, organizational learning, and human resource management.

Culture and competencies:

- Building teams
- Facilitating people
- Developing learning communities
- Encouraging commitment
- Creating a sense of cohesion in the organization
- Establishing shared values between people
- Listening with concern
- Facilitating conflict resolution

Table 4.4 Collaborate—Current Opportunities

	Advantages	Disadvantages
Competitors		
Customers		
Innovations		
Other		

Create

Value creation:
- Innovation:
  - Making new and better products and services. Common ways of achieving this are creative problem solving, new product development, and change management.
- Growth:
  - Prospecting for new and future market opportunities. Common ways of achieving this are strategic forecasting, trend analysis, and shared vision management.

Culture and competencies:

- Encouraging radical creativity
- Seeing the future first
- Destroying the old way of doing things
- Launching ambitious transformational initiatives
- Looking for emerging opportunities
- Stimulating people to think originally
- Conceiving significant new ventures
- Inciting revolution

Table 4.5   Create—Current Opportunities

	Advantages	Disadvantages
Competitors		
Customers		
Innovations		
Other		

Compete

Value creation:

- Speed:
  - Moving quickly to capture an opportunity. Common ways of achieving this are mergers and acquisitions, branding, and customer service.
- Profits:
  - Maximizing shareholder earnings. Common ways of achieving this are using goals and metrics, strategic resource allocation, and portfolio management.

Culture and competencies:

- Meeting objectives
  - Confronting problems as soon as they occur
  - Quickly eliminating underperforming initiatives
  - Overcoming barriers
  - Partnering with winners
  - Solving problems in real time
  - Focusing on performance
  - Driving for superior returns on investments

Table 4.6 Compete—Current Opportunities

	Advantages	Disadvantages
Competitors		
Customers		
Innovations		
Other		

Control

Value creation:

- Optimization:
  - Using resources in the best way possible. Common ways of achieving this are procedures, budgeting, and organizational design.
- Quality:
  - Eliminating errors. Common ways of achieving this are process controls, systems, and technology.

Culture and competencies:

- Conserving fiscal resources
- Implementing systems to control complex tasks
- Preventing people from making costly mistakes
- Complying with regulations
- Adhering to professional standards
- Making internal work processes routine
- Using continuous improvement processes
- Employing technology on a large scale

Table 4.7 Control—Current Opportunities	Advantages	Disadvantages
Competitors		
Customers		
Innovations		
Other		

Once the groups have completed the exercise, they will come back together and discuss and collapse their ideas by asking questions like, "What are the big trends?" or, "What are the big opportunities now?" The group will select and combine their ideas (Table 4.8).

Once the assembled groups have selected and summarized the company's current opportunities, they should discuss the following questions in order to focus on which current opportunities the strategy should address:

- What opportunities do we need to pursue now?
- What do we need to do (change, innovate, develop, etc.) to capture these opportunities?
- What symbols, stories, and metaphors can we use to express our point of view in a compelling way?

Table 4.8 Summary—Current Opportunities

	Advantages	Disadvantages
Competitors		
Customers		
Innovations		
Other		

Unanswered Questions

What questions did *identifying current opportunities* not answer or raise that must be answered to make it possible for key operational decisions to be made? (Be specific.)

1.

2.

3.

4.

How do we answer these questions?

Strategize Phase 2: Identify Current Core Competencies

Once the group has completed the first phase, identifying current opportunities, it will briefly review the strategic information and then focus in on the second phase, identifying current core competencies.

In order to test core competencies, the group is going to brainstorm. The group as a whole will come up with 20–25 items that members might consider core competencies. Once these items are listed, the group will need to ask itself, "Is this list true?" In order to determine this, the group will diagnose and assess core competencies (Tables 4.9 and 4.10).[4] Each potential competency will be taken through a series of tests, as shown below:

- The value test:
  - Is this core competency perceived as exceptionally valuable to customers?
- The rarity test:
  - Is this core competency unique within our industry and market?
- The imitation test:
  - Is this core competency extremely difficult to imitate?

- The future test:
  - How critical is this core competency likely to be in terms of future leadership within our industry?
- The organization test:
  - Are we better supervised and managed than our competitors to take advantage of this core competency?

Table 4.9   Core Competencies Diagnosis[5]

Is the core competency valuable?	Is the core competency rare?	Is the core competency difficult to imitate?	Is the core competency likely to be more valuable in the future?	Are we organized to exploit the core competency?
No				
Yes	No			
Yes	Yes	No		
Yes	Yes	Yes	No	
Yes	Yes	Yes	Yes	Yes

Table 4.10   Assess Core Competencies[6]

Perceived core competency	Is the core competency valuable?	Is the core competency rare?	Is the core competency difficult to to imitate?	Is the core competency valuable in the future?	Are we organized to exploit the core competency?

Once the group members have diagnosed and assessed the perceived core competencies, they must validate them. To do this, the group must ask "who" can validate them and "how" they can validate them:

- Who?
  - Peer organizations
  - Customers
  - Suppliers
  - Competitors
  - Experts: industry, technology, financial
- How?
  - Benchmarks
  - Peer review
  - Metrics
  - Trends
  - Surveys
  - Competitive intelligence

With the validated core competencies the group should ask which competencies could be exploited to press the advantage or overcome a disadvantage. In other words, "What do we have, and what can we do with it?" (See Table 4.11.)

Table 4.11 Current Core Competencies

Core competencies we *currently possess* and can exploit to press our advantage or overcome a disadvantage.

_____

_____

_____

_____

_____

_____

- What competencies do we need to exploit now to capture current opportunities?
- What additional current opportunities do these competencies create? (One of the values of a core competency is what you could do with it.)
- What do we need to do (change, innovate, develop, etc.) to exploit these competencies?
- What symbols, stories, and metaphors can we use to express our point of view in a compelling way?

Unanswered Questions

What questions did *identifying current core competencies* not answer or raise that must be answered to make it possible for key operational decisions to be made? (Be specific.)

1.

2.

3.

4.

How do we answer these questions?

Strategize Phase 3: Identify Future Opportunities

Once core competencies are in place, the group will be given the challenge of "seeing the future first." The group will need to review the strategic information at the beginning of the Strategize step before proceeding. The group will identify future opportunities by:

- Identifying the key drivers (big trends) of the future of your organization.
- Looking through the four perspectives and speculating on what opportunities will likely be created by these drivers.
- Focusing only on those opportunities that have a high impact on your organization and a high degree of probability of occurring.

- Discussing the implications of the drivers on the future of your organization and developing a point of view.

  Examples of drivers of the future include:

  - Economic trends
  - Political factors
  - Emerging technology
  - Market changes
  - Industry configuration
  - New products and services
  - Cultural shifts
  - Scientific breakthroughs
  - Information flow
  - Workforce dynamics
  - Education levels
  - Government regulations
  - Competitive landscape
  - Availability of materials
  - Weather calamities
  - Disease outbreaks
  - War and terrorism
  - Acquisitions and mergers
  - Value chain configuration
  - Loss of key leaders

Once drivers have been identified, the group should once again break into four groups to look at future opportunities from the perspectives of each of the four quadrants of the Innovation Genome—Collaborate, Create, Compete, and Control. Use Table 4.12 four times—once for each quadrant.

Table 4.12 Future Opportunities

Key drivers	The __ quadrant's view of opportunities

 Once the groups have completed their lists of future opportunities centering around the four different points of view, they should come back together and prioritize the ideas they have come up with according to the *impact* and *probability* of each idea (Figure 4.2).

Impact

	Low	Medium	High
High	III	II	I
Medium	IV	III	II
Low	V	IV	III

Probability

Figure 4.2 Impact and probability

After the drivers or ideas have been prioritized, the group should have a discussion around the four points of view in order to combine and summarize the future opportunities. Crucial to this exercise is making explicit that there are different points of view when it comes to the future. This will lead to powerful and important discussions. From that discussion will emerge a point of view about what the current reality is. When talking about the future, it's not just *what's* going to happen that's so important, but *when* it's going to happen. The company is going to have to pull the train into the station at the right time; this is key to success (Table 4.13).

- What opportunities do we need to pursue in the future?
- What do we need to do (change, innovate, develop, etc.) to capture these opportunities?
- What symbols, stories, and metaphors can we use to express our point of view in a compelling way?

Table 4.13   Summary—Future Opportunities

Drivers	Key opportunities

Unanswered Questions

What questions did *identifying future opportunities* not answer or raise that must be answered to make it possible for key operational decisions to be made? (Be specific.)

1.

2.

3.

4.

How do we answer these questions?

Strategize Phase 4: Identify Desired Competencies

The group must now identify desired competencies. Up to this point we've looked at where the current opportunities are, as well as the company's current abilities. We've also taken a look at tomorrow's opportunities. At this point we need to ask, "What does the company have to do to capture tomorrow's opportunities?" and, "What abilities does the company have to have today to accomplish this?" The key is not just where the opportunities are going to be, but what abilities the company can stretch and leverage to capture those opportunities (Table 4.14).

When talking about capturing these abilities, the group, after reviewing the strategic information, needs to think about the abilities from the four points of view of the Innovation Genome (Tables 4.15 and 4.16).

Table 4.14   Stretch and Leverage

4. Desired Competencies	3. Future Opportunities
•	•
•	•
•	•
•	•
2. Current Competencies	1. Current Opportunities
•	•
•	•
•	•
•	•

Table 4.15

Collaborate
- Building high-performing teams
- Hiring and staffing for values
- Developing thought leaders
- Creating a high-performing culture
- Establishing an idea lab
- Cultivating the workplace

Create
- Radical experiments
- Speculating new markets
- Changing leaders, offices, and practices
- Spinning off new companies
- Widening the array of products
- Exiting mature markets and products

Control
- Technology and information systems
- Controls and regulations
- Setting standards
- Continuous improvement process
- Quality processes
- Professional people

Compete
- Stretching goals
- Mergers and acquisitions
- Quick-strike problem-solving teams
- Focus on performance
- Decision-making processes
- Quick elimination of underperforming initiatives

There are only three things a company can do to develop a desired competency under any point of view:

1. *Build:* Acquire the desired competency by hiring people, or develop it by training people. Do things internally that you have control over. Building takes a lot of time, but is very sustainable.
2. *Buy:* A company can acquire a desired competency by outsourcing or by mergers and acquisitions. Buying is can provide the competency quickly, but it takes a lot of money, and sustainability is questionable.
3. *Barter:* A company can partner or share a competency with another company. Partnering does not take a lot of time or money, but will not create much value unless the partnership is manageable. Many partnerships fail because of the complex relationships they present.

Table 4.16 Developing Desired Competencies

Desired competencies	How to build	How to buy	How to barter

Once the desired competencies are listed, the group should discuss the following questions:

- What competencies do we need to exploit to capture future opportunities?
- What additional future opportunities do these competencies create?
- What do we need to do (change, innovate, develop, etc.) to harness these competencies?
- How does the new competency change the Strategize map?

Unanswered Questions

What questions did *identifying future core competencies* not answer or raise that must be answered to make it possible for key operational decisions to be made? (Be specific.)

1.

2.

3.

4.

How do we answer these questions?

Strategize Phase 5: Create a Story of Destiny

The final phase in Strategizing is to create a story of destiny. The role of the story of destiny is to create a sense of emotional connection that is owned and shared by everyone in the organization. A story of destiny requires three elements:

- It must be a metaphor or symbol that represents the collective and participative nature of the company's direction. It is a sense-making device for the vision of the company, and people need to be able to look at the symbol and interpret it in a meaningful way.
- It must precipitate a strategic document for the company.
- The story must be an anchor or a point of reference for all the performance management and operating rhythm aspects of the organization. Future steps of the Innovation Genome will be anchored from this point of reference because it personifies the vision of where the company is going.

There are many ways that a company can create a story of destiny. Many companies use visual images to do so and sometimes enlist experts such as Root Learning to help them in the process. Figure 4.3 is an example of a Root *Learning Map*® module that helps employees understand the strategic objectives of the organization and how they contribute to achieving company goals. In this particular case, the client, a Midwest energy services company, was focused on building a high performance culture. The Root *Learning Map*® module tells a story of destiny. It integrates a visual, data, and conversation and is rolled out to managers in small group sessions. The focus for this particular *Learning Map*® module is to help all employees understand the company's vision through learning and conversation on marketplace challenges and opportunities, both now and in the future, as well as how to build a high-performance culture.

In a general sense, a story of destiny should help people address the following issues:

- What are the current opportunities?
- What competencies are required to capture these current opportunities?
- What other opportunities do these current competencies create?
- What are the future opportunities?

Figure 4.3 Root *Learning Map®*

- What desired competencies are required to capture these future opportunities?
- What other future opportunities do these desired competencies create?

If you want to create your own story of destiny, use pictures and graphs to explain what and how the organization has become . . .

- An example of an organization that captured key opportunities.
- An example of an organization that missed key opportunities.
- Explain how the organization capitalized (or failed to capitalize) on its current opportunities and exploited its current competencies. Further describe what changes the organization made (or didn't make), and what competencies it developed to capitalize on future opportunities.

- Be creative. Have fun. Still, remember that this must not only be possible, it must also be probable.
  - ○ Stories should address: What happened? How did it happen? Why is it important? How did the organization overcome key barriers? How were opportunities captured (or not)? What changes did the organization have to make? What competencies did the organization have to develop?

Once this exercise has been completed, combine the two teams to create a story that integrates the best case and worst case. Make sure the story is clear:

- How is this relevant to the people in your organization?
- What does success look like?
- What do they need to do? What tools and support will they need?
- What's in it for them? For us?
- What happens next?

Polish the story. Put it in a hallway at the office and on the company Web site.

Create a forum for people to talk about the stories and give them a chance to clarify and improve them.

Conclusion

1. How do we determine our firm's competitive advantage?

Competitive advantage is determined by conducting an environmental scan of the firm in order to understand its competitive context relative to the firm's core competencies.

2. Who develops the firm's strategy, and who owns it?

The Strategic Think Tank consists of no more than 25 of the company's unit-level leaders who, collectively, have the ability to see the company's future direction and the ability to lead its strategic change. Strategy is developed by a team of leaders, but the whole organization has to own it.

3. How does innovation link with strategy?

Innovation means doing something new or doing the same thing a new way. Strategy is about seeing the future of the organization and taking it there. But don't ignore the past and present. Innovation is an enabler for moving a company strategically. The way a company embraces innovation is the way in which it will move forward strategically.

The 3-D View

Remember from Chapter 2 that innovation is typically a work in progress. Innovation always provides key insights into the past that will in turn provide some wisdom about the future. But, more importantly, it allows us a wider range of courses to speculate and navigate. Once the Strategize step is complete, it is important for the Creativizers and other appropriate people to ask in a separate meeting the Do, Doing, Done questions by thinking around the Innovation Genome. It is important that the meeting take place close enough to the Strategize step so that everyone remembers the experience but enough removed so that people have had time to think about what really happened.

Do . . .
Looking forward to future projects, communities, charters, and goals that will flow from the Strategize step, consider the questions in Table 4.18 from the four perspectives of the Innovation Genome.

Table 4.18 "Innovation Genome—Do"

Collaborate View	Create View
• What do I need to do?	• What do I need to do?
• How do I want to do it?	• How do I want to do it?
Control View	**Compete View**
• What do I need to do?	• What do I need to do?
• How do I want to do it?	• How do I want to do it?

Doing . . .
Looking at any current work taking place around the *Creativize Method* at your organization, consider the questions in Table 4.19.

Table 4.19 "Innovation Genome—Doing"

Collaborate View
- What's working and what isn't? Why?
- What changes should we make?

Create View
- What's working and what isn't? Why?
- What changes should we make?

Control View
- What's working and what isn't? Why?
- What changes should we make?

Compete View
- What's working and what isn't? Why?
- What changes should we make?

Done . . .

Looking back at what has taken place with the Strategize step and any projects that have been launched, consider the questions in Table 4.20.

Table 4.20 "Innovation Genome—Done"

Collaborate View
- What worked and what didn't? Why?
- What changes would we make if we ran this step or project again?
- What have we learned that can be applied to the current practices of the organization?

Create View
- What worked and what didn't? Why?
- What changes would we make if we ran this step or project again?
- What have we learned that can be applied to the current practices of the organization?

Control View
- What worked and what didn't? Why?
- What changes would we make if we ran this step or project again?
- What have we learned that can be applied to the current practices of the organization?

Compete View
- What worked and what didn't? Why?
- What changes would we make if we ran this step or project again?
- What have we learned that can be applied to the current practices of the organization?

CHAPTER
5

Step 3:
SOCIALIZE

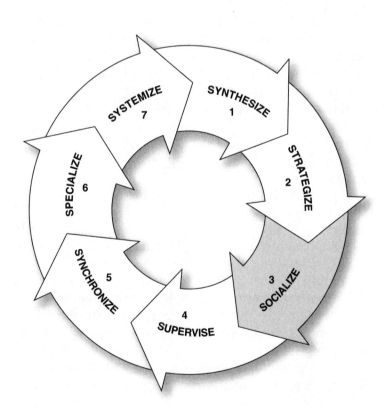

Socialize Overview

- Objective
  - Establish a shared vision and values in the Leadership Team.

- Participants
  - Leadership Team, Lead Facilitator, and Sponsor.

- Actions
  1. Sponsor communicates desired outcomes for this step and expectations for the Leadership Team.
  2. Lead Facilitator introduces the *Creativize Method* and the Innovation Genome to establish a shared mindset and language.
  3. Lead Facilitator presents the findings of the *Change and Innovation Assessment*.
  4. Leadership Team discusses the implications and impact of the assessment and develops a diagnosis of the current situation.
  5. Leadership Team reviews the organization's strategy and, if appropriate, the output of the Strategize step.
  6. Leadership Team creates a desired profile for the organization.
  7. Leadership Team, thinking creatively around the Innovation Genome, creates a road map and an action plan for the desired profile.
  8. Leadership Team resolves key issues and agrees on an action plan.
  9. Leadership Team identifies behaviors that they will have to change to make the action plan viable, and members publicly commit to making specific personal changes.
  10. Leadership Team codifies action plan into four strategic pillars that represent key enablers to the plan (e.g., improving customer service), for the Action Teams to work on.
  11. Leadership Team nominates Creativizers who will lead the process.
  12. Lead Facilitator produces a summary of the shared vision for review, revision, and distribution.

- Time
  - 2½ days. (Creativizer assessment takes an additional two weeks.)

This Chapter Will Help Me to Answer:

- What is the leadership vantage point, and why is this an important consideration?
- Is conflict good or bad?
- How do we get from ideas to action?

Introduction

The Socialize step is used to create a high-functioning project or senior team. This step is not about the project, but about the team. It is used to create a shared vision and shared values within the team. What does the team do? Where is the team going? Having a shared vision and shared values helps to create a high-performing team. If the project does not have a high-performing team, it doesn't matter what the strategy is or what the products are. If the team itself does not perform, the project will not work.

Socialize in Action—University of Michigan Health System

Marge Calarco is the chief nursing officer at the University of Michigan Health System which serves over 3,000 nurses. She's an optimist and has a profound belief in human potential. Calarco has committed herself to building a culture of empowered employees since she began at UMHS almost 20 years ago and most recently in her current leadership position in nursing over the past 5 years. In pursuing this end, Calarco was running a number of experiments and in so doing became connected to the Center for Positive Organizational Scholarship (POS) at University of Michigan's Ross School of Business. Calarco was impressed by many of the ideas presented and believed that they would help her to develop a strong foundation leading toward a culture of empowerment within UMHS.

The POS course included concepts and tools that would assist the team in creating an empowered and high-performing culture. One of the exercises the group participated in was called "The Reflective Best Self." This exercise involved receiving feedback from 10–20 people who shared three stories each, portraying each participant at his or her best. Participants then found themes and created a paragraph statement that described them at their best. They then shared their statements with the team, which allowed people to learn about one another and understand how they should be leveraging each person's strengths. As a result of this exercise people became more open to having difficult conversations that were previously too politically charged to conduct. Because team members felt appreciated, they were more open with one another and willing to work together on team challenges.

This and similar exercises increased trust and cohesiveness. The next challenge was for the team members to work together on creating a shared vision and then make commitments to move toward that vision. To assist in this process, the Innovation Genome was introduced as a way to give the group members new or different perspectives for thinking about their organization.

The common language created through the Innovation Genome helped individuals to communicate what it was like to work in their particular positions at UMHS. People shared honest comments and continued to have difficult conversations as they filled out an Innovation Genome assessment as a unit. In the end, members of each unit were surprised to find that they were on the same page as the others. The vision for each group, addressing both the current and desired culture, was almost identical. At this point, the question became, "Why are we all going in different directions when everyone wants the same thing?" These exercises led to three big breakthroughs.

First, the team members realized that they were not functioning as a team. There were many individuals who worked hard and were effective in their specific area, but there was nothing that was special being accomplished when they met together as a team. Loneliness also pervaded the group as individuals dealt every day with hard situations but felt that they had no outlet where they could share their experiences; when the group got together, members reported information and moved on. The nurses had been doing well at hitting their numbers, but they all believed they could be doing better as an organization. This team was filled with good people who had entered a profession that allowed them to affect people's lives. Hitting numbers meant that people's lives were being saved or improved. Somewhere along the way the nurses felt they'd lost their connection to people and had forgotten what really mattered. This loneliness and the inability to discuss the difficult issues had worked its way throughout the general nursing population.

Second, it brought an acknowledgment that the individual units and the overall nursing organization at UMHS were all trying to go in the same direction. This took people from being viewed as resistant to being viewed as "comrades," even though it acknowledged that they'd tried to reach their goals in different ways.

Third, it created ownership in the room for the vision. If a senior leader had come in and announced a new vision for the team, nobody would have owned the vision. Through the process of this course, the team members had a new vision of how they were supposed to work together and how the separate units were to work together; it began to be something they felt deeply about, something personal.

The next exercise required people to give feedback to everyone else in their group. Team members let individuals within their group know what they should continue to do and what they should do differently if the team was going to reach its desired future state. The room was very tense while people filled out cards and passed them out to one another. After making sense of what they had received, team members had to write down themes and report on what people needed from them and what commitments they were willing to make.

As the leader of the group, Marge Calarco was asked to go first. She described how she was a very innovative and flexible person who was also hard driving and liked to get things completed quickly and well. She would often start major initiatives, and then once they were moving, she would move on to something new and interesting. Calarco told the group that she wanted to stay focused and see this change initiative through. She recognized that there were a number of detail and implementation pieces to the project that she would need to be more patient and self-disciplined with so that she would be able to see the change through. In relating her commitments, Calarco was very honest and recognized some of her own misgivings. Her honesty and willingness to then commit to very specific areas of growth allowed the group to go on and have a very honest and open dialogue. Calarco modeled exactly the kind of honesty and openness needed from all members of the group as they made commitments and made sense of the feedback given to them. As the leader, Calarco did exactly what she needed to do to make this exercise successful and help the rest of the group to take it seriously.

With the final day of the course came the recognition that there were still a number of issues that had not been addressed. The morning action planning session was changed to a group discussion in which the team was coached on how to stay with and effectively communicate difficult topics. The group members were able to work through two significant issues in how they interact as a team. They knew they had more to deal with, but they now felt that they had an understanding of how to have conversations about real issues and begin building trust on the team. As trust grew, so would the ability to work across areas and create new solutions to difficulties that blocked the team from hitting its key indicators at higher levels.

Upon completion of the course, the group members continued to work on their commitments to build a strong and united team. Six months later the team met again as a follow-up and was pleased that individual behavior was continuing to change since the initial intervention. The group members stated that they were more open to giving specific feedback and making commitments that provide greater impact. Creating a shared vision and working together as a high-performing team are things that have to be a continual focus and that have great impact on changing culture and creating increased innovation and growth. However, trust and effectiveness do not come overnight, which makes revisiting and running the Socialize step a crucial part of a successful change and innovation process.

Getting Leaders to Act as a Team

In order to make the Socialize process work, it is important to get the leaders within the organization to act as a team. There are four levers to use in helping leaders to become a team; in order to reach everyone within the team and create a high-performing team, all four must be energized:

- Share values (Collaborate): This has to do with what people believe about the world and what people want from the world. One way to do this is to ask, "What do these different people want (i.e., People within the Collaborate quadrant want to go to work where they feel that they are part of a community, where there's not a lot of conflict, and where there is a lot of collaboration. Collaborate people want to feel like their personal lives and professional lives are aligned.)

Table 5.1   How the Innovation Genome Relates to the Socialize Step

Collaborate

Agree on shared values.
- What do we believe?
- How are we going to interact with one another?
- What are we going to be like on this journey?

Create

Create a compelling vision of the future.
- Using a story of destiny, tell me where we're going.
- Tell me where we're going in a way that's interesting and in a way that will make me want to go there.

Control

Establish a clear action plan.
- What's my program plan for next year?
- What's the process by which we are going to operationalize the plan every time we come to a meeting?

Compete

Decide on course of action.
- What specifically are we going to do?
- How are we going to make decisions going forward?
- What kind of things are we going to focus on and how do we go faster?

- Share vision (Create): Help team members to feel that what they are going to create is compelling.
- Set some basic goals that people are going to achieve (Compete): For example, "We are going to have 1,500 stores in a year."
- Set some processes to make the team come together (Control): What is the process by which things get done? How do decisions get made? How do we conduct meetings? Who decides?

It is very important that in creating a cohesive team we push on all four of these levers, not just one or the other.

Bringing Key and Hidden Issues to the Surface

The Socialize process will be ineffective if real issues are not brought forward and addressed. This makes it extremely important for the Lead

Facilitator to be able to bring key and hidden issues to the surface. There are a couple of reasons why some issues might not rise to the surface. For example, a group may seem to have little energy or an enormous amount of apathy. This could be an indication that people in the group do not want to discuss the issues. The reverse symptom might also be masking the same problem. A group with an enormous amount of energy might be covering something up—there is something group members are avoiding talking about.

In such cases an effective approach to bringing the hidden issues to the surface is to triangulate, or to get a third perspective involved. This approach brings up information learned from assessments and interviews and is intended to make the group more honest. For example, "Okay, you say you're all on the same page. You say you know everybody's good to go, but here are your results. Why do they say you don't get along?" When certain individuals in the group start discussing the issue, ask another member of the group who is being quiet whether he or she thinks the discussion or views are accurate. This exercise will often bring out the real issues.

Difference between the Leadership Team's View and the Organization's View

When you're running the Socialize exercises, you'll need to address two important issues. First, is the team a high-performing team and do its members have shared vision and values? Second, is the senior leadership team's view of where the organization needs to go the same as the view the organization has?

In some cases you will find that the view of the senior leadership team does not exactly match the organization's view. There can be a number of reasons for this. It could be that the senior leadership team has a clearer vision because its members have a better vantage point and can see things more readily. In this case, if the view of the leadership team and the view of the organization are different, it can mean that the senior leadership team hasn't done a good job of helping other groups see what it sees. The solution to this dilemma could be as simple as the team's providing information and creating opportunities for feedback.

It also could be that the senior leadership team is wrong. Its members may trust their own data or view more than that of different subgroups of employees throughout the organization who may be aware that the customer is not happy, that there is trouble on the assembly line, or that the product being developed is not going to come out right. In this case, the senior leadership team has to ask itself, "Why exactly are we so far out of the loop?" Solutions to this problem may include having people from the leadership team spend time with operations employees, having weekly or monthly town hall meetings, or conducting focus groups and interviews that are intentionally designed to bring out issues within the organization. The solution could also be as simple as having a "suggestions" box available where employees can provide anonymous feedback.

There is also the possibility that none of the above is correct. In this case the challenge is to come up with some way of melding these views together. It may be the members of the leadership team's job to lead the organization and lay out a path forward, but before they do that, they need to have a real knowledge of what's happening within the organization as well as other areas, such as Wall Street and the marketplace.

Redirecting Power and Influence

People within the organization have sensibilities about where they are going as well as sensibilities about what they can change and what they can't change. Some of those sensibilities are real because they are bound by factors such as processes, financial targets, or Wall Street. On the other hand, some are not nearly as entrenched as people think they are.

Almost inevitably when coming into a change situation, someone will say, "But we can't change X goal," or, "We can't change X process." What they really mean is that it's difficult to do. People can't change X and keep everybody's opinions and processes the same. Changing X would mean having to change something else. It doesn't mean that it can't happen. It just means having to change the scope and avenues they were pursuing to do it. In these situations it is often necessary to redirect power and influence within the organization.

Here are some ways that an organization can attempt to redirect power and influence within the organization:

> *Tap into personal power:* Who are the people with the unique ability to get things done? They could be powerful people who can sign checks and have great organizational authority, or they could be people who have great influence. Talk to these people before moving forward with any initiatives or change efforts.

Create connections: Often when redirecting power, it is helpful to find something that people care deeply about and connect it with what the organization is trying to do. This is how Congress works. One person wants an environmental bill, and the other wants a community college bill. They work together to make a deal so it becomes a win-win situation.

Make it personal: Another approach is to create personal and real stories about what's working and what's not working. Then use those stories to confront people with the truth.

Separate the idea from the issuer: When redirecting power and influence, it is also helpful to try to move the issue or issues away from individuals. For example, if there is a politician a person tends to dislike or disagree with, everything the politician says can be infuriating. However, if the politician's words were written down and the person reading the words was not told who said them, maybe only about 50 percent of what is said would be infuriating. Often 50 percent of what is creating resistance to change is not real. So, when talking about what's working and what's not working, the organization wants to move the issue of power and influence away from people and onto issues or onto things that it's trying to accomplish.

Ask for help: Finally, once the team has a shared vision, ask people how they can use their power and influence to accomplish the end goal.

Managing Conflict and Resistance

In every change and innovation project there is conflict. The important thing to remember is that the organization should not avoid conflict, but manage it. Conflict is inevitable and up to the point where it becomes very dysfunctional conflict, it is a good thing. Productive conflict means that the organization is vital and has energy; it is apathy that is the death of change and innovation. Resistance is also a very important thing. People who resist believe that they are protecting something very important. To effectively manage conflict and resistance it is important to try to understand what people are going through. (To learn a process for managing conflict see Step 6: Specialize, Phase 12: Manage Resistance.)

Establishing Consensus and Ownership

In an effort to create high-performing teams, it is important to establish consensus as often as possible within the group. However, different situations require different responses by the group, and so consensus will not always be possible. When teams have the opportunity to find a solution that everyone can agree upon, team members will all feel ownership of that idea and will be more likely to own their responsibilities and roles that are part of executing the idea developed by the group. Building consensus establishes high-performing groups that are able to make quick decisions when there is a pressing demand from a client, a leader, or any other source in the position to make demands or press for results because of the trust that has been developed in the group.

A good example of establishing consensus and ownership within an organization is found in a program implemented by JP Morgan. JP Morgan decided to create a CFO mindset in the controllers within the company. Company leaders wanted controllers to be more strategic so they developed a program called "CFO Mindset" in which Creativizers traveled around the world and taught the Innovation Genome that was oriented to the mindset. They got individual controller groups together in places like São Paulo and Singapore to create a shared vision about what the controllers could do to create strategic value in that organization. Ultimately, this created less reacting to reconciling the books and much more to being advisors and giving some kind of strategic advice to the firm.

When individuals take ownership for the success and failure of the group, organization, or community to which they belong, then the individuals in the group expand upon each others' success, and the group becomes more powerful than any one individual. It is important that teams have a shared vision and values and that each individual on the team takes ownership for the successes and failures of the team.

Preworkshop

The senior team is responsible for a set of exercises prior to the scheduled workshop—*The Change and Innovation Assessment* and *The Performance Management Assessment*.

Change and Innovation Assessment

Each senior team member needs to take the *Change and Innovation Assessment* one to two weeks before the scheduled workshop. (Note: Please refer to Innovation Genome, Step 1: Synthesize, Phase 2: Administer the *Change and Innovation Assessment*.)

Performance Management Assessment

The Lead Facilitator will need to contact the CFO or COO of the senior team to introduce the general idea of the *Performance Management Assessment* and discuss what information must be put together in order to help prepare for the Socialize workshop. In this meeting the Lead Facilitator will introduce examples of performance measures for each quadrant of the Innovation Genome (see Step 3: Socialize, Phase 3: *Performance Measures Assessment*). Once the senior leader gets an idea for the kinds of measures represented in each quadrant, the CFO or COO will then fill out the matrix presented in the table below based on the organization's current performance measures. (Table 5.2 is a sample; use Table 5.3 for your assessment.) The totals in each quadrant will vary based on the firm's needs, but the sum of all the quadrants must equal 100 percent.

The leader may find that there are few or no measures in certain quadrants. The senior leader is not required to fill in every cell under each quadrant but to hit on the key measures focused on in the organization and what weight the measure is given based on a total of 100 percent (e.g., under the Compete quadrant the leader might weight ROI as 15 percent of all measures). Once the senior leader completes the Performance Measures Matrix, he or she will pass the information to the Lead Facilitator so that the information can be incorporated into the presentation for the workshop.

Socialize Phase 1: Establish a Shared Mindset and Language

In order to build high-performing teams that are ready and willing to enact change, a company must first create and establish a shared mindset. Establishing a shared language, vision, and mindset is the objective of the first workshop in the Creativize change process. This workshop should

Table 5.2   Example Performance Measures Matrix

Current	Collaborate	Weight	Create	Weight
Measure	Employee retention rate	5%	Growth in total sales	10%
Measure		%	Growth in sales per person	5%
Measure		%	Total market share against competitors	5%
Total		5%		20%
	Control	**Weight**	**Compete**	**Weight**
Measure	Unit Cost	18%	Return on Investment (ROI)	20%
Measure	Percent of on-time deliveries	5%	Amount of cash on hand (cash flow)	15%
Measure	Number of product failure by product group	12%	Cycle time to market for new products and services	5%
Total		35%		40%

be made up of top organization leaders. It is during this workshop that the Innovation Genome is introduced and applied to the organization. Creativizers are chosen, and the teams for Step 5 (Synchronize) are created. The Socialize step also acts to affirm the master plan created in the Synthesize step in Chapter 3 or to readjust the master plan, if a major reve-

Table 5.3   Current Performance Measures Matrix

Current	Collaborate	Weight	Create	Weight
Measure		%		%
Measure		%		%
Measure		%		%
Total		%		%
	Control	**Weight**	**Compete**	**Weight**
Measure		%		%
Measure		%		%
Measure		%		%
Total		%		%

lation is made that affects the plan. (Note: This exercise is also used in Step 4: Supervise, Phase 2: Creating Shared Language and Mindset.)

Card Game

One of the most important steps in activating the change process is taking a look at how people interact: what are the dynamics of the different departments, employees, or functions within the organization? The Card

Game is the introductory exercise for the Shared Mindset workshop and functions by helping participants to begin to look at and understand interactions within their company.

To kick off the Card Game, each person will receive a stack of three or four different color-coded cards that are drawn randomly. All participants will then be able to walk around the room and engage in conversation with other attendees about which card is most descriptive of them, they will trade cards with others, and collect the cards which best characterize them. After a few minutes of conversation each person will return to his or her seat. All participants should have the same number of cards in their hand as they had when they started the exercise. The cards they are holding should more accurately describe how they would approach their work. The participants should then look to see which color they have collected most: which color best describes the way they perform their roles or functions within the company. Which one card best describes the way they perform?

After each person has decided on his or her color, the room will be divided into four corners according to color, following the model. This is done by asking everyone with a yellow card to raise his or her hand. Once the participants have raised their hands, send them to the corner of the room that will represent the yellow quadrant of the Innovation Genome. Do the same thing with the other three colors of the quadrant.

Once everyone has moved to one of the four corners of the room, start with the yellow group and have the participants in the yellow corner read their cards aloud to the rest of the group. Next ask the participants with yellow cards to stay quiet while the rest of the groups answer questions about that group. With the view that the organization will devote one year to work toward making changes in the firm, each group will begin analyzing the other groups within the room by answering the following types of questions:

- How do they (i.e., participants in the yellow quadrant) interact with each other?
- How do they decide who becomes the leader?
- What tools, methods, and processes do they use?
- For what offenses do they fire people?
- For what purpose do they create?
- Are they fast or slow?
- Are their approaches breakthrough or incremental?
- Where do we typically find these people in your firm? In what other types of firms?

Once the group has answered all the questions about the yellow quadrant, you would follow the same process with the other three quadrants.

It is during this exercise that stories of workplace wars begin to emerge; people begin to see the different mindsets and philosophies that exist within the company. The Card Game also functions as an important introductory exercise in teaching the Innovation Genome model, which will be used to put the change and innovation process in operation.

Teaching the Innovation Genome

Upon completion of the Card Game exercise, the Innovation Genome is introduced. The reason that organizations have workplace wars is that there are tensions within the company. The Innovation Genome helps to explain these tensions and is broken down into four categories. You can refer to Chapter 1 for the full description of each of the four categories, or four quadrants, of the Innovation Genome model.

When considering the Innovation Genome, two important questions a company should ask itself when preparing for the change and innovation process are "How much?" and "How fast?" The question of how much is asked to determine how radical the change needs to be. The more radical the change, the greater the risk and potential reward will be. In this case the organization would need to take on a Create approach to change. If the organization doesn't need a radical a change and doesn't want to take on much risk, it will shift more toward a Control approach to change. The faster the change needs to occur, the more the company will need to shift toward a Compete approach to change. The problem with moving quickly is that speed is not sustainable. If the organization has the time to take the Collaborate approach, the change will be more sustainable. Answering these questions will help the company to better decide which direction it needs to move toward in the Innovation Genome.

Framework Levels

The Innovation Genome exists in what could be compared to an ecosystem. There is always a larger situation that will determine what the company has to do, but there are also underlying structures, world views, and philosophies within the company that determine its actions. The company may be compared to a boat leaving on a voyage. The boat's crew can make choices such as choosing the sail, its sailors, the routes it will take, and the provisions it will have on board (the structure), but the ship cannot control the ocean or the weather (the situation). The underlying structure of the company is what provides the ability to navigate according to the map. It can be divided into three categories:

- *Purposes:* The destinations we seek.
- *Practices:* What all the people on board do, their beliefs, how they act.
- *People:* It is the people who create practices to create purposes.

So, the Innovation Genome value creation formula is

$$People + Practices = Purposes$$

The underlying philosophical belief of the Innovation Genome is that we have the ability to affect the universe, but the universe also has the ability to affect us. It is important not to confuse situation and structure. A situation (Table 5.4) is driven by outside forces such as market force and trends, whereas the structure (Table 5.5) is composed of the company's core values and beliefs. The Innovation Genome takes into account both the situation and the structure and looks at how these affect the company's People, Practices, and Purposes. Once the situation and the structure are understood and defined, there are a number of strategies the organization can take. The strategies will be informed by the situation.

There's an underlying philosophy to each view, and the power center for each view is different. The power center for each category helps to form the structure:

- *Collaborate's power center is the* heart. A Collaborate person often takes people's feelings into account when embarking upon a new project.
- *Create's power center is* intuition *or* spirit. A Create person is intuitive and often uses flipcharts or draws pictures to explain or map out ideas.
- *Compete's power center is the* head. A Compete person is logical and highly analytical. This is often the person explaining "how this creates that."
- *Control's power center is the* hands. In the Control category people tend to "get stuff done." A Control person likes to see an example and then get to work.

Table 5.4 Situation: External Conditions such as Market Forces and Trends

Collaborate
When . . .
- A community united by shared beliefs defines the organization, such as environmental concerns.
- Competency is closely linked to unique individual abilities, such as an entertainer.
- Lifestyle identification determines the product or service, such as motorcycles.

Create
When . . .
- Differentiation creates significantly higher margins, such as consumer electronics.
- Start-ups compete with incumbent firms through radical innovation.
- An industry is situated around blockbuster invention, such as pharmaceuticals.

Control
When . . .
- Scale and scope of organizational processes are very large and complex, such as automobile manufacturers.
- Government regulations and standards determine business practices, such as medicine.
- Failure is not an option, such as aerospace.

Compete
When . . .
- Shareholder demands are the primary driver, such as financial institutions.
- Aggressive competition changes the market dynamics through mergers and acquisitions.
- Investors demand quick financial results.

Time is also structured or experienced differently within each category:

- *Collaborate:* In the Collaborate category time is developmental and progressive, the way forming a relationship of trust takes time.
- *Create:* Within the Create category time is structured as emerging in multiple streams; time is consistently in flux.
- *Compete:* Within the Compete category time is considered to be artificial or imposed. Deadlines are very important. If a project is said to take nine days to accomplish, it will take nine days.

Table 5.5 Structure: Underlying World View such as Core Values and Learning

Collaborate
- Power center: heart
- Experience of time: natural (developmental)
- Experience of space: balance
- Experience of energy: gathering
- What collaborators seek: harmony
- How they seek it: reflection
- Their gift: empathy
- What they value: integrity
- How they learn: dialogue
- How they change: values

Create
- Power center: intuition (spirit)
- Experience of time: emerging (multiple streams)
- Experience of space: variety
- Experience of energy: expanding
- What they seek: transcendence
- How they seek it: experimentation
- Their gift: imagination
- What they value: novelty
- How they learn: synthesis
- How they change: vision

Control
- Power center: hands
- Experience of time: sequential (fixed)
- Experience of space: structured
- Experience of energy: focused
- What they seek: perfection
- How they seek it: observation
- Their gift: discipline
- What they value: standards
- How they learn: analysis
- How they change: process

Compete
- Power center: head
- Experience of time: artificial
- Experience of space: alignment
- Experience of energy: pursuing
- What they seek: power
- How they seek it: challenge
- Their gift: courage
- What they value: winning
- How they learn: competition
- How they change: goals

- *Control:* Within the Control category time is experienced as fixed and sequential; 8 is followed by 9, 9 by 10, and so on. People often use to-do lists, Outlook calendars, and/or Palm Pilots. In the Control category time is all about order.

The structure of an organization is made up of Purposes, Practices, and People.

Purposes (Table 5.6) are defined by the outcome or value that the organization intends to create:

- *Collaborate:* Community and knowledge
- *Create:* Innovation and growth

Table 5.6 Purposes: Outcomes, or the Value the Organization Intends to Create

Collaborate
- *Community:* Establishing and maintaining shared values and culture. Common ways of achieving this are networking, empowerment, and team building.
- *Knowledge:* Developing understanding and skills. Common ways of achieving this are training, organizational learning, and human resource management.

Create
- *Innovation:* Making new and better products and services. Common ways of achieving this are creative problem solving, new product development, and change management.
- *Growth:* Prospecting for new and future market opportunities. Common ways of achieving this are strategic forecasting, trend analysis, and shared vision management.

Control
- *Optimization:* Using resources in the best way possible. Common ways of achieving this are procedures, budgeting, and organizational design.
- *Quality:* Eliminating errors. Common ways of achieving this are process controls, systems, and technology.

Compete
- *Speed:* Moving quickly to capture an opportunity. Common ways of achieving this are mergers and acquisitions, branding, and customer service.
- *Profits:* Maximizing shareholder earnings. Common ways of achieving this are goals and metrics, strategic resource allocation, and portfolio management.

- *Compete:* Speed and profits
- *Control:* Optimization and quality

Practices (Table 5.7) are defined as the culture, competency, and pro-cesses of the organization. To define Practices, we ask, "What do we do at the organizational level to create value?"

Table 5.7 Practices: Culture, Competency, and Process of the Organization

Collaborate
- Developing learning-building teams
- Facilitating people communities
- Encouraging commitment
- Creating a sense of cohesion in the organization
- Establishing shared values among people
- Listening with concern
- Facilitating conflict resolution

Create
- Encouraging radical creativity
- Seeing the future first
- Destroying the old way of doing things
- Launching ambitious transforma-tional initiatives
- Looking for emerging opportu-nities
- Stimulating people to think orig-inally
- Conceiving significant new ventures
- Inciting revolution

Control
- Conserving fiscal resources
- Implementing systems to control complex tasks
- Preventing people from making costly mistakes
- Complying with regulations
- Adhering to professional standards
- Making internal work processes routine
- Using continuous improvement processes
- Employing technology on a large scale

Compete
- Meeting objectives
- Confronting problems as soon as they occur
- Quickly eliminating underper-forming initiatives
- Overcoming barriers
- Partnering with winners
- Solving problems in real time
- Focusing on performance
- Driving for superior returns on investments

Practices include:

- *Culture:* What does the organization believe? What are its values?
- *Competencies:* What are the abilities of the organization?
- *Processes:* What is the strategy? How does the organization allocate resources?

People (Table 5.8) are the individuals within the organization at all levels. However, for organizational change purposes the leaders will be looked at very closely because it is the leaders who create practices within the organization.

To review, these are the basics of the Innovation Genome:

- Four quadrants—Collaborate, Create, Compete, and Control
- Framework levels:
  - Situation—External conditions

Table 5.8   People: Individuals in the Organization, at All Levels

Collaborate	Create
• Sees potential	• Visionary dreamer
• Builds commitment and trust	• Clever
• Is sensitive and caring	• Optimistic
• Is a patient listener	• Enthusiastic
• Encourages participation	• Quick on their feet
• Respects differences	• Expressive
• Empowers people	• Big-picture thinker

Control	Compete
• Pragmatic	• Goal- and action-oriented
• Supervised and methodical	• Impatient
• Scientific or technical	• Assertive
• By the book	• Driven
• Problem solver	• Decisive
• Objective	• Challenging
• Persistent	• Competitive

○ Structure—Underlying world view made up of:
  – Purposes (Outcomes or value the organization intends to create)
  – Practices (Culture, competencies and processes)
  – People (Individuals in the organization, at all levels)

Differentiate and Integrate

The Innovation Genome represents four views of the world. The challenge of the change process is to think about each view and then successfully integrate the views in a way that will optimize each quadrant and create a high-performing organization moving in its direction of choice. This is often done through an exercise in which all the participants attending the workshop are divided into four groups, each representing one quadrant of the Innovation Genome. The four groups representing each quadrant are then asked to think about the problem, opportunity space, or project through the lens of the quadrant they are assigned to. Once the four groups have each created ideas they feel good about, they will be asked to join the opposite group (Compete versus Collaborate or Control versus Create) to take their ideas and generate new and better ideas that will take into account both perspectives represented from the Innovation Genome. In other words, the group in the Collaborate quadrant will join with the group that created ideas from the perspective of the Compete quadrant. They will then need to take both sets of ideas and create new, better ideas that take into account perspectives from both quadrants.

Once opposites integrate, real innovation and change occur. Because the opposing quadrants represent opposite approaches, when an idea can be created that takes both viewpoints into account, innovative ideas are more likely to follow. The same is true when two groups learn to work effectively together even though their tendencies and approaches are very different. Figure 5.1 illustrates the objectives of the Differentiate and Integrate process.

To help make the Differentiate and Integrate process more effective, it is important to first diverge and then converge at each step in the process so that the entire range of operations is explored before a solution is developed. This means that each group representing a different perspective from the Innovation Genome would first need to create as many ideas as possible (diverge). There would be no questioning about whether an idea is good or bad. Rather, the group would try to build on ideas and

Differentiate
- Consider the issue by thinking around the four perspectives
- Use breakout groups to divide and conquer

Integrate
- Integrate the perspectives and develop hybrid practices
- Integrate the breakout groups to create agreement

Figure 5.1   Differentiate and Integrate

create as many new ideas as possible. Once the group has a strong list of ideas, it would need to begin to ask questions to determine which ideas it will focus on (converge). The group might want to know whether any of the ideas it created could be combined, or whether an idea is possible, what resources would be needed, and other questions that would narrow the large number of ideas down to the two or three the group will move forward on. When the groups with opposite perspectives are brought together to integrate ideas, they will want to start by diverging again before they begin to converge ideas.

- Diverge:
  - Ask open-ended questions.
  - Tell stories to share experiences.
  - Create visions and symbols.
  - Launch experiments.
  - Engage the mind.
  - Create energy and momentum.
  - Explore the art of possibility.
- Converge
  - Ask closed-ended questions.
  - Consult experts to understand the facts.
  - Develop systems and measures.
- Validate through tests.
  - Engage the hands.
  - Create processes and plans.
  - Integrate the science of reality.

There are three Change and Innovation Teams that should be assigned to carry out the organization's change process. These teams will be made up of:

- *Leadership Team:* Made up of key leaders.
- *Creativizers:* Made up of key people within the organization who are committed to the change process and cognizant of the organization's situation, purpose, and people. These are the people responsible for seeing the change process through.
- *Action Teams:* Managers and other key people within the organization who can effect change.

The Leadership Team is the smallest team, but it plays a vital role because it is the leaders who establish practices in the organization. The Creativizer's role is extremely important because he or she will be responsible for follow-through. The Action Team is made up of people who can make or break the project. For these reasons, it is imperative that the right people be on the right teams.

Socialize Phase 2: Diagnose the Purposes, Practices, and People

At this point the themes from the assessment are reported, and the senior leadership group is presented with diagrams that represent what the organization looks like currently, as well as diagrams of what it will look like according to assessment results. There are three diagrams, one that addresses Purposes, one that addresses Practices, and one that addresses People. Figure 5.2 is an example of what an organizational diagram could look like.

The power of the assessment diagram is that it can be used to show the path to the future, and it can become a symbol of the organization's shared mindset. It gives the company a visual image of where it's at and where it wants to be, which can be powerful in gauging the differences between the quadrants within the Innovation Genome.

The group has been presented with the organizational diagrams and must now diagnose the situation by having a discussion that includes the following topics. Note that in order to create an effective shared vision, it is important that the *group* diagnose the situation, not the Creativizer.

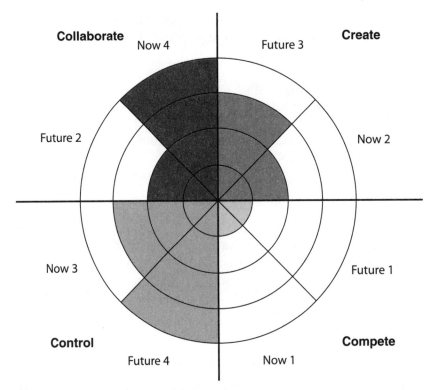

Figure 5.2 Sample organizational diagram

Diagnose the Situation

- Where are there major differences in the profiles? Why do these differences exist?
  - Purposes, Practices, and People
  - Between our business unit and your operating unit
  - Between our operating units
  - Within our unit
  - Other surveys
- What are the strengths and weaknesses?
  - Our unit
  - Others
- Where are the biggest gaps between the current and desired situation?

Once the situation has been diagnosed, the group must focus on creating a shared vision. It is important to ask questions relevant to the organization's desired picture. Once the group knows where "there" is, it should draw a picture of what the organization will look like when it has achieved its vision. It is important that the group not limit its thinking to the chart; the group is free to adjust the current and desired profiles as appropriate; it should think freely within each quadrant. The company may not want to necessarily change quadrants, but it might prefer to improve the quadrant it's already in.

Create a Shared Vision

- What is our desired organizational profile?
  - Moving toward what and away from what?
- What potential challenges does this create for our organization?
  - Obstacles, organizational development, people, strategic positioning, etc.
- What does this organization look like?
  - Use stories and visual imagery to describe how it works.
- Adjust the current and desired profiles for culture and competency as appropriate.
  - In the next phase, we make the desired profile operational.

Socialize Phase 3: Performance Measures Assessment

Once the group has consensus and creates a final desired profile from the *Change and Innovation Assessment*, it is ready to translate the Purposes results into specific Performance Measures. The *Change and Innovation Assessment* is a sociometric assessment and is based on perceptions of those who take the assessment. Tying the *Change and Innovation Assessment* Purposes results into specific measures will allow the group members to determine more concretely how much they really want to shift toward other quadrants in the Innovation Genome.

The list of measures is based on a study presented in the upcoming book *Competing Values Leadership: Creating Value in Organizations*.[1] The study looked at two key measures in each quadrant of the original Competing Values Framework and studied the Fortune 2000 over the last 10 years based on these measures. There were a number of interesting findings on the kinds of value produced based on these eight key measures. The list of measures shown in Tables 5.9–5.12 gives examples of measures that are similar to the eight used in the study in an attempt to lead the group toward picking the appropriate measures in its particular industry and organization.

The steps to follow now are

1. The Lead Facilitator shows the group the Current Performance Measures Matrix prepared by the CFO or COO to remind group members of the measures currently being used and how much weight is given to each measure (refer to the Current Performance Measures Matrix from the preworkshop, just before Phase 1).

Table 5.9   Collaborate

Measures of Community
- Employee satisfaction and morale survey ratings
- Employee retention rate
- Turnover rate due to poor performance
- Absence rate
- Reduction in employee grievances and complaints
- Headcount as a percentage of forecasted needs
- Job posting response rate
- Percent of job offers accepted
- Percent of employees promoted
- Customer satisfaction survey ratings

Measures of Knowledge
- Percent of training requirements fulfilled
- Number of training days per employee
- Training expenditures as a percent of operating budget
- Training investment per employee
- Percentage of employees with career development plan
- Number of employee suggestions approved
- Number of best practices communicated and applied across departments
- Skill targets achieved through training and development
- Impact and value evaluation of training and development
- Average experience level of personnel

2. The Lead Facilitator asks the group participants if the information presented seems accurate to them or if there are any glaring issues they would like to discuss and adjust. Once the group members feel comfortable with the current measures, they review a list of potential measures that fall into each quadrant.

3. The Lead Facilitator breaks the group into three smaller groups and has them review the measures.

4. Once the groups have reviewed the potential measures, they will then select a few measures from each quadrant or create their own measures that relate to the examples and place them in the Desired Performance Measures Matrix below. (See Tables 5.13 and 5.14.)

Table 5.10   Create

Measures of Innovation
- The number of new products or services launched
- Number of new sources of revenue
- New products or services development investment as percentage of sales
- Revenues derived from new products or services as a percentage of total revenue
- Return on investment for new products or services
- Investment in R&D as percentage of total expenditures
- Ratio of R&D expenditures in core research versus development of applications
- Diversity of innovation portfolio mix
- New product and service process pipeline flow rate
- New product and service survival rate

Measures of Growth
- Growth in total sales
- Total market share against competitors
- Growth in sales by segment
- Growth in sales by channel
- Growth in sales by geography
- New market growth in sales
- Growth in sales through joint ventures
- Growth in sales through new applications of existing products and technology
- Measures of brand recognition
- Growth in sales per person

Table 5.11 Compete

Measures of Speed	Measures of Profit
• First to market with products and services	• Return on assets
• Cycle time to design and develop products and services	• Total revenue
• Cycle time to market for new products and services	• Net present value
• Time to profitability for existing products and services	• Gross profit
• Time to profitability for new products and services	• Stock price
• Number of projects launched ahead of schedule	• Shareholder value
• Number of projects delivered ahead of schedule	• Operating income
• Ratio of projects launched to projects advanced through review gates	• Earnings per share
• Time to new market penetration achieved through acquisitions	• Amount of cash on hand (cash flow)
• Number of employees qualified to jump-start projects	• Bid and quote success rate

5. Each measure is given a specific weight of importance based on the Purposes (Desired Future Outcomes) Profile from the *Change and Innovation Assessment*.

If the group on average gave the highest score to the Compete quadrant, the second highest to the Create quadrant, third to the Control quadrant, and the lowest score to the Collaborate quadrant, then each quadrant will receive a certain value. For example, if the Compete quadrant has four cells filled in, it would have a total weight of 40 percent; if Create had three cells filled in, it would receive 30 percent; if Control had two cells filled in, it would receive 20 percent; and if Collaborate had only one cell filled in, it would receive 10 percent. If the group selects three measures in each quadrant, they would have to divide the allotted per-

---

Table 5.12 Control

Measures of Efficiency
- Unit cost
- Target versus cost achievement
- Actual versus planned production
- Days' supply of finished goods inventory
- Percentage of back orders
- Percentage of milestones achieved
- Percentage of on-time deliveries
- Total internal cost savings
- Labor productivity variance
- Throughput time

Measures of Quality
- Initial quality at the release of a product
- Percentage of scrap
- Safety violations
- Regulatory violations
- Number of product failures by product group
- Improvement on error or defect rate
- Percentage of reduction in redundancy or waste
- Number of engineering changes after release (manufacturability)
- Percentage of certified suppliers
- Number of warranty claims

---

centage in each quadrant to the three measures (i.e., the three measures in the Compete quadrant may receive 20 percent weight, 12 percent weight, and the final measure 8 percent weight, so the total comes to 40 percent weight). The process is completed for each quadrant in the matrix.

6. The groups report on the measures they selected and the weight given to each measure.
7. Once all three groups have reported on their measures and weights, the group as a whole has to decide how to combine the results into one matrix they can agree upon. Because the matrix will help determine a number of decisions that the group will make throughout the workshop, it is important that the group be allowed to have vigorous and productive discussion so that people are clear and can feel good about moving forward.
8. Once the matrix is filled out, the Lead Facilitator will ask the group if there are any final thoughts or push the group to make sure members are comfortable and committed to their decisions. Once the group is in agreement, the Lead Facilitator can move on to the next exercise in the workshop.

Table 5.13 Example of a Desired Performance Measures Matrix

Desired	Collaborate	Weight	Create	Weight
Measure	Employee retention rate	5%	The number of new products/ services launched	13%
Measure	Training investment per employee	5%	Investment in R&D as percentage of total expenditures	5%
Measure		%	Growth in total sales	12%
Total		10%		30%
	Control	**Weight**	**Compete**	**Weight**
Measure	Unit cost	10%	Return on Investment (ROI)	20%
Measure	Percentage of on-time deliveries	5%	Amount of cash on hand (cash flow)	15%
Measure	Number of product failures by product group	5%	Cycle time to market for new products and services	5%
Total		20%		40%

Table 5.14   Desired Performance Measures Matrix

Desired	Collaborate	Weight	Create	Weight
Measure		%		%
Measure		%		%
Measure		%		%
Total		%		%
	Control	**Weight**	**Compete**	**Weight**
Measure		%		%
Measure		%		%
Measure		%		%
Total		%		%

Socialize Phase 4: Integrate the Strategy

Every organization has a strategy, which is the plan it is trying to pursue. How does the shared vision support or change this strategy?

Relate the Shared Vision and Strategy

- What are our current opportunities?
- What are the key ways in which we are pursuing them?
- What capabilities do we need to succeed?
- How does our diagnosis of the organization's culture and competencies support this strategy?
- How does it change it?
- What are our future opportunities?
- What are the key ways in which we are pursuing them?
- What capabilities do we need to succeed?

Socialize Phase 5: Organizational Change and Innovation Actions

The group must now decide what needs to be changed within each quadrant in order to reach its desired picture. To do this, the group will be divided into teams, once again according to quadrants: Collaborate, Create, Compete, and Control. Each team will fill out the chart for the quadrant it is assigned to. It is important that team members seek to see the answers through the lenses of each particular quadrant and keep the company's shared vision at the forefront of their decisions. Teams will need to list what each quadrant should do more of, do less of, and do differently. They should also list what actions they should start and what actions they should stop, and they should provide specific boundaries about what the actions mean and don't mean (Table 5.15).

In filling out Table 5.15, it is important for the teams to recognize that if they are going to start something, they must also stop something. The group members must also realize that if they create too many actions, they will be less likely to do any of them. Once the group creates a number of actions, they must select the best four or five ideas to implement.

Translate Ideas into Actions

Once each group has agreed on the ideas it intends to implement, the groups must translate their ideas into actions. They must be able to see how each idea can be implemented and achieved within the workplace. Table 5.16 is a guide for mapping out an action plan.

Table 5.15   "Start, Stop, Do Differently" Practices

Start, Stop, or Do Differently	Means:
•	•
•	•
•	•
•	•
•	•
•	•
•	•
•	•
•	
•	**Doesn't mean:**
•	•
•	•
•	•
•	•
•	•
•	•
•	•
•	•

Socialize Phase 6: Change Behavior

In the change process it is important to focus not only on "how" but also on "who." The group has now mapped out what the organization is going to be and how it's going to get there. Now it needs to turn its focus to "who's going to do what?" In this exercise each person is going to receive a note card in order to write a short evaluation of each person in the room. What value does each person currently contribute to the group? What new behaviors are needed from each person in order to accomplish the task at hand? What does each person need to do to make change work? For this exercise to be successful, it is essential that each person be completely honest in his or her evaluation of one another. Each person should follow the directions provided below.

Table 5.16 Translate Ideas into Actions

What are we doing?	Who is doing it?	Why are we doing it?	How are we doing it?	Where are we doing it?	When will it be done?

Behavioral Change

- You have created a shared profile of the desired future. This profile cannot be realized unless everyone begins to behave in ways that are aligned with the desired future. This exercise is designed to bring about such a change.
- Steps:

    1. You will write an evaluation of every person present. For each person select a sheet of paper and write his or her name at the top right.
    2. On the front of the sheet list the things you most value about what the person currently contributes to the group.
    3. On the back list the answers to this question: "What new behaviors do we need from this person in order for us all to get to the desired future?"
    4. Deliver the evaluations to the respective recipients.

5. Read the evaluations you have received and Synthesize the themes on both sides. Be prepared to report the themes from both sides and to indicate what personal commitments you are willing to make to bring about the desired future.

- The senior-most person will be asked to report first.
- The future of the organization depends on your integrity and courage in this exercise.

Commitments

Upon completion of the evaluations, all participants will Synthesize their feedback and indicate the themes they've drawn from each side of the evaluation sheet, as well as make commitments about changes they will make. All participants will indicate what assistance they feel they need from others to make these changes, and how they're going to follow up on these commitments. Essentially, each person is making both a social contract and a personal commitment (Table 5.17) about how he or she is going to behave differently in order to promote the change process in moving forward.

Table 5.17   Behavior Change Commitments

Themes	
Changes you are committed to making	
Assistance you need from others	
Follow-up	

Socialize Phase 7: Select the Creativizers

The next part of the process is the development of Creativizers who can take these actions forward in the organization at large. This is an extremely important phase because the role that Creativizers play is so vital to the change process. The people selected must be able, ready, and willing to see the process through. In order to select the proper people for this role, it is important to understand the functions of the Creativizers, as well as their roles and responsibilities. (*Note:* Use the following to expand upon the function of Creativizers in Step 5: Synchronize, Phase 1: Rollout Preparation.)

Function of Creativizers

- Develop sustainable internal competencies for facilitating change and innovation.
- Create a community of change practitioners that share best practices and regularly add new knowledge and tools to the organization.
- Leverage the skills of a few unique individuals to liberate the potential of the entire firm.
- Establish a legitimate forum, agenda, and pro-change and innovation community in the organization.

Creativizer Development Process

1. See one:
   - Observe a workshop.
   - Provide feedback and action planning.
2. Do one:
   - Assist in running a workshop.
   - Run a workshop.
   - Provide feedback and action planning.
3. Teach one:
   - Assist a developing Creativizer in running a workshop.
   - Provide feedback and action planning.

Creativizer Roles and Responsibilities

- Keep the process on track.
- Focus the group on the desired results.
- Create a positive environment.
- Establish a group identity.
- Encourage participation, mutual respect, and listening.
- Stimulate group energy.
- Give feedback on group dynamics.
- Structure and clarify issues.
- Resolve conflicts.
- Challenge boundaries and habit-bound thinking.
- Confront hidden problems.
- Solve problems when appropriate.

Assess Potential Creativizers

In discussing roles and responsibilities of the Creativizers, people in the group should begin to think of possible candidates or people in the organization who can perform these roles. In thinking about each possibility, the following questions should be asked in order to assess which people are appropriate for this role:

- How does the organization view the Creativizer's competency to undertake this challenge?
- Does the Creativizer have sufficient understanding of this challenge?
- Is the Creativizer capable of helping the organization successfully plan, design, develop, and implement this challenge?
- Does the Creativizer have adequate organizational credibility to help the organization implement the challenge?
- Does the Creativizer have a vested interest in the success or failure of the challenge?
- Is the Creativizer capable of advising the challenge team?
- Is the Creativizer viewed as professional and ethical by the organization?
- Does the Creativizer have the interpersonal skills to motivate and communicate effectively with the organization?

- Does the Creativizer have a track record of producing results?
- Is the Creativizer willing to develop herself or himself and others in order to expand capabilities?

Picking Creativizers

Deciding who is chosen as the Creativizers to help lead the change process is one of the key decisions made throughout the Creativize Method. The best process can be created, but without the right people running the process, things can go awry quickly. Creating change within an organization will cause people in the organization to resist when they see that the changes are actually going to be implemented. The Creativizers must believe in the cause they are pursuing in order to effectively lead the change process through difficult times. These Creativizers must also have the right relationships and knowledge of the organization to understand what truly needs to occur if change and innovation are ever going to take hold in the organization.

With this in mind, the senior leaders are responsible for narrowing down the group of potential Creativizers to the *Creativize Method*. To begin, they should list a number of potential candidates. The senior leaders should then go through and give each person a score from 1 to 5 on each of the following criteria (1 being the lowest and 5 being the highest). Once the senior leaders have ranked everyone they originally selected, they should narrow the list down to the top 15 people. After these 15 are interviewed by the Lead Facilitator, the final 10 Creativizers will be chosen, These are the people who will lead the change and innovation process with the help of the senior team.

The criteria for the selection of these Creativizers are as follows:

1. Highly creative thinker.
2. Strong bias toward action and results.
3. Methodical.
4. Highly credible and influential with key stakeholder groups.
5. Knows how to energize a group.
6. Is able to unearth and resolve difficult conflicts.
7. Is able to engage everyone into a participative process.
8. Is able to make connections and see new possibilities.
9. Understands the organization and key challenges.
10. Puts the organization's interests before their own.

Sponsor Creativizers

Once the group has assessed the Creativizers and agreed upon certain individuals within the organization, it should formally go through the process of sponsoring the Creativizers. There should be a sponsor assigned to each Creativizer who formally agrees to take responsibility for seeing that the Creativizer is following through and that the person chosen for the role is performing the role as necessary for the change and innovation process to be successful in the organization (Table 5.18).

Socialize Phase 8: Define Strategic Pillars

By this point, the organization has already created a shared vision of where it is now and where it wants to go. Before proceeding with rolling out the strategy, the group must decide what the strategic pillars are. *Strategic pillars* are the key issues that will enable the strategy to happen or stop it from happening. A flexible technology platform, a high-performance culture, and being a low-cost provider are all examples of strategic pillars. To identify strategic pillars, review the action plans that were created earlier in the Synchronize step and adjust them as necessary so that they could be considered strategic pillars. There should be no more than five strategic pillars selected (Table 5.19).

Table 5.18   Creativize Method Role Chart

Sponsor	Facilitator	Action Team

Table 5.19 Five Strategic Pillars

Strategic Pillars	Creativizer	Action Team
1.		
2.		
3.		
4.		
5.		

Conclusion

1. What is the leadership vantage point, and why is this an important consideration?

The Leadership Team sees the organization from a perspective that is different from everyone else's. As part of that perspective, leaders need to be especially mindful of the past, present, and future of their company's innovative projects (remember to ask the "do, doing, done" questions). Because the Socialize step is about the people and not the project, the goal is to get the Leadership Team's future vision to be shared by the organization. It is important to recognize these differences and keep them in perspective because this is likely to explain why there is conflict within the organization when people are faced with any change process.

2. Is conflict good or bad?

Conflict is inevitable when embarking on organizational change. The key is to effectively manage it so that it can be good for the organization's learning process. Otherwise, poorly managed conflict is bad.

3. How do we get from ideas to action?

People. This step is about the people of the organization and getting everyone focused on tapping into his or her creativity in order to move the organization forward toward a common, shared vision. It starts with getting the leadership team to agree on a shared vision. Changes in the organization's behavior will occur when senior leaders begin to act on a shared vision.

The 3-D View

Remember from Chapter 2 that innovation is typically a work in progress. Innovation always provides key insights into the past that will in turn provide some wisdom about the future, but more importantly it allows us a wider range of courses to speculate and navigate. Once the Socialize step is complete, it is important for the Creativizers and other appropriate people to ask in a separate meeting the Do, Doing, Done questions by thinking around the Innovation Genome. It is important that the meeting take place close enough to the Socialize step so that everyone remembers the experience but enough removed so that people have had time to think about what really happened.

Do . . .
Looking forward to future projects, communities, charters, and goals that will flow from the Socialize step consider the questions in Table 5.20 from the four perspectives of the Innovation Genome.

Table 5.20   Innovation Genome—Do

Collaborate View
- What do I need to do?
- How do I want to do it?

Create View
- What do I need to do?
- How do I want to do it?

Control View
- What do I need to do?
- How do I want to do it?

Compete View
- What do I need to do?
- How do I want to do it?

Doing . . .
Looking at any current work taking place around the *Creativize Method* at your organization, consider the questions in Table 5.21.

Table 5.21   Innovation Genome—Doing

Collaborate View	Create View
• What's working and what isn't? Why? • What changes should we make?	• What's working and what isn't? Why? • What changes should we make?
Control View	**Compete View**
• What's working and what isn't? Why? • What changes should we make?	• What's working and what isn't? Why? • What changes should we make?

Done . . .

Looking back at what has taken place with the Socialize step and any projects that have been launched, consider the questions in Table 5.22.

Table 5.22

Collaborate View	Create View
• What worked and what didn't? Why? • What changes would we make if we ran this step or project again? • What have we learned that can be applied to the current practices of the organization?	• What worked and what didn't? Why? • What changes would we make if we ran this step or project again? • What have we learned that can be applied to the current practices of the organization?
Control View	**Compete View**
• What worked and what didn't? Why? • What changes would we make if we ran this step or project again? • What have we learned that can be applied to the current practices of the organization?	• What worked and what didn't? Why? • What changes would we make if we ran this step or project again? • What have we learned that can be applied to the current practices of the organization?

CHAPTER 6

Step 4: SUPERVISE

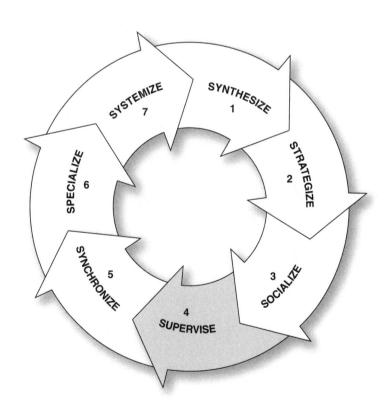

Supervise Overview

- Objective:
  - Prepare participants to help run an organizational change process.

- Participants:
  - Selected upper-midlevel employees who are believed to have necessary skills to lead change.

- Actions:
  1. Sponsor communicates desired outcomes and expectations of participants for this workshop.
  2. Lead Facilitator introduces *Creativize Method* overview and the Innovation Genome in order to establish a shared mindset and language.
  3. Participants participate in a team-building experience that is processed by the participants as the Lead Facilitator guides them through the process.
  4. Participants discuss the implications and impact of the *Change and Innovation Assessment* and diagnose the current situation.
  5. The team members discuss what they learned from the team-building experience and previous team experiences and begin to create norms and expectations for the new group.
  6. Participants create action plans that will move the organization from the current to the desired state.
  7. Participants learn to manage resistant employees and groups who could block the change process.
  8. Participants practice facilitating one of the exercises they participated in earlier in the workshop and discuss what they will need in order to be more effective at running the workshops on their own in the future.

- Time:
  - Three days with an optional one-day follow-up workshop. (Note that developing Creativizers is an ongoing process that takes much more time than the three or four days allotted here.)

- Set assignments

This Chapter Will Help Me to Answer:

- What does it take to be a Creativizer?
- What's the best way to communicate any change process to people in an organization?
- How do you develop buy-in for a change process?

Introduction

The purpose of the Supervise step is to develop a community of highly practiced Creativizers who can apply their knowledge and skill in a cascading way throughout the organization. In other words, by creating small groups who develop skills through being trained and experimenting, the Creativizers begin to develop an understanding of what works and what doesn't work in their organization. The Creativizers are then able to share with one another what they have learned so they can create new innovative practices for the organization. They can then spread this knowledge by forming new groups and teaching them what they have learned. The Supervise step becomes a cyclical process for learning throughout the organization.

Supervise in Action—DSM

Wim Vorage looks like he plays football (soccer to Americans) for Feyenoord, Rotterdam—the fabulously great blue-collar team of the Netherlands. It fits his character: focused, honest, hands-on, and collaborative like the captain of a winning team. Vorage is the antithesis of a business magazine pretty-boy who whips up a perfect strategy on a PowerPoint presentation with the last slide that reads "implement." He is Captain Implementation, the go-to guy for Dutch chemical giant DSM's plant operations. He is a Creativizer in one of the most uncreative places in the world—the floor of a chemical plant.

Vorage is big on freedom: freedom to think new thoughts; freedom to try new things; freedom to speak the truth to those who don't want to hear it. But he also believes in responsibility in a big way: responsibility to your team, company, and community; responsibility to own your work; responsibility to get it done. In fact, over the nearly 30 years that he's been with DSM, Vorage has made a career out of solving one tough, ugly, and complex problem after another. Along the way, he also reinvented many of DSM's core manufacturing processes and operating strategies, and he developed a legion of future leaders for good measure.

Vorage started as an engineer, and, like all real engineers, he loves to make things work. His first assignment was as the maintenance engineer at a humongous petrochemical complex at Geleen in the Limburg region in the south of the Netherlands. Ten years earlier the sister plant blew up killing 13 people. Although a rookie, Vorage realized that his cracker (a cracker is a gigantic array of furnaces, tanks, and tubes) was on a crash course to repeat history. The problems cut across all departments and functions, so no one wanted to own it. Vorage went to the site manager and division manager and spelled out his concerns. They all agreed the cracker needed to be operated and maintained differently, and they gave Vorage their full support. The three of them worked hard for four years to fix the problem. There was nothing glamorous about the solution—no revolutionary invention that changed the game. Instead, as is so often the case, it required painstaking incremental improvements to get things working while keeping everyone safe.

Vorage moved up through the ranks and went on to manage a polymer plant where DSM customers required a lot of specific changes to chemical formulations. He developed flexible processes to meet these changes. This would become a Vorage trademark—take a mundane assignment and find ways to increase value.

Next, Vorage was sent to manage a plastic conversion plant in Luxemburg that made industrial plastic bags and plastic pallet covers—a commodity product manufactured in one of Europe's most expensive regions. This was a real challenge for Vorage. He was the only Dutch-speaking person at the plant; most of the workers were immigrants from scountries where work was scarce (Portugal, Belgium), and nearly 50 percent of the workers were women, which was quite unusual at that time in this industry. Vorage and the workers did their best to develop new processes and practices to significantly reduce the costs associated with operating the plant, but it wasn't enough and they had no choice but to close it down. This was a traumatic experience for everyone, Vorage included, and many of the people at the plant had no place to go.

Vorage decided that it was important to close the book on the plant with some type of event that would ease the pain and bring closure for the displaced workers. On the advice of several Portuguese women from the plant, Vorage and the workers conducted a funeral for the plant with all the workers in attendance. The symbolic significance of the experience brought tears and hope to the workers. At the end of the services they held a football competition and a farewell dinner. Every year for the next three years, Vorage held reunions in order to check up on people and make sure they were doing okay.

Vorage went on to improve or close other plants. His next stop was the south of Germany and Berlin. Each time he demonstrated his fierce resolve to do things differently, engage the people, and make tough choices. All the while, DSM was entering fine chemical and life sciences businesses and moving away from commodity petrochemicals. At this point Vorage was sent to manage DSM's phenol plant in Rotterdam. The workers had been through a terrible explosion that killed seven people, and some years later a bitter cold winter had closed the plant for six weeks. The plant was of strategic significance because it produced a significant amount of benzaldehyde in the world. However, the price of phenol was falling, and the operation needed to be scaled back. Vorage had to find a way to turn a liability into an advantage for DSM. He assembled a team to work on the problem, and it quickly developed co-products that became the mainstay of the plant. The plant became so successful at producing these co-products that over time the co-products became more valuable than the main product.

Everything old is new again. Vorage was brought back to the Geleen site where he started his career with DSM to manage a project that would be leveraged to re-create the site. He called the project "Copernicus" because just like its namesake he had to find a new center for DSM. Geleen was the heart of DSM, and Vorage was now faced with the challenge of changing the mindset of the people on the site from the past to the future: from one large chemicals complex belonging to DSM to dozens of smaller and flexible plants belonging to several owners. The six business groups that occupied the Geleen complex had been operating separately for some time. Vorage's first challenge was to create synergies in manufacturing processes. Then he had to remove layers of support services. His way of weaving processes, systems, and people together now became of strategic importance.

Shortly before Copernicus, the petrochemical division of DSM and its largest and historically core business group was sold to the Saudi Arabian company SABIC which overnight became the largest producer in the

Geleen complex. Vorage didn't make the deal to sell the business or create the strategy; instead he made SABIC operational by reimagining outdated visions, revising operating practices, and re-creating the culture of a site that viewed its universe as revolving around the operations (manufacturing excellence) of the plants on the site.

After the sale of its petrochemicals division, DSM acquired the vitamins and fine chemicals business of F. Hoffman—La Roche AG of Switzerland, the world's largest vitamin manufacturer. Vorage's new challenge will be to figure out how to make a commodity such as citric acid in Belgium, an expensive place to manufacture, cheap enough to compete with markets such as the Chinese market, where it was much less expensive to produce. The outcome is unsure, but of one thing there is no doubt. Vorage and the team of future leaders he assembles will be there trying stuff and working things out. Through their experiences and experiments, they will develop incredible capabilities for making necessary changes happen as well as the feeling of ownership, which will help propel DSM's Citrique Belge into the future.

There are several key lessons in this example. The first is, *show, don't tell.* Vorage was an expert at getting things done and achieving results, not just talking about getting things done. In doing so, he showed and he created opportunities for experiential learning. As a teacher, Vorage embodied the second lesson—*see one, do one, teach one*. Vorage's strongest capability was his ability to turn liabilities into assets. The secret to which is to *leave room for the emergent stuff that you don't know now* and to let yourself be open to the possibility that the ride may yield more than the destination ever intended. In looking to be creative at traditionally noncreative places such as chemical plants, Vorage discovered new ways to create growth out of old methods as well as how to share those ways with others so that he could move throughout the company to discover more.

Range: Differentiation (Favoritism) to Integration (Acceptance, Accommodation, and Assimilation)

One of the key abilities Creativizers need to expand is learning to differentiate their thinking and the thinking of the group they are developing. *Differentiation* means that the Creativizer learns to understand and appreciate the approach of people representing different strengths on the

Table 6.1   How the Innovation Genome Relates to the Supervise Step

Collaborate	**Create**
Do things together.	*Do things first.*
• Create team and organizational community.	• Speculate about new opportunities.
Control	**Compete**
Do things right.	*Do things fast.*
• Establish a work process.	• Set challenging goals.

Innovation Genome. We all have a certain style with a tendency to show favoritism toward specific types of ideas, practices, and behaviors that hit our "sweet spot." Creativizers need to stretch past these natural tendencies so they can appreciate and implement differing views in the project group.

View from the Balcony

When Creativizers help form and develop new project groups, they need to play a role similar to that of an effective coach. An appropriate phrase that we use symbolically is that a Creativizer must have a "view from the balcony." This phrase is often used by Ronald Heifetz of Harvard's Kennedy School of Government. The focus is not on the result the team is creating but on helping the team to work together more effectively. To do this the Creativizer must be close enough to the group to understand what is needed by the group so that members can reach their goals, learn from each other, and become high performing, but separate enough to remain objective. The following questions can be asked by the Creativizers to help them in this process:

- Is this team on the right track?
- What's working and what's not working? Why?
- How can this team become higher performing?

- Will this project create value?
- Will this project create any breakthroughs?

Performance Dialogue

As Creativizers work with different Action Teams, gain new competencies, and effectively move groups toward productivity, learning, and growth, the team members may start expecting the Creativizer to solve their problems for them. The Creativizer must resist this temptation so that the group can learn to solve its own problems and gain new competencies. Performance Dialogue is an approach that can be used to get groups or individuals to learn how to solve problems on their own.

When approached with a problem, the Creativizers should say that they will help the person or group only if they can do the Performance Dialogue together.

Following are steps in the Performance Dialogue process (questions will need to be adjusted if working with a group rather than an individual):

- At the first meeting the Creativizer guides the individual or group through creating ideas and making decisions around the following questions:
  - What's the mission of your team and how do you support it?
  - What goals do you need to achieve to help the team reach its mission?
  - How do you plan to achieve your goals?
  - What assistance do you need to achieve your goals?
  - Set a new date to meet and review goals and plans (90 minutes approximately every six weeks).
- During all the remaining meetings the Creativizer discusses the following questions with the individual or group:
  - What's the mission of your team and how do you support it?
  - What have you accomplished over the last six weeks since we talked?
  - What goals have succeeded and failed?
  - What roadblock prevented you from completing the goals last agreed upon?
  - How do you plan to achieve your goals?

○ What assistance do you need to achieve your goals? (You are being an advisor to support them in their ideas.)
○ What are the new goals and plans for our next dialogue?
○ Set a new date to meet and review goals and plans (90 minutes approximately every six weeks).

Scouting Report for Black Belts

The Socialize step ends with the senior team creating a list of potential Creativizers based on ten criteria. The same ten criteria are used as an assessment filled out by three to five colleagues of each potential Creativizer. Based on the results of the assessment, the potential Creativizers are ranked and interviewed to determine the final group of Creativizers. Below you will find an example of the Creativizer Criteria Assessment and potential interview questions.

Creativizer Criteria Assessment

1. Highly creative thinker
Lowest   1   2   3   4   5   Highest

2. Strong bias toward action and results
Lowest   1   2   3   4   5   Highest

3. Organized and methodical
Lowest   1   2   3   4   5   Highest

4. Highly credible and influential with key stakeholder groups
Lowest   1   2   3   4   5   Highest

5. Knows how to energize a group
Lowest   1   2   3   4   5   Highest

6. Is able to unearth and resolve difficult conflicts
Lowest   1   2   3   4   5   Highest

7. Is able to engage everyone in a participative process
Lowest   1   2   3   4   5   Highest

8. Is able to make connections and see new possibilities
Lowest   1   2   3   4   5   Highest

9. Understands the organization and key challenges
Lowest   1   2   3   4   5   Highest

10. Puts the organization's interests before their own
Lowest   1   2   3   4   5   Highest

Potential Interview Questions

1. What are the key challenges that are keeping your organization from becoming as successful as possible?
2. What are the key challenges you are facing in your role within the organization that keep you from being as successful as possible?
3. What drives you to being the best employee you can be? Please give an example that you have experienced to illustrate this point.
4. Please give an example of a recent project you took part in. What went well? What needed to change so that greater success could have been achieved? How did you know whether you were successful or not? What challenges did you face and how did you get past those challenges?
5. Can you give an example of a time when you had to be creative or create a new way of doing things that led to your having success in your job?
6. When you need to draw on the influence of others in the organization to help you fulfill your responsibilities, who are some of the people you turn to in order to help you be successful?
7. What steps would you take to move your organization toward having greater success?

Selected Creativizers are then trained on the *Creativize Method* and how to facilitate the process. One area that the Creativizers will need to begin working on immediately is the selection of innovation project leaders. These leaders will eventually select groups around projects created during Step 5 (Synchronize), which will be launched during Step 6 (Specialize). Creativizers will want to use the same process that was used to select them for selecting innovation leaders while focusing more specifically on finding people with expertise in the area the project is set up for. One way to find people with the right expertise is to learn where the opportunity spaces in the organization are. One way to find opportunity space is by having the potential innovation Project Leaders take the *Assessment of Organizational Strengths and Weaknesses*. By learning what is working and what is not working, you will see where projects can be launched in order to fix a problem or to further enhance the success already occurring in the organization.

The *Assessment of Organizational Strengths and Weaknesses*

Please read each of the following possible concerns and circle the number that best describes how well the area mentioned works or doesn't work in your organization. A 1 means not working at all, while 5 means it is working at a high level.

1. Attracting, developing, and keeping good people	1	2	3	4	5
2. Maintaining work and life balance	1	2	3	4	5
3. Obtaining cross-boundary cooperation	1	2	3	4	5
4. Maintaining effective interpersonal relationships	1	2	3	4	5
5. Empowering people	1	2	3	4	5
6. Thinking and planning	1	2	3	4	5
7. Aligning vision, strategy, and behavior	1	2	3	4	5
8. Stimulating innovation	1	2	3	4	5
9. Leading culture change	1	2	3	4	5
10. Growing the organization	1	2	3	4	5
11. Improving the bottom line	1	2	3	4	5
12. Improving customer satisfaction	1	2	3	4	5
13. Stimulating high performance	1	2	3	4	5
14. Managing time	1	2	3	4	5
15. Staying ahead of the competition	1	2	3	4	5
16. Improving internal processes	1	2	3	4	5
17. Producing high-quality goods and services	1	2	3	4	5
18. Succeeding with constrained resources	1	2	3	4	5
19. Improving organization decision making	1	2	3	4	5
20. Controlling projects	1	2	3	4	5

Are there any pressing problems that are consuming your attention that are not on the above list? Please describe them here.

_____

_____

_____

_____

Once you are clear on the opportunity spaces available, you can find employees who are high on the 10 selection criteria, along with having expertise in the potential project areas targeted.

As the list of potential innovation project leaders narrows, it will be important to have each person on the list take the *Change and Innovation Assessment* reviewed in Step 1 (Synthesize). By understanding the tendencies of the innovation project leaders, the Creativizer can more effectively coach them as they select a team, form the team, and create differentiation and integration on the team.

Ways of Getting Buy-in

Innovation, culture, and *organizational practices* are all words that are general and big. Throughout the book we've noted that individuals rarely want to own problems in organizations because it's hard to discuss the problems, get your mind around them, and to resolve them. Yet, creating innovation and changing culture and practices are keys to greater success in organizations, and it's important to find ways to create buy-in at different levels of the organization around these issues. The problem is that the minute you bring up one of these topics, you will often get shut down by certain leaders or by the organizational practices and processes that are already in place.

One of the best ways to get buy-in is by working on existing projects. There are a number of reasons why this approach is effective. One is that existing projects have resources committed to them and individuals who own them. By linking the initiative you are working on to a project in existence, you can get the buy-in needed to create the results you are seeking. As long as the project comes in on time and creates the desired result, you can try new ways of doing things and experiment to find out what works and what doesn't. From there you can incorporate what you've learned into other projects throughout the organization.

Another point to keep in mind regarding buy-in with respect to innovation is that return on investment does not come immediately. It often takes a number of failures before you finally have a success. In many cases, innovation projects are terminated early in their development because the resources spent on the potential innovation do not bring the quarterly returns the organization requires.

There are several actions you can take to overcome these problems. First, you can get sponsorship from a powerful member of the senior team. Having this person on your side will help you fight off the forces that seek to shut down your project. This is helpful unless political pressure gets too strong for the sponsor, the sponsor leaves the company, or the sponsor has a change of mind and wants to shut down the project. A problem with this approach is finding a powerful person who wants to see the project through to the end, no matter what happens. In addition, it's also possible that you may not know powerful people in your organization well enough to even get their attention.

Another way to get buy-in is to take the project offline. Find a place for the group to meet away from the organization. Treat the operation like a stealth project. However, be sure to get permission from the right people so that you will have the resources you need. By keeping the project offline, you can keep it around long enough to know if you are on to something. You can nurture the project until it is ready to be introduced back into the organization.

Teachable Point of View[1]

Innovations are developed through experience and experiments. The failure cycle can lead to success, but only if individuals and groups take the time to learn from both their successes and failures. Discussing what is working and what is not working is just the first step. You also need to incorporate the lessons learned back into the day-to-day activities of the organization. One of the best ways to do this is to use the idea of the "45-second elevator" speech.

The purpose of the elevator speech is to paint a compelling picture for someone in 45 seconds that communicates the insights you have learned, why those insights matter to the organization and to the person you are talking to, and how those insights can be implemented in the organization.

To create the elevator speech, you need to ask yourself what you've learned through your experiences and how you can communicate those insights to the organization. You also will want to consider what would happen if your insights were implemented in the organization and what potential barriers there might be to getting them implemented.

The elevator speech helps you clarify what you've learned and how it might be applied throughout the entire organization. Once you have an idea of the basic concept you want to spread, you need to put that information into a format that creates excitement and commitment. One way to do this is by telling a story in your elevator speech.

There are several important factors you need to think about when you create your story. For example, you should ask yourself how your story relates to what the listeners are trying to accomplish. Put yourself in the shoes of these other individuals and consider their interests and problems as well as what they might want from you.

To help guide your thinking and structure your story, you'll also need to consider the listener's point of view based on the Innovation Genome. Table 6.2 shows the different forms of communication in each of the four quadrants. This information can be useful to you for developing the right format for the story.

While learning to run the *Creativize Method*, it is important to master an understanding of yourself and those you will lead through the change and innovation process. After running the process a number of times and helping teach others to run the process, you will begin to more naturally understand yourself and others, and you will be able to see complexities beyond the use of the *Creativize Method*.

Becoming a Learning Community

Because innovation occurs through experiments and experience, the group has to think of failure as an opportunity to learn. Whenever a team or organization is trying to accomplish something it has not done in the past, it needs to learn what it takes to create the new desired outcome. One of the key functions of Creativizers is to form a community of learning. Learning the Innovation Genome along with learning how to run and customize the *Creativize Method* is a process. You must first be taught the concept, then teach or run the concept, and finally meet with others who have tried to teach or run the concept and share what worked, what didn't work, and how to move forward more effectively. Through this hands-on learning process, the Creativizers quickly get smart and

Table 6.2 How Do They Communicate?

Collaborate
Communicates by:
- Using experiences that relate to the audience.
- Using examples to illustrate the point.
- Being helpful and user-friendly.
- Acknowledging emotional issues.

Expect them to:
- Have an animated face—eyes flash, etc.
- Use expansive, nonverbal gestures.
- Use stories to illustrate points.
- Talk out loud or to themselves to learn.

Create
Communicates by:
- Looking at the big picture.
- Making things colorful and visual.
- Using metaphors.
- Looking at the future.
- Making things conceptually sound and clear.

Expect them to:
- Ask questions that lead to other questions: Why? How?
- Speak in phrases.
- Stop in midsentence thinking that others obviously know what they mean.

Control
Communicates by:
- Providing details.
- Being neat.
- Following a sequential order.
- Using a recognizable "appropriate" form.

Expect them to:
- Ask questions that have answers: Who? What?
- Speak in sentences and paragraphs.
- Complete their sentences and paragraphs.

Compete
Communicates by:
- Using facts.
- Showing clear analysis.
- Coming to the point.
- Being logical.
- Being quantifiable.

Expect them to:
- Use facts to illustrate points.
- Be very matter-of-fact.
- Express emotions abstractly.
- Appear to display little or no emotion.

start to adjust the method to fit the needs of their organization. It will also become clear through this process what resources and help they will need both internally and externally.

Creativizers who are willing to meet together often to learn from one another and make adjustments will be more likely to succeed. Creativizers also need to lead other learning communities throughout the organization through projects that are launched. By meeting regularly with those working on the projects and asking them the right questions, Creativizers quickly "get smart" as they determine what is working and what is not. It will rapidly become clear whether there are any simple rules or best practices that need to be implemented at a larger scale in the organization. It will also become clear how the current culture, competencies, processes, measures, and projects are either helping or killing the needed innovation in the organization.

Supervise Phase 1: Roles and Responsibilities

In running a workshop, it is important that the Creativizer gauge the audience. The Creativizer must be aware of the expectations and agenda of those attending the workshop. It is also very important for the workshop participants to understand that they also are responsible for their experience at the workshop because it is an interactive process. To get a good feel for the group, the Creativizer should begin by asking the following questions.

What's Your Agenda?

- Directions: Break into groups and discuss the following questions (30 minutes):
    - Why are you here?
    - What result would you like to create over the next three days?
    - What do you need from outside consultants?
    - What do you need from your peers?
    - What's your role and responsibility in making the three days more meaningful?
    - How will you know if we are successful as a group?
    - Who shares your agenda?

The group attending this workshop is responsible for leading the change process within the organization. Because of this, it is important that each person understand what his or her individual role is. The following exercise aids in helping the Lead Facilitator to understand the group's expectations in becoming a change agent for the organization.

What's an Internal Creativizer?

- Directions: Break into groups and discuss the following questions (30 minutes):
  - What is your role as a Creativizer?
  - What are the pitfalls or dangers of being a Creativizer?
  - What are the keys to success of being a Creativizer?

Once the group members have discussed what they believe the roles of Creativizers to be, the Lead Facilitator will discuss other possible functions of Creativizers.

Function of Creativizers

The function of Creativizers is to:

- Develop sustainable internal competencies for facilitating change.
- Create a community of change practitioners that share best practices and regularly add new knowledge and tools to the organization.
- Leverage the skills of a few unique individuals to liberate the potential of the entire firm.
- Establish a legitimate forum, agenda, and pro-change community in the organization.

In order to accomplish the functions above, the Creativizers should understand the development process, or the way in which they will be trained to become a Creativizer as well as the roles and responsibilities they will have to fulfill upon becoming a Creativizer.

Creativizer Development Process
Roles and Responsibilities

The roles and responsibilities of a Creativizer are to:

- Keep the process on track.

- Focus the group on the desired results.
- Create a positive environment.
- Establish a group identity.
- Encourage participation, mutual respect, and listening.
- Stimulate group energy.
- Give feedback on group dynamics.
- Structure and clarify issues.
- Resolve conflicts.
- Challenge boundaries and habit-bound thinking.
- Confront hidden problems.
- Solve problems when appropriate.

Supervise Phase 2: Creating a Shared Language and Mindset

It is important that the group members understand the foundation of the *Creativize Method* change process and that they understand the basic tenets of the Innovation Genome. It is also important for group participants to be able to communicate effectively in order to accomplish the aim of their respective units within the organization.

When running the Innovation Genome Card Game, it is important to remember that this is a learning experience for the group. Learning is a process, and when the group members have to think about, make sense of, and communicate back what they are learning, the process becomes more effective. Create time after the Card Game to have the group members think through what they have learned and to allow for questions and conversation. (Please refer to "Step 3: Socialize, Phase 1: Creating a Shared Language and Mindset" in order to run Step 4: Supervise, Phase 2.)

Supervise Phase 3: Diagnosing the Change and Innovation Assessment

In becoming Creativizers for the organization, the group must learn how to understand and diagnose the *Change and Innovation Assessment*. (Please refer to Step 1: Synthesize.)

Facts about the *Change and Innovation Assessments*

The following includes facts that the Creativizers need to be aware of when they are dealing with an assessment within the organization.

- The assessment assumes feedback is useful, valuable, and actionable.
- It acts like a mirror because it measures "perceptions," not necessarily the "truth."
- It focuses on development, not performance appraisal.
- It provides a road map to change that must be carried out through leadership behavior and business practices.

Initial Reactions

People's reactions to the assessment vary. A Creativizer must understand what some of these reactions may be so they have time to figure out how they want to deal with these reactions. Looking through the following list can help a Creativizer be aware of and be ready to deal with the varying reactions which may include shock, anger, resistance, and apathy.

- Our respondents really don't know the organization that well.
- The wrong people filled out the surveys.
- Our job makes us act this way. We're really not like that.
- Some of our respondents really have it in for our boss.
- Our respondents didn't understand the questions.
- This was just a bad time to do this.
- The computer must have scored this wrong.
- Our respondents don't understand the situation we are in.
- All our strengths are right, but our weaknesses aren't.
- We used to be this way, but we've changed recently.
- This survey is based on choices we can't make.
- This must be some other group's report.
- It's all accurate but we just don't care.

Showing this list to a group before you share their data will help minimize their use of these statements. Using specific and recent examples gleaned from the interview data and reminding participants that people's perceptions are their reality can also be helpful approaches to dealing with these responses. Even if the perception is wrong, you still have to meet people where they are at in their minds.

(See example profiles in Step 1: Synthesize, Phase 2: Administer the *Change and Innovation Assessment*.)

Create a Shared Meaning

Once the assessment has been completed, it is the Creativizer's responsibility to help groups within the organization create a shared meaning around the assessment. This is done by using questions such as the following to create ideas about what the results might mean. As the discussion progresses, it is the Creativizer's responsibility to help the group focus on a shared meaning.

- Where are there major differences in the profiles? Why?
  - Purposes, Practices, and People
  - Between your business unit and your operating unit
  - Between your operating units
  - Within your unit
  - Other surveys
- What are the strengths and weaknesses?
  - Your unit
  - Yourself
- Where are the biggest gaps between current and desired?
- What pressing problems does this create for your business?

Supervise Phase 4: Team-Building Exercise

One purpose of this workshop is to help the selected Creativizers begin to form as a team. The Creativizers will be responsible for running the *Creativize Method* and giving support to the action teams. As they lead the process, they will begin to learn from their attempts to lead change and will need to have a group with which they can share what they are learning, what's working, and what's not working and where they can give support to one another. Having a team of Creativizers who know how to work well together, who trust one another, and who support each other will be a key to the Creativizers leading change and innovation in their organization.

Many successful managers, coaches, team leaders, and others believe that an important part of becoming a successful team is going through challenging experiences together. Because you do not want to create a crisis in your organization just to strengthen your team, many team-building exercises have been created for newly forming teams to help them learn how to work with one another, develop trust, and experience something difficult together. The following exercise is just one of many that can be used when a group begins to form.

Team-Building Exercise

One of our colleagues, Professor Robert Quinn, learned of a team-building exercise created by an executive who participated in one of his courses about leading change. The executive didn't know how to introduce the concepts he learned with his team during the one-week period of time he had for getting them up to speed. The executive created this exercise to teach that change means going somewhere you have not been before and that you have to try new things, fail, learn, and make adjustments until you figure out how to be successful. The executive told Professor Quinn about the exercises, and Quinn has used this exercise with thousands of executives around the world who have found it helpful in teaching a group about change. This exercise not only helps the team members learn about themselves, but it teaches them what it will mean to lead change and innovation.

To run this exercise, follow the directions below:

Break the workshop participants into groups containing anywhere from 6–8 people.
- Based on the number of groups you have, you will need that many breakout rooms and a tents for each room. Buy smaller tents and use the same kind of tent for all of the groups. Spread all of the equipment in different places across the floor.
- Each group has three minutes to generate a set of guidelines on how to operate as a high-performing team.
- While the groups are planning their guidelines, select people on each team and ask them if they will be your "volunteers" (one volunteer for every four team members).
- At the conclusion of the three minutes, distribute blindfolds and instruct all the nonvolunteers to put them on.
- Instructions to the group:
  ○ Everything you do will be as a team.

- You will be told a destination, and you will travel there as a team.
- There will be equipment on the floor.
- Find the equipment and build the object with quality. (Do not divulge what the object they are building is.)
- When it is complete, return here as a team.
- When everyone is sitting in the chairs you are now sitting in, you may take off your blindfolds.
- Instructions to the volunteers:
  - You are a safety engineer.
  - Your job is to hover over these people at every moment and prevent any kind of physical safety problem.
  - Your job is not to help them solve any problem. Do not lead them. Do not talk to them.
  - Your job is also to be a historical observer. Note all the key events so that you can discuss them later.
- Instructions to the entire group:
  - You have three more minutes to plan. Do not leave your chair.
  - Give instructions on how to get to the destination.
  - Clearly answer the participants' questions.
  - Tell them to begin.

Once all the participants have returned to their seats and removed their blindfolds, you will begin to process their experience with them as a group. To process this experience, follow the directions below:

- Each team should spend five minutes recounting the history of its group experience.
- When the five minutes are up, everyone is asked to think alone for five more minutes about the following questions:
  - What worked? What didn't?
  - Who played what role?
  - How well did the team members work together?
  - Was there any conflict? How was it resolved?
  - How were decisions made?
  - Were any norms or rules set during the process?
  - What would you do differently if you could do the exercise together again?
- After the five minutes are over, the Lead Facilitator should bring the whole group together and lead a discussion about the above questions.

- ○ The Lead Facilitator will guide this discussion and help the group members be as specific as possible when discussing their experience.
- ○ Once the group participants have decided on the key learning points from their experience, they should divide into their groups again and fill in Table 6.3 concerning the roles each individual played in the group.

Once the teams are done processing the tent exercise, they should spend five minutes writing in a journal what they learned about themselves and their team members. It is important that the Lead Facilitator remind the group that what everyone experienced happened in one setting, around one situation, and does not mean that this is necessarily the role and behaviors that should be expected of each group member throughout his or her time as a team.

Team members should remember their key learning points as a resource to help them in the creation of norms, rules, and expectations in the next part of the Supervise step.

Table 6.3   Individual Roles

Collaborate	**Create**
Person/role:	Person/role:
1.	1.
2.	2.
3.	3.
Control	**Compete**
Person/role:	Person/role:
1.	1.
2.	2.
3.	3.

Supervise Phase 5: Creating Team Norms and Expectations

During this part of the Supervise step in the *Creativize Method*, it is important for the team members to gain a basic understanding of team development along with the tools to create clear norms, rules, and expectations as they begin to work together as a group. Participants also need to experience this development process so that they are able to run the same process with groups they will help form during later steps of the *Creativize Method*.

A Theory of Group Development

Many studies have been done to generate theories on the formation and development of groups. One of the most basic and core ideas is summarized in Table 6.4.[2]

Whenever people are involved in something new and feel uncomfortable in the situation, it is important for them to recognize that they are not alone. When the group is in the storming phase of the group development process, it can be helpful to know that other groups go through this same process. If participants keep working at creating relationships, resolving concerns, and talking openly about challenges, they will begin to find energy by being part of the group.

To help the group move through the four phases with greater speed, it is important that clear norms, rules, and expectations be set. By answering the following questions; having a clear vision and clear goals; by making rules, processes, and boundaries; and by resolving concerns together as a group, the team will move toward high performance.

Norms, Rules, and Expectations

In preparing to set norms, rules, and expectations for the group, the Lead Facilitator will ask each group member to think back to a time when he or she was part of a high-performing team. Group members will then individually answer the questions below based on their experience of being part of that high-performing team:

- How did the group resolve conflict?
- How did the group make decisions?

Table 6.4   Theory of Group Development

Forming
- Team depends on leader for guidance.
- Little agreement.
- Roles and responsibilities unclear.
- Lots of questions.
- Processes ignored.
- Members test tolerance.
- Leader directs.

Norming
- Agreement and consensus forms.
- Roles and responsibilities become clear and are accepted.
- Big decisions are made by entire group, small decisions by sub-groups.
- Strong commitment is made.
- Working process and style established.
- Mutual respect emerges.
- Leader facilitates.

Storming
- Decisions difficult to make.
- Team focuses on goals.
- Members vie for power.
- Clarity of purpose increases.
- Factions emerge.
- Compromise on emotional issues required to make progress.
- Leader coaches.

Performing
- Team strategically aware.
- Shared vision and values emerge.
- Focus turns to overachieving goals.
- High autonomy established.
- Conflicts resolved by team.
- Relationships and teamwork strengthen.
- Team members develop personal skills.
- Leader oversees.

- How did the group make sure all members felt involved?
- How did the group communicate during and between meetings?
- What roles did each member of the group play?
- In what ways did the group remain open to feedback?
- What did the group do to keep everyone aware of the group process?
- What measures were needed to determine if the group was making progress?
- What were the key ground rules the group followed?
- What else took place with this team to make it high performing?

The Lead Facilitator will then bring the group together and have the members answer the following questions while remembering their experience of being on a high-performing team and what they learned while participating in the tent exercise. The Lead Facilitator should help guide the discussion but should not lead this discussion. The group will be making decisions based on how they answer these questions together. The group roles, norms, and expectations will begin to get set as the group has this discussion, and the facilitator should point things out to the group only to help move them forward. Below are some of the many questions the group may choose to answer together:

- How will the group resolve conflict?
- How will the group make decisions?
- How will the group make sure all members feel involved?
- How will the group communicate during and between meetings?
- What roles can each member of the group play?
- In what ways will the group remain open to feedback?
- What can the group do to keep everyone aware of the group process?
- What measures are needed to determine if the group is making progress?
- What are the key ground rules the group will follow?
- What else needs to be discussed as a group?

Just a few of the many ideas and tools the group may want to use to help them answer some of the above questions appear below. There are also many facilitation books available on the market that the Lead Facilitator may choose to share as a resource for the group.

A Basic Approach to Resolving Conflict

There are five general ways that groups and individuals use to deal with conflict.[3]

Avoid: An individual or the whole group ignores the issue, changes the subject, or does anything to avoid confronting the conflict.

Accommodate: One individual or many in the group will seek to keep peace above all else. This may mean convincing one side to give in or to give in to the other side.

Compromise: This is when all sides in conflict look for common ground and are willing to give up some of what they are seeking as long as they get some of what they want.

Compete: An individual or group of individuals will do whatever it takes to win through arguing their point and making the other side seem wrong.

Collaborate: Everyone involved uncovers and faces the issue, discusses and understands all the points, wants everyone involved to win.

All five of these approaches to conflict resolution have their strengths and weaknesses. Table 6.5 will help you understand when to use each approach and what the drawbacks are for using that approach. The group needs to realize that conflict is necessary for high-performing teams as long as it is handled appropriately.

Having a general understanding of approaches for resolving conflict may be enough to help a group make decisions about how it wants to approach conflict. Some groups may need tools and processes to follow when conflict arises. Problem and outcome structuring are two of many processes that can be used to help a group resolve conflict.

Problem Structuring

- What's wrong? (Can you be specific?)
- Why do you have this problem?
- How does this problem limit you?
- What does this problem stop you from doing?
- Whose fault is it that you have this problem?
- How long have you had this problem?

Outcome Structuring

- What do you want?
- When do you want it?
- How will you know when you are getting (or have gotten) what you want?
- When you get what you want, what else in your life will change?
- What resources, internal and external, do you have to help you get what you want?

Table 6.5   Approaches to Conflict Resolution

Approaches to Conflict	When to Use	Drawbacks
Avoid	Problem can't be solved, issue is trivial, need time to calm emotions.	Conflict is never addressed, no diversity or creativity allowed, can allow conflict to get worse.
Accommodate	One side is wrong, issue isn't as important to one side as it is to the other, relationship is most important.	Issues are unexplored, one side dominates decisions and doesn't seek others' opinions.
Compromise	Sides can't agree, decision needs to be made.	Process most adversarial, all sides lose something.
Compete	Right decision is more important than relationship.	Sides harbor bad feelings, will struggle working together in the future.
Collaborate	Arrive at decision, if there is time and the appropriate skill.	Takes a great deal of time, commitment, and skill.

- How can you use the resources you have?
- How can I help you begin to get what you want?

When all sides concerned have answered these questions together, they will have a better understanding of where others are coming from. The group will then find that there are clear ways for moving forward.

Listening Basics for Resolving Conflicts

When conflict is not effectively dealt with in a group, it often leads to failure of group members to listen to one another. The idea of listening seems basic, yet many people and groups have a hard time being effective listeners. Here are some dos and don'ts that will enable the group to move more quickly toward becoming a high-performing team.

Do . . .

- Probe for clarification.
- Listen for a story and unvoiced emotion.
- Empathize.
- Summarize.
- Get rid of distractions while listening.
- Ask appropriate questions that provide detail.
- Establish eye contact, nod your head, and smile.
- Ask how you can help.

Don't . . .

- Interrupt.
- Respond too soon.
- Editorialize.
- Jump to conclusions.
- Judge the person.
- Try to solve the person's problem too quickly.
- Take calls or interruptions in the course of the meeting

Types of Decisions

It will help the group think about how it will approach decision making by understanding the following six general approaches.[4]

Power structure: The person deemed the leader of the group, whether formally or informally, can state at any time what he or she thinks the decision should be and the group follows.

Group silence: Certain individuals make their opinions known and assume that if everyone is silent, the group agrees with them (which may or may not be true).

Minority: A small number of people agree on a decision and start moving forward with the decision without waiting or checking in with other group members to find out if they agree.

Compromise: When there are two or three choices and the group cannot agree on any of them, a new choice is created in which each side gives up and receives part of their desires and the group moves forward with the newly created option.

Voting: There are multiple ways of voting, but in the end this is a technique in which all the options are presented and people choose the one or more options they like best. The option with the most votes wins.

Consensus: Participants feel they had their say and a fair chance to influence the final decision. Adjustments are made so that participants feel good about the end decision and are willing to support the decision as their own.

These decision-making approaches have strengths and weaknesses, which are discussed in Table 6.6.

A Tool for Decision Making

There are many tools and processes that can be followed by groups to help them create consistency in their decision making. One of many tools that can be used to help the group make decisions is laid out in the following list and in Table 6.7.

Directions:
- Create three ideas representing each quadrant from the Innovation Genome.
- Select the best idea from each quadrant.
- Try to integrate ideas from the opposing quadrant (create a new idea that is better than any single idea).
- Integrate the two remaining ideas into one final decision, or select the idea everyone feels best about.

Developing Roles

When the group thinks about creating roles, it is important to understand that each group member has strengths and that his or her time will be

Table 6.6   Approaches to Decision Making

Types of Decisions	Strengths	Weaknesses
Power structure	Fast, easy, expert in the group, minor decisions.	People might not own decision or feel heard.
Group silence	Fast, easy, helps when decisions are minor.	No time to think or discuss, may feel unheard or cared about.
Minority	Fast, easy, helps when decisions are minor.	People are not heard, can divide the group.
Compromise	Lots of discussion of key points, everyone wins.	Everyone loses, can divide the group.
Voting	Everyone participates, democratic, clear outcome.	Some lose, losers may seek to undermine decision.
Consensus	Collaborative, people own decision and are committed.	Slow, requires appropriate skills from group members.

used most effectively when taking advantage of those strengths. When creating roles people will play in the group, members may want to share their results from the "People" portion of the *Change and Innovation Assessment*. Table 6.8 will also help the group gain a quick understanding of what tendencies people have that lean toward certain quadrants in the Innovation Genome.

Table 6.7   Decision Making through the Innovation Genome

Collaborate	Create
Idea:	Idea:
1.	1.
2.	2.
3.	3.
Pros	Pros
Cons	Cons

Control	Compete
Idea:	Idea:
1.	1.
2.	2.
3.	3.
Pros	Pros
Cons	Cons

What Competencies Need to Be Developed within Your Team?

Whether a group is trying to become high performing or has already accomplished high performance, it will need to continue to improve if it is going to stay successful. With an ever-changing external environment every organization is put into a situation where it must change or it will eventually fail. Groups within organizations in turn are faced with the same problem.

Table 6.8 Individual Tendencies around the Innovation Genome

Collaborate
- Needs people
- Good listener
- Status quo/dislikes change
- No risks
- No pressure
- Counselor/helps others
- Questioning
- Insecure/needs reassurance
- Supportive
- No conflict

Create
- Dreamer
- Unrealistic goals
- Creative; ideas flow
- Needs approval and compliments
- Generalizes
- Persuasive, outgoing
- Off the cuff
- Innovative
- Excitable
- Enthusiastic

Control
- Planner/superviser
- Details/technicalities
- Slow decisions
- Must be right
- Conservative/cautious
- Low pressure
- Precise/critical/logical
- Problem solver
- Persistent
- Follows procedures/compliant

Compete
- Goal-oriented/results-oriented
- Impatient
- Task-oriented/high achiever
- Workaholic
- Decisive
- Opinionated/stubborn/blunt
- Fast decisions
- Tough/firm in relationships
- Power conscious
- Competitive/loves challenges

One important discussion the group needs to have should focus around the areas of both individual and group development. By now the group should be clear about what goals it needs to accomplish and what general culture, competencies, and practices are needed to get the group to accomplish the goals. The following questions will help the group further clarify what competencies it needs to develop and an approach for doing so.

Review the agreed upon outcomes and answer the following questions:

- What are the key goals that will move the group toward the accomplishment of its desired outcomes?
- What skills are required to accomplish the goals that will move the group toward these outcomes?
- What help, training, and tools will each individual and the group need in order to accomplish these goals?
- Are there experts we may need to call on for help?

Once the group has set basic norms, rules, and expectations, it will have taken an important step toward becoming a high-performing team. However, becoming a high-performing team is a process, and the group needs to be open to discussing regularly what's working, what's not, and how it needs to adjust the norms, rules, and expectations it has set. Setting expectations helps the team when decisions need to be made and conflict arises, but expectations will be more fully formed and understood after the group goes through those processes a few times.

Supervise Phase 6: Action Planning

At this point the group will develop actions around the Innovation Genome quadrants based on the shared meaning created by the group in the previous phase. (See Tables 6.9 and 6.10.) (To review this process, please use the following tools and refer to Step 3: Socialize, Phase 5: Organizational Change and Innovation Action.)

Create a Shared Vision

- What is our desired organizational profile?
  - Things to move toward and away from.
- What potential challenges does this create for our organization?
  - Obstacles, organizational development, people, strategic positioning, etc.
- What does this organization look like?
  - Use stories and visual imagery to describe how the vision works.
- Can we make these changes?
  - Adjust the current and desired profiles for culture and competency as appropriate.
  - In the next phase, we will make the desired profile operational.

Table 6.9   Leadership Profiles

Collaborate
- Teachers
- Communicators
- Counselors
- Listeners
- Conflict resolvers
- Community builders

Create
- Dreamers and visionaries
- Fashion trendsetters
- Creative actors
- Big-picture thinkers
- Experimenters
- Energizers

Control
- Planners
- Supervisers
- Analysts
- Technicians and scientists
- Methodical problem solvers
- Professionals

Compete
- Competitors
- Decision makers
- Goal-oriented achievers
- Sprinters
- Political game masters
- Deal makers

Table 6.10   Potential Pitfalls of Types

Collaborate
- Group think
- Irrational enthusiasm
- Isolation from external pressures

Create
- Unrealistic vision
- Poor methodology
- Lack of discipline

Control
- Excessive deference to expertise
- Scientific thinking
- Right-way and wrong-way thinking

Compete
- Overemphasis on competition
- Short-term focus
- Autocratic decision making

Supervise Phase 7: Behavior Change

Remember that if individuals throughout the organization don't change their behavior, the projects that are launched will slowly turn into the same kinds of projects that already are occurring in your organization. Innovation will not occur in new ways if everyone is behaving in the same way. By individuals committing to behaving in new ways, the organization will begin to change and create new kinds of innovation.

Below are a few items that Creativizers need to consider when running the Behavior Change Exercise with a team in their organization.

- People need to have a history with one another.
- The leader must be prepared to engage with authenticity.
- When possible, interview participants prior to the event.
- Feedback should be centered on the proposed vision.
- Feedback should be centered on actionable items.
- Participants should own their statements.
- Help the group express their feelings and come to emotional closure.

(Please refer to Step 3: Socialize, Phase 6: Behavior Change.)

Supervise Phase 8: Gaining Buy-in

When dealing with change in organizations, Creativizers will inevitably meet some resistance, even from those who verbally and logically support the change. Change often requires people to step out of their comfort zones, and this may cause certain individuals or groups to resist in order to prevent the change from moving forward. When things get difficult, people often go back to things that worked in the past. The combination of these things requires Creativizers to gain buy-in from these resisters in order to move the process forward. In leading the change process, Creativizers will need to be able to pinpoint the people in the organization who are creating resistance and be able to influence them to cooperate. (Please use the following tools and refer to Step 6: Specialize, Phase 12: Manage Resistance.)

Supervise Phase 9: Learning to Facilitate Using the Innovation Genome

At this time the group is attending a workshop, which is the first step to members becoming Creativizers. However, over the next several months the Creativizers-in-training will be experiencing and experimenting with the steps and tools they learn in this workshop. This will ready them to assist the Lead Facilitator in running the *Creativize Method* steps that their respective organizations have selected. Below are charts (Tables 6.11–6.17) that map out this Creativizer development experience as well as present ideas for effectively accomplishing these tasks.

Discussing the "People" Section of the Assessment

In preparation for this workshop, participants will have taken the *Change and Innovation Assessment* (Step 1: Synthesize) in which they will have learned their individual profile within the Innovation Genome. The following exercise and discussion will help participants gain an understanding of their profile and how they influence and are influenced by others.

- What did you learn from taking this assessment?
  - What specific hypothesis did you come up with?
- What quadrant are you strongest in?
  - How do your strengths sometimes present themselves as weaknesses?
- What might this mean for someone who is facilitating the steps of the *Creativize Method*?

Tables 6.13 and 6.17 will help participants to understand people who fall into different quadrants within the Innovation Genome. This will allow participants to communicate effectively with groups they facilitate; it will also aid them in creating and adjusting exercises, which will help groups get the most out of their experience.

Table 6.11   Practicum/Postpracticum Experience

During the Workshop

Learn how to run specific modules from Steps 1 and 3
- Learn your Innovation Genome profile and how it will affect you while running these modules.
- Learn how to use the Innovation Genome to more effectively run these modules and influence those you lead through this experience.

Practice the modules
- Each participant will be videotaped while running one of the modules.
- The group you work with will discuss what went well, what didn't, and what other tools will be needed.
- The small groups will come together with the Lead Facilitator to discuss what was learned.
- Questions and concerns will be addressed by the Lead Facilitator.

Over the Next 90 Days

Running the modules
- Select an intact group in your organization.
- Help group members take the *Change and Innovation Assessment*.
- Run the Card Game with them and discuss the key learning points.
- Help the group create a shared meaning from the survey.
- Work with the group to think around the Innovation Genome and create specific action plans.

Learning from running the modules
- Videotape yourself running the modules.
- Review the videotape, receive feedback from participants and write a two-page case on what worked, what didn't, tools needed, how the modules can be improved, and what progress is being made on the action items.
- Send videotapes and cases to Lead Facilitator for review.
- Plan an optional follow-up workshop on new tools, feedback, and next steps

Table 6.12   What Do You Need to Run the Modules?

Selecting a Group
- Try selecting a group that is doing really well and is willing to experiment or a team that is struggling and needs help accomplishing desired results.
- Try keeping the group size to between 8 and 20 people.
- Make sure group members have specific goals or a specific problem in mind and that are ready to be worked on when they participate in the modules.

Workshop Preparation
- Find a room with good lighting, high ceilings, and good space for the workshop.
- Make sure there are breakout rooms or that the room is large enough to have small groups meet in different corners of the room.
- Have any refreshments and meals thought through and planned ahead of time.
- Think through the outcomes you are trying to create in each module and practice any parts you are uncomfortable with.

Assessment
- Collect all the names and e-mail addresses of the group members.
- Decide if there are ways to break the group into smaller groups (functional, level, etc.).
- Set up a call with the Lead Facilitator and ThinkTroop (delivers assessment online) 3–4 weeks prior to the workshop.
- Review the results and create hypothesis before you lead the group in real time toward creating a shared meaning.

Materials
- Have PowerPoint slides ready and printed for participants.
- Add the overall results of the survey to the presentation.
- Have a projector, computer, and slides on a disk, CD-ROM, or hard drive.
- Be prepared with flip charts, markers, and other helpful tools for breakout groups.
- Have someone record the workshop on videotape.

Table 6.13   Who Are You Facilitating?

Collaborate
- Needs people
- Good listener
- Status quo/dislikes change
- No risks
- No pressure
- Counselor/helps others
- Questioning
- Insecure/needs reassurance
- Supportive
- No conflict

Create
- Dreamer
- Unrealistic goals
- Creative; ideas flow
- Needs approval and com-
  pliments
- Generalizes
- Persuasive, outgoing
- Off the cuff
- Innovative
- Excitable
- Enthusiastic

Control
- Planner/Superviser
- Details/technicalities
- Slow decisions
- Must be right
- Conservative/cautious
- Low pressure
- Precise/critical/logical
- Problem solver
- Persistent
- Follows procedures/compliant

Compete
- Goal-oriented/results-oriented
- Impatient
- Task-oriented/high achiever
- Workaholic
- Decisive
- Opinionated/stubborn/blunt
- Fast decisions
- Tough/firm in relationships
- Power conscious
- Competitive/loves challenges

Table 6.14   How Do You and Team Members Communicate?

Collaborate

Communicate by:

- Using experiences that relate to the audience.
- Using examples to illustrate the point.
- Being helpful and user-friendly.
- Acknowledging emotional issues.

Expect them to:

- Have an animated face—eyes flash, etc.
- Use expansive nonverbal gestures.
- Use stories to illustrate points.
- Talk out loud or to themselves to learn.

Create

Communicate by:

- Looking at the big picture.
- Making ideas colorful and visual.
- Using metaphors.
- Looking to the future.
- Making ideas conceptually sound and clear.

Expect them to:

- Ask questions that lead to other questions such as Why? How?
- Speak in phrases.
- Stop in midsentence thinking others obviously know what they mean.

Control

Communicate by:

- Providing details.
- Being neat.
- Following a sequential order.
- Using a recognizable "appropriate" form.

Expect them to:

- Ask questions that have answers such as Who? What?
- Speak in sentences and paragraphs.
- Complete their sentences and paragraphs.

Compete

Communicate by:

- Using facts.
- Showing clear analysis.
- Being to the point.
- Be logical.
- Being quantifiable.

Expect them to:

- Use facts to illustrate points.
- Be very matter-of-fact.
- Express emotions abstractly.
- Appear to display little or no emotion regardless of the situation.

Table 6.15 What Do They Respond To?

Collaborate
Feeling:
- Experiential
- Sensory-involving activities
- Movement
- Music
- Listening to and watching people
- Group interaction

Create
Open-minded:
- Experimental
- Visual
- Having a lot of space
- Individualized learning designs
- Selling ideas
- Designing products, practices, etc.

Control
Controlled:
- Structure
- Sequential formats
- Lectures
- Textbooks
- Case discussion
- Programmed learning
- Behavior modification learning designs

Compete
Fact-based:
- Formalized lecture
- Case discussions
- Textbooks
- Programmed learning
- Behavior modification learning designs
- Working solo
- Being challenged

Table 6.16 How Do They Act?

Collaborate
- Expressing ideas
- Interpersonal
- Teaching
- Training
- Writing to others to further a relationship

Create
- Causing change
- Conceptualizing
- Generating ideas
- Integrative
- Trusting intuition
- Visualizing

Control
- Administrative
- Implementation
- Organizational
- Planning
- Regulatory
- Supervisory

Compete
- Analytical
- Financial
- Problem solving
- Scientific
- Statistical
- Aggressive

Table 6.17   How Do You Develop Your Weakest Quadrants?

Collaborate
- Volunteer to be part of a company project.
- Lead a group toward making a decision by consensus.
- Find one nice thing to say to a colleague each day.
- Help two colleagues in conflict and help resolve their concern.

Create
- Set a time each week to brainstorm about important issues.
- Make a decision based on intuition.
- Conceptualize a new program, service, or product for your organization.
- Keep a small notebook and jot down new ideas you have.

Control
- Create and follow a to-do list each day.
- Plan a project in detail and follow through with it.
- Read a manual you own and follow it often.
- Supervise your filing systems and desk.

Compete
- Clearly define work and goals for the next quarter.
- Read and understand a finance and budget report.
- Calculate your salary per hour.
- Create a contest based on similar goals with fellow employees.

Communicate Clearly

Personally answering the following questions will prepare you to more effectively communicate with and facilitate a group through the Innovation Genome.

- What's the best way to communicate with group members?
- What are you suggesting?
- What does success look like to them?
- What's in it for them?
- How is this relevant to what they do?
- What would you like them to do?
- What changes will they have to make?
- How will you support them?
- What are the next steps?

The following two exercises will assist in enhancing individual understanding of the above internal discussion.

What Quadrant Do You Relate To?

- Directions: Break into groups based on your strongest quadrant and discuss the following questions. (You have 30 minutes.)
  - If you were running this workshop, how would you use your strengths to reach the objective you set?
  - What weaknesses do you often run into, and how would this block you from reaching your objective?
  - How can you use techniques from the different Innovation Genome quadrants to complement your natural tendencies?
  - How would you facilitate groups from the other three quadrants (what are their strengths, weaknesses, tendencies)?

- Directions: Spend 15 minutes with each group in the other three quadrants discussing the following questions. (Round 1: Control/ Collaborate, Compete/Create) (Round 2: Control/Compete, Create/ Collaborate) (Round 3: Control/Create, Collaborate/Compete.)
  - What do we need to understand about your group to more effectively facilitate or influence people in your quadrant?
  - What do we do that is least effective in facilitating or influencing people in your quadrant?
  - How can we most effectively benefit each other when we are working together?

Tricks of the Trade

- View from the balcony:
  - Let's look at ourselves. What's working; what isn't?
- Advocating the opposite point of view:
  - Think of someone not in the group who is widely known and has an opposite point of view. What would [name here] do?
- Connecting the how to the what:
  - What are some other ways to think about this issue?
- Change reaction to pro-action:
  - What would you do?
- Make it clear:
  - Can you give me an example of where this works?
- Open alternatives:
  - Can we think of a few options?

- Focus on the purpose
  - Is this helping us get to where we need to go?

Supervise Phase 10: Running Steps 1 and 3

The participants will now be broken into groups of three where they will be given the opportunity to run a portion of one of the steps they have learned in this workshop. Within this process, each person will be videotaped while running a portion of the assigned step. The group will then watch the video and give feedback to the individual on what went well and what didn't. Each person within the group will go through this process, each running a different step. They will then discuss as a group what further tools they need or concerns they may have about running these steps within their respective organizations. The groups will reconvene at the end of the exercise, and the Lead Facilitator will address issues and present further tools to assist participants in becoming ready to run these workshops.

Learning to Run the Workshops: Exercise 1

- Directions: Break into groups and do the following:
  - Select a member of the group to lead the first 10–15 minutes of the Card Game.
  - Have a different member of the group videotape the member who is leading the Card Game.
  - Watch the video together as a group and discuss what went well, what didn't, and what tools or help the person needs to be more effective.
  - Return to the larger group to discuss what each group learned from the exercise.

Learning to Run the Workshops: Exercise 2

- Directions: Break into groups and do the following:
  - Select a member of the group to lead the first 10–15 minutes of creating meaning from the results of the culture and competencies assessment.
  - Have a different member of the group videotape the member who is leading the discussion of the assessment results.

- Watch the video together as a group and discuss what went well, what didn't, and what tools or help the person and other group members would need to be more effective.
- Return to the larger group to discuss what each group learned from the exercise.

Learning to Run the Workshops: Exercise 3

- Directions: Break into groups and do the following:
  - Select a member of the group to lead the first 10–15 minutes of creating action plans from the assessment results.
  - Have a different member of the group videotape the member who is leading the creation of action plans.
  - Watch the video together as a group and discuss what went well, what didn't, and what tools or help the person and other group members would need to be more effective.
  - Return to the larger group to discuss what each group learned from the exercise.

The final exercise within the Supervise Workshop encourages the participants to think through what it will take to prepare themselves to lead their own workshop. Once again breakout groups will create ideas for how to prepare and generate questions and will reconvene, presenting these ideas and asking questions of the Lead Facilitator.

Workshop Preparations

- Directions: Break into groups and discuss the following questions. (You have 30 minutes.)
  - If you had to run this workshop next week, how would you prepare for it?
  - What tools would you use to help you run this workshop?
  - What questions would you want answered before you could run this workshop?

To conclude the workshop, the Lead Facilitator describes the post-workshop assignment in more detail and answers the questions the participants may have regarding fulfilling the assignment.

Postworkshop Assignment

- Assignment:
  - ○ Run a one-day workshop using tools and processes presented during this workshop:
    - – With an intact team at a lower level in the organization.
    - – Must videotape workshop and send it to Lead Facilitator.
  - ○ Write a one- to two-page case study about what worked, what didn't, and what tools you would need to be more successful at running another workshop.
    - – Send case study to the lead consultant for review in preparing a one-day follow-up workshop.

Conclusion

1. What does it take to be a Creativizer?

A Creativizer must be an integrator of all four quadrants of the Innovation Genome, regardless of the Creativizer's own tendencies. Being a Creativizer requires an appreciation of all four quadrants and being able to teach others how to appreciate and work within all four. Creativizers are like coaches. They must resist solving problems for their teams, but they must help the team solve problems for themselves. Creativizers are people whose success is measured by the effectiveness of their team's ability to work together toward achieving the needed change and innovation in their organization.

2. What's the best way to communicate any change process to people in an organization?

The best way is to recognize the different ways in which people communicate. In this model, the four quadrants differentiate people and groups. The Creativizer has the role of determining the best way to reach these different groups. Remember that innovation and change are works in progress that also require alignment to the past, present, and future. Creativizers must be able to communicate along this dimension.

3. How do you develop buy-in for a change process?

Just as communicating change requires the ability to see differences, developing buy-in requires the ability to get everyone on the same track. Having senior organizational leaders on board is critical for adding legitimacy to the change. It is critical because failure and resistance are possible when trying new things. If people see the change process as legitimate, then resistance can be effectively managed and the failure cycle can be managed until it becomes a cycle of innovative wins.

The 3-D View

Remember from Chapter 2 that innovation is typically a work in progress. Innovation always provides key insights into the past that will in turn provide some wisdom about the future, but more importantly it allows us a wider range of courses to speculate and navigate. Once the Supervise step is complete, it is important for the Creativizers and other appropriate people to ask in a separate meeting the Do, Doing, Done questions by thinking around the Innovation Genome. It is important that the meeting take place close enough to the Supervise step so that everyone remembers the experience but enough removed so that people have had time to think about what really happened.

Do . . .
Looking forward to future projects, communities, charters, and goals that will flow from the Supervise step, consider the questions in Table 6.18 from the four perspectives of the Innovation Genome.

Table 6.18

Collaborate View
- What do I need to do?
- How do I want to do it?

Create View
- What do I need to do?
- How do I want to do it?

Control View
- What do I need to do?
- How do I want to do it?

Compete View
- What do I need to do?
- How do I want to do it?

Doing . . .

Looking at any current work taking place around the *Creativize Method* at your organization, consider the questions in Table 6.19.

Table 6.19

Collaborate View
- What's working and what isn't? Why?
- What changes should we make?

Control View
- What's working and what isn't? Why?
- What changes should we make?

Create View
- What's working and what isn't? Why?
- What changes should we make?

Compete View
- What's working and what isn't? Why?
- What changes should we make?

Done . . .

Looking back at what has taken place with the Supervise step and any projects that have been launched, consider the questions in Table 6.20.

Table 6.20

Collaborate View
- What worked and what didn't? Why?
- What changes would we make if we ran this step or project again?
- What have we learned that can be applied to the current practices of the organization?

Control View
- What worked and what didn't? Why?
- What changes would we make if we ran this step or project again?
- What have we learned that can be applied to the current practices of the organization?

Create View
- What worked and what didn't? Why?
- What changes would we make if we ran this step or project again?
- What have we learned that can be applied to the current practices of the organization?

Compete View
- What worked and what didn't? Why?
- What changes would we make if we ran this step or project again?
- What have we learned that can be applied to the current practices of the organization?

CHAPTER
7

Step 5:
SYNCHRONIZE

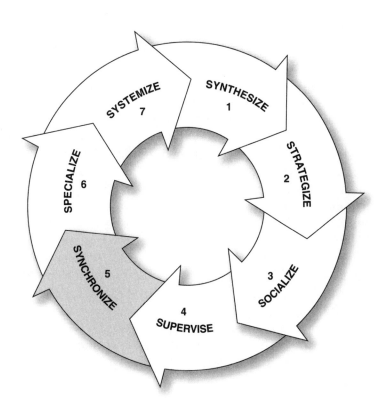

Synchronize Overview

- Objective:
  - Engage leaders throughout the organization to operationalize the vision.

- Participants:
  - Action Teams, Leadership Team, Creativizers, Lead Facilitator, Sponsor, and other appropriate leaders and experts from throughout the organization. (This step requires the participation of a large number of participants and needs to be held in a setting of significant size.)

- Actions:
  1. Select Leadership Team members, Action Team members, and Creativizers who are assigned to guide one of the strategic Action Teams and work in this group for the duration of the Synchronize step.
  2. Sponsor communicates desired outcomes for this step and expectations for the Action Teams.
  3. Each Action Team discusses the meaning of their subject and determines what currently works and what doesn't in meeting the challenge of this subject in their organizational units.
  4. Each Action Team, thinking creatively around the Innovation Genome, creates an action plan for changing relevant organizational practices or inventing new ones.
  5. Each Action Team presents its action plans to all the other Action Teams, gets feedback, and reconvenes in the individual teams to modify plans.
  6. Each Action Team identifies quick wins, key measures, resources required, and assigns responsibility for these actions to make them operational.
  7. Each Action Team presents its action plans to the Sponsor and/or senior executive officer for questions, modifications, and acceptance.
  8. Creativizers integrate action plans into a master plan and track their progress.

- Time:
  - Three days.

This Chapter Will Help Me to Answer:

- How do organizational leaders begin to operationalize a vision?
- What's more important—big wins or small wins?

Introduction

 Once the organization has a vision of where it wants to go, how does it enlist people within the organization to implement and own the vision? This is where Synchronize comes in. The Synchronize step is the launching pad for the core work streams and projects that will be jump-started in order to create small wins and make the larger vision realizable. Synchronize engages the group intelligence of the organization in order to create ownership and gain traction on the strategy. In Synchronizing we translate the vision or strategy into operation.

Synchronize in Action—Reuters

Reuters was created as a news agency for the British Empire. Reuters provided the service of reporting back to the United Kingdom what was going on in India, Singapore, and other parts of the world. Reuters became the world's premier news agency. In the 1970s it built one of the premier financial service companies. It was the first to provide information on buying and selling of financial services, stocks, and pricing around the world. Reuters still had a strong news organization, but it really built an enormous empire around making information about financial services available to investment banks, investors, hedge funds, risk managers, and the like. Reuters was virtually uncontested in the financial market until Michael Bloomberg created a more simplified platform in the 1990s. Bloomberg was incredibly aggressive in both sales and pricing, and in a very short period of time, at the end of the 1990s, Reuters found that Bloomberg had taken half its market share.

In 2002 Reuters appointed its first American CEO, Tom Glocer. Glocer had the very difficult task of downsizing Reuters because it had too much cost overhead. In the process, Tom changed a lot of senior management, which was also very difficult, and developed a new strategy for Reuters— a strategy with which he thought Reuters could more effectively compete. The problem was that Reuters didn't know how to execute or implement the strategy. It was around this time that Reuters was looking for a management program to teach its senior managers how to effectively create value in this new environment. Reuters partnered with the University of Michigan (U of M) to create this program, called "Leading Edge," around the Innovation Genome.

Anne Marie Bell, head of employee communications at Reuters wanted to have consultants come to London in order to preview the Leading Edge course. When the consultants started talking about what they were going to do with respect to teaching, implementing, and executing this course, Bell began to see a wider role for Reuters' yearly Managing Directors Conference. She came up with a concept to make the Managing Directors Conference a way to implement or start getting traction on Glocer's strategy. Bell worked diligently to find an environment in which executives would be able to actually operationalize the strategy. In the end she found an old tram (streetcar) warehouse in Camden Town, a more or less working-class part of London, and created a program called "Fast Forward" with the CEO, Tom Glocer. The program was a way to very quickly implement the strategy that Glocer and his senior group had been working on. It was a way to implement a strategy of efficiency, which also created a way to reduce cost and improve productivity while giving Reuters a roadway or pathway to growth.

Meanwhile, David Ure, the head of strategy at Reuters, called the consultants from U of M and laid out what he thought the key enablers were to making the strategy work. Ure had worked very hard to limit the key enablers to five key things, which included issues such as the technology and platform on which Reuters delivered its product, the segmentation in which Reuters sold its product, the leadership and culture in which the people at Reuters need to perform their duties, and so on.

One hundred of the top leaders from Reuters were invited to come to the Managing Directors Conference as well as 25 people who were considered to be the "best and the brightest." These were the "change and innovation activists" who were not necessarily in the top 100 of Reuters, but were there in order to change the thinking a bit and loosen up the group. The conference gave attendees the feeling that they were on the floor of the New York Stock Exchange. It was very dynamic, energetic, and at times slightly chaotic. There was also a very strict timetable in that there were only two days to have an operating plan for the Fast Forward strategy which included projects, work flows, assignments, and due dates.

At the beginning of the conference there were five senior leaders who talked about five particular areas (strategic pillars). They talked about what their view of those pillars was, what kind of projects they were currently working on, and what they were trying to do with them. After these leaders finished, the group of 125 was carefully divided into five prechosen groups, geared around the five topics. Every group had a senior leader who was the Sponsor of that group, a project leader whose job it was to take projects forward after the conference, as well as a Creativizer (somebody from U of M or from Reuters).

The first thing asked of the group members was that they identify what they thought a strategic pillar meant. This was done in order to create an operational definition because everybody had a different idea about what the pillar actually was or what it meant. So, the first piece consisted of getting everybody on the same page. For the second piece the group talked about what was working and what wasn't working with Reuters in the particular area that the group was focusing on. This gave people a forum in which to have a difficult conversation, which would ultimately lead to making an insightful decision. The third thing the Creativizers did was ask the group, "What are some incredible ideas that we've got about how to implement or operationalize this particular concept?" This led to highly creative thinking, and what came out of this part of the session was a whole host of incredible ideas. The smaller group then had to take these ideas and pick a few of them to report to the collective group.

The groups then came back to the plenary session where an environment had been created that was very exciting. There was high-tech video and music playing in the background, and everyone was in a big center bay of the old tram warehouse. All the chairs had been taken out of the room, and people were standing as if at a rock concert.

Each group then brought all 25 members up, and they made their presentation. Upon completion of each presentation, rather than doing a question and answer session, they had 10 minutes to rush out into the audience and become self-supervised. Every person from the presenting group had to find four people from other groups and talk about two things: The first was potential improvement points for the ideas: where an idea might be polished up, or any holes in the idea that needed shoring up. The person giving feedback was directed not to give criticisms, only contributions. The second thing they talked about was possible overlap because many of these groups were working on similar challenges; this helped the groups to decide who had the right-of-way in these cases. The last thing they did on the first day was go back to their groups, talk about what they heard, and make revisions on their ideas.

That night at dinner the energy and anxiety were palpable. Some people were upset because they felt that months' worth of work were being undone, some felt that they didn't have enough data, some felt like they weren't being heard, and some felt that their point of view was not properly being taken into account.

The second day the groups focused on how to operationalize the ideas they came up with on the first day by asking questions like: What are the key projects that would come out of these work streams? What are the metrics or measures that we're going to put on these projects to see if they are working or not? Which project management process were we going to use? Who's going to do what? How are we going to make revisions as we go along? So on the second day the groups were very quickly getting traction on their projects. Again the groups reported to the plenary group at times and would once again go into the audience working out potential improvement points and overlap. Finally, all the groups had an operating plan and came in to make a pitch to the plenary session. The CEO sat in the middle of the room, asked hard questions about plans, and decided whether each plan was a go, a no-go, or a go with qualification. Within each of the groups a real decision was made, and a project was launched by the end of this session.

At the end of the conference some extraordinary things happened. One member of the audience came up and said that he was personally very ambivalent about the organization and had even considered resigning. He thought that one of the things he might do at the conference was resign because he was not optimistic about the organization. This person said that he was so optimistic after what he saw in the organization—the great intelligence, willpower, and incredible culture—that he was now so confident that he was going to buy some shares of Reuters. He asked if anyone else wanted to buy shares, and they passed the hat. That day, at the end of a two-day Synchronize summit, a room of 125 people had bought 1 million shares of Reuters. At the time, Reuters was trading at the lowest rate it had been since the 1970s, but the group was so optimistic about its plans that they bought. The chairman of the board, Sir Christopher Hogg, was so moved that he was asked to come up and talk. He said that this was the most extraordinary experience he had ever been through as a manager and was deeply committed to supporting Reuters as it went forward with its Fast Forward plans.

Months passed after the conference. Many of the plans were implemented, and some of them didn't work. The conference attendees then asked to do a project like this throughout the company, and it called the project, "Follow the Sun." It picked a day six months after Fast Forward, and all 16,000 people in the Reuters organization worldwide participated so that they could also own the projects. In reality about half the projects actually panned out. Although this may sound low, it's actually a very high number. It's an incredible yield rate because most strategies never even get implemented. In trying these projects, both those that worked and those that didn't, the organization became incredibly intelligent very quickly and made great progress on its plans.

About a year later there was an article in the *Daily Mirror* written about how the year before all the senior executives at Reuters got together and bought Reuters' stock. The article intimated that it was because they were ashamed of how the stock was doing. However, it said that instead of backfiring, the stock greatly appreciated and the executives made an extremely large profit on their investments.

This success was made possible because Anne Marie Bell understood that Reuters wasn't getting traction on its strategy, and she also understood that she could use the Managing Directors Conference to create that traction. David Ure brilliantly understood that part of the reason the strategy wasn't getting traction was that there were four or five areas that Reuters needed to get right in order to make the strategy tenable, and he identified these areas. It was these senior leaders who basically gave the ownership of the strategy back to the other 125 leaders in the organization, and they trusted the organization to do it. Most importantly, three things were generated: First, there was an enormous amount of energy and momentum generated. The strategy went from something that people couldn't get traction on to something with great traction. Second, ownership—the ownership of the strategy—now resided not just in the senior leadership but also in everyone. And finally, group creativity—the genius of the group got unleashed in a very short time.

An important lesson learned here is *create more ugly pots*. This idea is applicable when understanding the yield of Reuters' ideas into real projects. The more ideas (either good or bad; ugly or beautiful) that are

Table 7.1   How the Innovation Genome Relates to the Synchronize Step

Collaborate
Getting organizational buy-in
- Lessons people learn for themselves are much deeper than what they're taught by others.
- A strategic document will provide little motivation if the people involved had nothing to do with the creation of it.

Create
Creating new approaches
- Operationalizing strategy in highly creative ways.
- Allows organization to realize the high creativity within its employees.

Control
Building on systems and technology
- How do plans meet current reality?
- Plans need to fit into how people are paid, how products are manufactured, how products are sold, etc.

Compete
Focusing on key goals
- Plan should attain a certain cost efficiency, margin, growth, etc.
- People need to be not only creative but also results driven.

generated, the more workable ideas will actually emerge. The company is then able to grow more because it has more workable ideas that are creating value.

Selecting Who Will Attend the Summit and Establishing Action Teams

In selecting attendees for the summit like the one presented in the Reuters case, the organization needs to look for four types of players: Executive Sponsors, Project Leaders, Creativizers, and Action Team members. In considering who will fill these positions, the organization should look for three things:

Power: A Sponsor should be in a position of power, specifically, organizational power. A sponsor should be someone who can take responsibility for getting things done.

Influence: The Project Leaders, Creativizers, and Action Team members should all have some influence within the organization. In other words, they should have the ability to influence the organization to go one way or the other.

Expertise: The other thing to look for is expertise, someone who has a deep knowledge of something. The organizational chart can be a very poor predictor of expertise. There may be someone a few levels down who has more expertise about a certain type of technology, for example, than a higher-up.

In selecting people for the summit, it is essential to include the best and brightest. The collection of these three attributes will provide an extremely sound basis for some very good decisions and very good actions. A final intangible to take into account when deciding on a team is a propensity or proclivity toward action. The teams have got to have some doers, people who are actually going to take the projects forward. The teams cannot be composed only of people who are studiers or hold a great amount of information. They must include people who are actually going to go out and experiment.

Prepping Leaders and Creativizers

In prepping leaders and Creativizers, there are two important things for them to understand. The first is their role. For example, the role of a Sponsor is to keep the work stream on track and sanction it. The role of a project leader is to make sure that there's a clear project plan for determining who will do what and that it will be viable. The role of a Creativizer is to keep the process moving, to honor and listen to all different points of view, to make sure that time commitments are met, and to make sure that there are creative answers and deliverables at each point in the process. Because each role is so defined, it is extremely important that people understand the role they will be playing before coming to the summit.

The second thing that has to happen in prepping the leaders and Creativizers is that they must be aware that the summit can be a messy, emergent process; they may feel like they're on the floor of the stock exchange. The leaders must be warned not to overreact and not to worry; it is a process in which revisions may need to be made as the process progresses. It may be that at the end of the day when everyone's going to dinner, certain leaders have to meet again if they didn't get through a certain piece, or they may have to borrow somebody from another team, or have to caucus with other senior leaders because there's a very key strategic initiative that they've agreed upon previously at the executive team meeting and now realize that it's the wrong decision and maybe they should change it. All this is going to go on, and conflict is inevitable. People who are personally invested in their work believe that they are protecting something sacred, and they are going to argue. The leaders must be made aware that this will happen and that these kinds of events must be expected.

Establishing a Sense of Excitement and Momentum

Establishing a sense of excitement and momentum should start at the very beginning of the process. From the time attendees are invited to the summit, it is important to emphasize that they are the best and the brightest; emphasize that this is not a planning meeting but a doing meeting where they're going to have a say in what the organization is going to do. The senior executive or whoever is going to kick off the summit should begin by making it clear to the attendees that this is their meeting. Decisions are going to be made, projects are going to be launched, and they are the people who are going to be in charge of these projects. The senior executive should make it clear that those who were invited to the summit are there because they have her or his trust, and that she or he believes in their intelligence as well as in their commitment to the organization. This will add to the excitement and momentum created for the summit.

Other things that can be done to encourage a sense of excitement may include such things as creating an environment where people have to stand, putting rubber balls on the tables so people can throw them at each other, playing music in between sessions, making sure that people get a chance to mill around and talk to others, and making sure that there are places where people in the group can go and have fun. The whole summit should be arranged less as a comfortable meeting space and more as an active, co-participating space. The point is that this is not just another meeting but a working session; it should feel more like a studio, workshop, or garage where people are working together.

Real-Time Decision Making

At the summit there is a very short time to make real decisions. Materials should be prepared ahead of time and be available at the summit so that if there is a question or debate about financials, segmentation, or whatever the group may be working on, participants can pick up the informational materials at a table somewhere and thumb through them. It is also very important that there be enough expertise within the individual groups so that if there's a question, the group has an expert to turn to; this will contribute greatly to making real-time decisions possible. There should also be enough power and influence within each group to make important decisions.

Most importantly, the Creativizer should keep emphasizing the amount of time that people have to make decisions so that groups keep their conversations nice and crisp and keep debates to a minimum. The group must be held to the time limit! It should also be made clear that, if the group doesn't make a decision within the time allotted, then the senior Sponsor will make the decision. In the end, the group is free to decide what's right, but it has to meet the set deadlines.

Harnessing Conflict and Managing Crises

It is extremely important to have people with differences of opinion in the various groups, but it is also very important to quickly harness the conflict and get to a point where people understand what the key issues are. When group members are discussing certain issues they may have with a project or possible problems they foresee, the Creativizer should see if they can start bundling those issues together in order to find the root cause of those concerns. For example, "I'm hearing two themes here. One is that we currently don't have the money to do it, and two, we don't have a culture that will support it." Recognize conflict and rather than saying which side is right, start working with the Innovation Genome model and ask, "What are some alternatives that could make this conflict go away?"

It is important to have conflict because conflict will lead to creative ideas and will get momentum going, but it is also vital that the Creativizer use the conflict to help come to a purposeful decision. Resolution, how-ever, doesn't mean that everyone agrees. There will always be groups of people who have points of view that will not be included in the final analysis. While this can be frustrating for certain individuals, it is not bad; it's necessary to the process. The worst-case scenario would be to have a "group think" where everyone agrees on something that's quite ordinary or the status quo. If you're going to really implement an insightful strategy, something with a sense of destiny, there are always going to be people who are in dissent. In this case the Creativizer should point out that it's okay to be in dissent, but that the individual has agreed to go forward for the greater good of the organization.

Engaging Expertise and Relevant Facts

For a Creativizer running a group, the key is to recognize that "not everybody knows." For example, if the group is working on a medical center kind of issue and has 10 people in the room but only one world authority on a particular part of the practice, everybody's voice may not have an equal weight. It is very likely that the expert knows more about this particular issue, and the Creativizer may want to listen to this person because he or she has some expertise and relevant facts that other people don't. The other side of this, however, is that the collective group doesn't bring all the biases to the situation that the expert might bring, and therefore may be able to provide some additional insight or creative ideas through alternative approaches.

What is important for a Creativizer to think about when people get in a room is, "Who actually knows?" and "How do we give that person a voice?" Often there are nine or ten people in the room who have one point of view, but the person or expert who really knows has an alternative point of view. In this case the Creativizer needs to really listen to this person and give this person's voice greater weight than everyone else, because this person has the expertise. That's why it's critical that when the teams are formed, there are experts in the room or available to be consulted.

Creating Transformational and Operational Action Plans

Upon conclusion of the summit, there are two important things to look at regarding the projects:

1. People need to understand what they're doing and why they're doing it. There should be a clear operations management piece, which includes milestones. Who will do what? When? What are the outcomes we're looking for? Who's responsible for this? It's important that the milestones are not long milestones; they should be

small win milestones. Leaders should plan to check up on projects every two weeks or every two months. Projects should be able to be measured in short increments so the company can get traction on them and start learning what works and what doesn't work. What the organization doesn't want to do is create something for which they don't see an outcome for a year, because that project will never get traction. The basic rule is "The quicker we can see an outcome by segmenting a project, the faster we're likely to do it."

2. When deciding upon action plans, the Sponsor must ask the question, "How is this different from the way we do things now?" If somebody cannot articulate how it's significantly different, it's not different enough to be done at the summit. It has to be differentiated enough from the way things are normally done or there would be no reason to bring together the best and brightest throughout the organization. There may be things that the organization continues to do the same way, but those things do not need to be the focus during this summit.

In the end, if the company is successful with this project, it will create some dissidence or some discord, some friction with the way the organization runs with its current operating plan. That's okay; this is something that will happen whenever there is a change within the organization. What we're trying to do with the projects is to create new, innovative ways of doing things, while proving viability.

Summit Pre-Work

The objective of the summit is to make the strategy operational. The summit is a three-day conference consisting of various leaders from across the organization. Teams should be Supervised prior to the conference and should consist of the following:

Leadership Team Member: The Leadership Team member is a top executive in the company. This person may have responsibilities for leadership at the highest level for this organization, unit, or team. The Leadership Team member is essential because he or she will be the one who has a voice in the final approval of the action plans.

Creativizers: The assignment of Creativizer is the single most important assignment within the Synchronize step. The team of Creativizers must consist of leaders from the company dedicated to the change and innovation process. The Creativizers guide the Action Teams through the strategy rollout process follow-through. The Creativizer's primary responsibilities will be: (1) *to keep the process on track*, and (2) *to create energy, ownership, and drive within the groups*. The function of the Creativizer is discussed in greater detail below.

Action Teams: Action Teams are made up of staff members within the company who must "buy in" to the change and innovation process in order for it to be successful. The Action Teams will be made up of company leaders such as department managers, Supervisers, and team leaders. There is an Action Team for each of the strategic pillars.

(The function of Creativizers is further discussed in Step 3: Socialize, Phase 7: Select the Creativizers.)

Strategic Pillars and Pressing Problems to Identify and Codify

In the Socialize step, the senior leaders select three to five strategic pillars, which the Action Teams will be assigned (Table 7.2). These pillars need to address the current and desired aspirations of the organization. Examples of pillars may include targets like:

- Improving customer support
- Breakthrough product development
- More effective hiring

The objective in identifying these strategic pillars is to make the strategy operational and integrate it with speed and ownership at all levels.

Each pillar must have a(n):

1. *Sponsor:* Having a Sponsor from the Leadership Team will ensure that decisions made are real and lasting.
2. *Creativizer:* A Creativizer is needed in order to ensure sustainable capability and help move the project forward.
3. *Action Team:* An Action Team is selected according to members' knowledge, influence, and power to enable them to integrate their specific strategic pillar.

Table 7.2   Five Strategic Pillars

Strategic Pillars	Sponsor	Creativizer	Action Team
1.			
2.			
3.			
4.			
5.			

Synchronize Phase 1:
Opening Comments from the Senior Leader

The session will begin with a strong opening from the most senior leader whose role is to clearly outline the purpose of the event. To begin the summit, this key leader will give opening statements and share a brief overview of the purpose of the summit.

Within the opening statements the leader should talk about:

- What the new strategy is and what the new strategy means to the people at the summit.
- Why the new strategy is being rolled out this way.
- What the participants can expect over the next three days. Also, group members should be informed of what is expected of them.

The opening statement should prepare participants to:
1. Own the strategy.
2. Make decisions.
3. Add valuable ideas.
4. Make the strategy operational and integrate it into their operating plans.

Synchronize Phase 2:
Agenda, Activities, and Breakout

The first activity will include a look at the summit agenda, a review of the strategic pillars that were generated in Step 3 (Socialize), and confirmation of the assigned Action Teams to each of the pillars. One of the most important actions prior to the summit is to pick the right people to be working on the right pillars in the right groups. Which people are able to make decisions for each pillar? It is essential that the pillar each team is working on is relevant to its function and that team members have some real experience or expertise in the area of the particular strategic pillar. Action Team members can include:

- Anyone who is an expert on the way the process or strategic pillar is operationalized.

- Anyone who is an expert in how the strategic pillar is consumed.
- Any key stakeholder, which includes anyone who can make the process happen or anyone who can stop it from happening.

Synchronize Phase 3: Defining Meaning and Implications

Defining the meaning of the strategic pillar can often be one of the hardest steps to accomplish. Members of the Action Team will have their own idea about the meaning of the pillar based on the individual's experiences with the pillar. Vital to this step is having a discussion about what the strategic pillar means—that is, a common definition of the challenges. The discussion must not be abstract, but concrete with specific examples. People in the room must clearly define what the pillar means and what it doesn't mean within their organization.

During the discussion the Creativizer listens for collective points of view or "schools of thought." The Creativizer then summarizes or joins the schools of thought together—for example, financial view of performance management. This is followed by a discussion of where the views can be combined and where they can't. Compatible views are then pooled, and incompatible views must be resolved within the group through focused discussion.

The end result of this exercise must be an agreed-upon definition of the strategic pillar.

Synchronize Phase 4: Define Best Practices

In determining best practices, each Action Team member will share a failure associated with the general subject of the strategic pillar, followed by a personal success story. After each story the person will discuss what worked and what didn't.

Once again the Creativizer breaks the responses down into themes. Using these themes, the group determines what works and what doesn't. The ones that worked are "best practices," the ones that don't are to be avoided as action plans are developed.

Synchronize Phase 5: Action Plans

In the Action Plan section each Action Team will think creatively around the possible solutions to meet the challenges of the particular strategic pillar. The best of these ideas for each quadrant will be translated into actions.

- What should they do more of?
- What should they do less of?
- What should they do differently?
- What should they start?
- What should they stop?

Once the Action Team has brainstormed around the Innovation Genome and translated its best ideas into actions, it must prioritize the items. Action items should be specific in terms of what the organization does.

Once the issues are stated in terms of actions, the groups will be pushed to:

- Stop programs, processes, and practices.
- Integrate action items into existing processes.

One of the keys in determining whether the Action Team is ready to make decisions lies largely around what the Action Team is willing to stop. Is it willing to stop anything?

The objective is *not* to start a series of new projects. The objective is to make modifications or changes to existing projects and practices, and to launch as *few* new projects as possible.

Once actions are identified, the Action Team will prepare a presentation to be delivered to the entire assembly that spells out its course of action.

For the presentation of action plans, Action Teams will come back together with the entire assembly. The presentation of the action plan should include what the team is going to do more of, less of, start, and stop, but should also include an explanation of what the action plan means and what it doesn't mean. For example, more emphasis on creating a positive workplace could mean that the company strives to be a desirable place to work, but doesn't mean that it will take focus off profitability.

"Means" and "doesn't mean" are a good way to create a ground-level view of what is really going to take place; this helps to establish guidelines and boundaries for the Actions step (Table 7.3).

Upon completion of presentations, groups within the audience will self-organize in order to join forces with the other groups in discussing questions and answers, as well as challenges or issues that the group may not have considered. They do this by forming teams of three to five people, depending on the number of strategic pillars. If there are three strategic pillars, there should be three people in the group representing

Table 7.3 Actions

Action

Do more

Do less

Do differently

Start

Stop

Means

Doesn't mean

each of the pillars. This is also a good vehicle for new ideas to be proposed or to collaborate with other groups with similar ideas.

After the presentation, Action Teams reconvene and talk about what they learned from the feedback of the other groups. The key will be to identify "hot spots" and list any goods ideas they got from meeting with other groups. The Action Team will then have a discussion about how to integrate the feedback, and whether it needs to make modifications to the action plan. For the most part, Action Teams will find that it is necessary to make at least a few modifications.

Synchronize Phase 6: Identify Quick Wins and Managing Resistance

Once the group has discussed the modifications or changes it will make to its plans, it will identify "*quick wins.*" In order to identify quick wins, the group must ask itself how to make the actions operational, powerful, of high impact, and functional as quickly as possible.

High-impact and easy-to-implement actions are *big wins*. Moderate-impact and easy-to-implement actions are *small wins*. High-impact but hard-to-implement actions are *long-term projects*. Actions that are not high impact or easy to implement are labeled *time wasters* (Table 7.4).

Once quick wins are identified, Action Teams will develop operating plans in order to implement the quick wins. Each Action Team will create metrics or quantifiable measures of success, as well as create a time frame and resource requirements (Table 7.5).

In this step the group is looking for, "Who will do what, when, why, where, and how?"

Once the Action Team has identified quick wins and the plans for implementing them, it is necessary to determine if there is any resistance to that implementation. (Please refer to "Step 6: Specialize, Phase 12: Manage Resistance" for the exercise on how to manage resistance.)

Synchronize Phase 7: Questions, Modifications, and Acceptance

Finally, Action Teams will once again meet in front of the collective group for final presentations. The Action Team's final presentation should include:

Table 7.4 Identify Quick Wins[1]

	Easy to Implement	Tough to Implement
Small payoff	Small wins	Time-wasters
Big payoff	Big wins	Special cases

Table 7.5 Translate Ideas into Actions

What are we doing?	Who is doing it?	Why are we doing it?	How are we doing it?	Where are we doing it?	When will it be done?

- Modifications to the plans presented at the previous planning session.
- Quick wins.
- Action and implementation plans.

- How to overcome key obstacles.
- Resources needed to proceed.

Upon completing its presentation, each Action Team will be given 10 minutes for questions or suggestions from the senior leader who should:

- Cross-examine the idea.
- Present challenges and concerns.
- Offer suggestions for improvements.
- Commit to providing needed resources.

Groups will then respond and commit to making adjustments as necessary.

The purpose of this exercise is to produce a definite outcome. There are two things that it should accomplish:

1. It should gain the approval and resources of senior leaders in order for the plan to move forward.
2. It should provide all four groups with actual work streams that they will be required to carry through and follow up on.

Synchronize Phase 8: Wrapping up the Summit and Moving Forward

In the wrap-up the senior leader will talk about disseminating the decided strategies throughout the organization. The senior leader should conclude his or her statement by leaving a positive and inspirational message with the audience.

After the summit each Action Team must gather all the action items needed for implementation and lay them out in a master project plan. This will be relevant to tracking the progress of the project and enabling the team to pinpoint what's on schedule, what isn't, and why.

Creativizers will be responsible for tracking the projects. The master project plan should be a simple diagram that groups can look at collectively, as displayed in Table 7.8.

Table 7.8 Manage Initiatives

Initiative	Purpose	Stage	Resources	Decision	Priority

Conclusion

1. How do organizational leaders begin to operationalize a vision?

The Innovation Genome shows how a leadership summit can be an effective tool for operationalizing a change vision. The key is to hold a summit that emphasizes doing rather than just meeting or talking. People with organizational power, influence, and expertise should attend the summit, and the purpose of the summit should be to choose projects that will create wins for the organization.

2. What's more important—big wins or small wins?

Big wins are great, but they're often difficult to achieve. Small wins are just as effective at moving the organization forward because they are easier to achieve and they build momentum. Remember that small wins over time contribute to big wins in the long run.

The 3-D View

Remember from Chapter 2 that innovation is typically a work in progress. Innovation always provides key insights into the past that will in turn provide some wisdom about the future, but more importantly it allows us a wider range of courses to speculate and navigate. Once the Synchronize step is complete, it is important for the Creativizers and other appropriate people to ask in a separate meeting the Do, Doing, Done questions by thinking around the Innovation Genome. It is important that the meeting take place close enough to the Synchronize step so that everyone remembers the experience but enough removed so that people have had time to think about what really happened.

Do . . .
Looking forward at future projects, communities, charters, and goals that will flow from the Synchronize step, consider the questions in Table 7.9 from the four perspectives of the Innovation Genome.

Table 7.9

Collaborate View
- What do I need to do?
- How do I want to do it?

Create View
- What do I need to do?
- How do I want to do it?

Control View
- What do I need to do?
- How do I want to do it?

Compete View
- What do I need to do?
- How do I want to do it?

Doing . . .
Looking at any current work taking place around the *Creativize Method* at your organization, consider the questions in Table 7.10.

Table 7.10

Collaborate View
- What's working and what isn't? Why?
- What changes should we make?

Create View
- What's working and what isn't? Why?
- What changes should we make?

Control View
- What's working and what isn't? Why?
- What changes should we make?

Compete View
- What's working and what isn't? Why?
- What changes should we make?

Done . . .

Looking back at what has taken place with the Synchronize step and any projects that have been launched, consider the questions in Table 7.11.

Table 7.11

Collaborate View
- What worked and what didn't? Why?
- What changes would we make if we ran this step or project again?
- What have we learned that can be applied to the current practices of the organization?

Create View
- What worked and what didn't? Why?
- What changes would we make if we ran this step or project again?
- What have we learned that can be applied to the current practices of the organization?

Control View
- What worked and what didn't? Why?
- What changes would we make if we ran this step or project again?
- What have we learned that can be applied to the current practices of the organization?

Compete View
- What worked and what didn't? Why?
- What changes would we make if we ran this step or project again?
- What have we learned that can be applied to the current practices of the organization?

Step 6:
SPECIALIZE

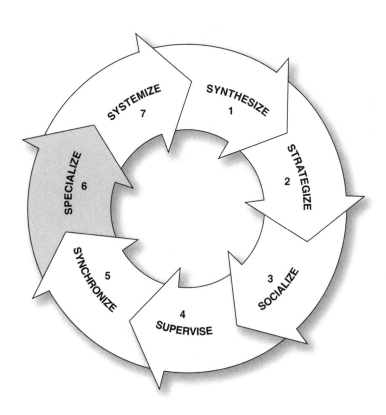

Specialize Overview

- Objective:
  - ○ Jump-start change and innovation Action Teams.

- Participants:
  - ○ Action Teams, Creativizers, and other appropriate leaders and experts from within and outside the organization.

- Actions:
  1. Sponsor communicates desired outcomes for this step, which should relate to an action plan developed in the Synchronize step, and expectations for the Action Team.
  2. Creativizer introduces the Innovation Genome to establish a shared mindset and language.
  3. Action Team meets with leaders and experts, gathers and Synthesizes data, and identifies the key challenges of the project.
  4. Action Team, thinking creatively around the Innovation Genome, identifies better and new ways of meeting the challenge.
  5. Action Team identifies potential obstacles, resisters to the solutions it has developed. and creates plans for gaining buy-in.
  6. Action Team develops key measures and project and development plans.
  7. Action Team jump-starts action items created around the strategic pillars.
  8. Action Team tests its creative ideas through a diverse array of experiments, prototypes, and market tests.
  9. Action Team meets on a regular basis.

- Time:
  - ○ Three days for jump start (Action Team meets regularly until project is completed or eliminated).

This Chapter Will Help Me to Answer:

- How can I use data to help me innovate?
- What's the best way for an organization to try something new?
- How do we integrate our project ideas into the organization?

Introduction

In the Specialize step we launch individual change and innovation projects, or projects that come out of the Synchronize step. The Specialize step is used to create results and set up practices that will lead to successful outcomes in the final phases of the change or innovation process.

Specialize in Action—ProQuest

The ProQuest Information and Learning Division offers data pulled from thousands of publishers worldwide to libraries and schools around the nation. This service has the ability to index and search across all these different sources in one place, and is therefore a very attractive service for academic libraries.

In 2001–2002, ProQuest was redeveloping its core platform or core offering in response to two challenges. The first was that ProQuest had some financial trouble during the dot-com bust because it was considered by many investors to be a dot-com even though it wasn't. It had been mixed up with dot-coms because it was in the information services arena, and, at the time, there were a number of dot-com information service providers. The second challenge was an aggressive new competitor in a market that ProQuest formerly had the corner on. A competitor made a series of bold moves that significantly changed the market landscape. In order to remain strong and successful, ProQuest had to respond quickly to these challenges. The solution was ProQuest 2, the follow-up to ProQuest. The project was a very complex task that required a tremendous amount of coordination.

Elliot Forsyth, the head of human resources (HR) for ProQuest Information and Learning was new to the company, and his concerns were twofold. First, he felt that ProQuest needed to understand the customer requirements of the data product in order to build it the right way, and he was concerned that a lot of engineers in the group might not be collaborating enough with customers. Second, he was concerned about the process of getting very different groups of people together for the first time in years and helping them to operate seamlessly and effectively as a cross-functional group. Forsyth teamed with some consultants in order to manage these processes.

Tom Hamilton was head of the group in charge of creating ProQuest 2. Hamilton had been very successful on other projects but understood that this was a key project for the entire organization, and so running it was a huge responsibility. Hamilton had direct reports from the various areas including the technical area, the licensing area, and the content design area to help him in his efforts.

In embarking upon this project there were a number of things that happened right away. The first move included a number of meetings that focused on what exactly the group members knew about the customers and what kind of information they needed to know. The group broke into subteams that studied specific parts that needed to be investigated in order to build ProQuest 2. For example, one group gathered information on the new technologies that needed to be integrated into ProQuest 2; another looked at how the needs of academic libraries were going to change. The groups hit the road and went to a number of different places around the planet. Within roughly a two-week time period, these teams had collected an enormous amount of data about their customer groups and emerging technologies that needed to be included in ProQuest 2.

The next sessions were really about trying to do two things at the same time. The first was to sort through the data. What were the priorities that needed to be included in the product? A whole host had been created, but there were too many priorities to manage. The group wanted every feature, flexibility, and market that could possibly be added. The key at this point was trying to figure out what the customers really wanted. The group was looking for buyer utility levers, attributes that clients really wanted. At the same time the groups were benchmarking what the ProQuest 2 product looked like against some of its competitors. The second thing that the group was trying to do was think creatively about what they could do to meet market needs but also to combine ideas that would enhance the product and catapult them in front of their competitors.

There was also a sense of urgency around launching this project. The project was begun in the fall of 2001 and needed to be ready by the summer of 2002 because it needed to be shown at the American Library Association meeting where key buyer groups and first adopters would be looking at the new product. It was absolutely essential that the group meet this deadline.

During this period of time, there were other critical factors. The group was trying to figure out, "What, in fact, are the strategic ramifications of this product?" In this case ProQuest 2 was not just a product; it was a product that would allow for other types of information services and publishing products to be developed on this platform and be bundled or combined with the ProQuest 2 product. ProQuest 2 would act as a bridge by which a number of products would come together.

After the group did the initial data finding and a lot of creative thinking about the project, an Action Team of around 80 people was assembled and given its own place to work. It rented an office building, and the only job in that building was to create ProQuest 2. The group's new workspace was well capitalized and well staffed, but some challenges soon emerged. The division president abruptly left the company. Cost cutting kicked in, and some parts of the product development team experienced staff reductions. Every time the engineers talked to a customer, it was both exhilarating and exasperating. They learned about what the customers wanted, but it became incredibly hard to manage. Because of these challenges, the product timeline began to slip, and the team began to flag.

When spring hit, the team had been working incredible hours through the winter and sorted out the product requirements. It had taken months to get to the baseline of what those requirements were. At this time the team was taken off-site to be reenergized at a session where a lot of time was spent talking about the team itself. "What kinds of things are working on the team, what isn't working, how do we work more collaboratively, what things are personally going to energize us or make our life better?" This session was important because it was the antithesis of what an engineer would do because it had no functional outcome. However, what it did do was help the team begin to operate and function more like a high-performing team. The team began to remember why it was doing this project, and it remembered the creative nature of the project. It's very easy to get drawn into the project timelines and the everyday drudgery when working through a difficult project.

During the session the CEO came in and talked about how important the project was, how proud he was of the team, and how confident he was that the team would bring the project in on time. That alone was extremely energizing for this team. The high confidence of and a thank you from the senior leader goes a long way with a team that feels like it's been through battle and feels like their effort hasn't been fully recognized.

In the end, the product came out just in time for the library show and played to rave reviews. More importantly, it created an avenue by which future products and enhancements could be created. ProQuest 2 is not a product that has been created and left on the shelf, but a product that's created with a number of elaborations and a road map forward for adding innovation.

As in many jump-started projects, ProQuest 2 was not really about the project itself but about what the project brought along with it. In this case, ProQuest 2 was a project with a very ambitious timeline. It was about creating a new product, a central product that established the direction of the company. But, once into the project, the group realized that the product was really more than a single product, it was a platform on which a number of other products were going to be situated or built. A whole array of products could be built on this platform or this kind of technology. The group also learned that the process or practices that go into making that type of platform needed to be different from the customary organizational practices or methods.

More important than the project itself is the fact that ProQuest developed a handful of practitioners under Tom Hamilton and Elliot Forsyth, while also developing practices that are now leveraged and used in other parts of the organization. It developed a lot of its own unique and new innovation practices including practices for jump-starting projects, managing projects, managing a portfolio of projects, making decisions, allocating resources, and following those projects through the development phases and Stage-Gate systems that accompany the development phases. All those things made innovation more resilient, dynamic, and sustainable within ProQuest.

Two lessons emerge from this example. The first is *develop a community of highly practiced Creativizers*. The practitioners under Tom Hamilton and Elliot Forsyth had to develop ProQuest 2, but, in doing so, they actually learned how to practice and manage creativity in their organization. The development of ProQuest 2 highlights the second lesson: *hide inside "Trojan horse"* projects. This means to create projects that will provide opportunities for innovation practitioners to learn what practices work and what practices don't. The ProQuest 2 project gave them those opportunities. Other companies can benefit from giving their people the same opportunities to develop their creativity. ProQuest 2 was about responding to competitive pressures in the market and sustaining the growth of the company. In this case, ProQuest's growth was realized through creativity and innovation. The ProQuest 2 project actually embedded the creative mindset into the organization, thus positioning it to adjust to its customers' needs and positioning it for future growth.

Selecting and Prepping the Action Team

One of the most important aspects in the Specialize step is selecting and preparing the Action Team because its members are the people who are going to be working on the project. In creating an Action Team, it is im-

---

Table 8.1 How the Innovation Genome Relates to the Specialize Step

Collaborate
- Keeping the team working together effectively.
- Resolving conflicts; establishing and maintaining a high-performing team.

Create
- Experimenting with diverse approaches as opportunities emerge; trying new approaches.
- Being creative; trying things that are very different from the way things are currently being done.

Control
- Identifying and integrating best practices into processes that can be scaled across the organization.

Compete
- Achieving project goals on time.

---

portant to remember that this is an ongoing process that requires people to come and go from the team, depending on the needs of the various phases and the situation.

The following is a list of questions geared around the four quadrants of the Innovation Genome. These questions are useful in determining the Action Team members and ensuring that the right players are on the team.

The following questions address how team members are going to work together and how effective the team will be.

- Collaborate—Do we have the right . . .
  - People?
  - Influence?
  - Culture?

It's important to have radically diverse arrays of work streams or projects that are going to provide the company with some new avenues for exploration.

- Create—Do we have the right . . .
  - Vision?
  - Creative ideas?
  - Experiments (projects)?

Answering these questions ensures that the projects will produce the kind of value the company is looking for, verifies that the power is in place to accomplish that value, and makes certain that the Action Team includes the people who have the abilities to get things done.

- Compete—Do we have the right . . .
  - Goals?
  - Power/resources?
  - Competencies?

These questions confirm that teams are supervised in the right way, help the company to understand what the teams know and what they don't know, and ensure that there are processes in place that are going to allow the teams to go forward with the project.

- Control—Do we have the right . . .
  - Structure/design?
  - Information?
  - Systems/processes and technology?

When organizing teams, these questions are relevant because they require the company to ask, "What kind of people, vision, goals, and structure are we going to have?" This may lead to adding to or subtracting players from the team that had not been anticipated. People in various segments or phases of the project may be more effective or less effective. For example, early in a project, people who are anchored to the Create quadrant may be more effective because the early stages are often about strategizing and creating ideas. However, as the project progresses, people anchored to the Control quadrant may be more effective because they have a lot of systematic ideas about how to scale the project.

Establishing a Team Charter

One of the first jobs of the Action Team is to establish a team charter. The charter is a mini business plan, and like a regular business plan, it needs to lay out who's going to do what and when they're going to do it, what people get for their investment, and what kind of return they're going to have. The plan needs to spell out how it's going to motivate people to be effective on this project. Big improvements will not be free on any project.

The plan has to actually have something in it, whether it's money, freedom, or something that's exciting for people to work on; there has to be something in the plan that inspires people to move it along.

Create a definition of the Action Team and what specific work it has to accomplish. In establishing a team charter, the following details should be discussed:

- What are the desired outcomes to be achieved by the Action Team? Talk about what kinds of goals need to be met, and by when.
- What are the deliverables? What will people get for their investment and time on the team?
- What resources are going to be provided?
- What is the length of this assignment?
- What are the team mission and values?
- What is the formal authority of the team? Will it be able to tell the company what to do, or will it have to use influence to accomplish its aim?
- What is the design and development plan? What is the schedule?
- What is the ongoing management reporting and feedback process? As the project moves along, how will everyone know what's working and what's not? How will team members get direction?
- What are the performance measures and incentives? What do people get for effectively making progress on this team?

It's important that people understand that the charter the group is creating provides a different way to get the project done. If it could be accomplished through the normal avenues, it would be. It's critical to view this charter as a special assignment, and it should be treated as such. The standard, organizational, institutional rules may not apply here, and, in many cases, there needs to be a separate space created for the Action Team in order to get the results it needs.

Gathering Data Quickly

Action Teams need to gather data before moving forward. By collecting and analyzing data, Action Teams can determine their best opportunities for success. This section explains the ways in which data should be collected.

1. General guidelines for collecting data:
   - *What do we know, need to know, and want to know?* The first thing a company should ask is, "What do we know?" There are many ways of knowing. We can know through hard data, imagination, questions, intuition, or experience. The people in an organization should be able to distinguish among these three questions on an ongoing basis. People must use the knowledge that they already have about their own work experiences. For example, if you work at a restaurant and you regularly experience a certain complaint from customers, you know that something is not working. This knowledge is tacit, meaning that it is internal to you and guides your actions in alleviating the source of the complaints. In generating this knowledge, you are using a heuristic approach to data gathering, which means you are learning for yourself as you do your work. You might also have hard data to support what you already know. Customers put their comments on comment cards, and food critics review restaurants and publish their opinions. Knowledge and information can be found in a variety of places. The key is in knowing where to look.
   - *Look for people at the center of the network—people who either know or who can find the people who do:* It may take a few degrees of separation, but using your contacts can usually help you to find the right person. For example, if you need to find someone in the pharmaceutical industry who develops drugs, you might call a contact you have in the marketing department of a pharmaceutical company who can lead you to the expert you're seeking.
2. Sources of data:
   - *Quality and efficiency data:* Quantitative data are relatively easy to find. They can come from complaints, failure rates (how many parts do we have to scrap?), warranty data (what percentage of tires did we have to replace?), or utilization statistics (how many pieces did we make last month?). Companies usually gather these kinds of data on a regular basis because they're closely related to performance data.
   - *Customers:* These data often come from sales force reports, surveys, focus groups, and one-on-one interviews.
   - *Anthropology:* Companies can gather these data through field observation, through customer clinics for lead adaptors, or by building prototypes and seeing how they work and how potential customers like them. For example, Sony often makes short production runs of consumer electronics and tests them by selling them in the con-

sumer electronics district of Tokyo; it's what Sony calls *expeditionary marketing*. The company takes the products out and sees what this very sophisticated market likes and what it doesn't like.

- *360:* The 360 approach involves interviewing and surveying staff, customers, and suppliers and gathering competitive intelligence. This is used in order to create a more complete picture of what's happening around you in a 360 degree way (imagine your organization as the center of a circle, with the circle being the context in which it exists) in both the competitive space and the buying and selling space.
- *Futuring:* Futuring uses data that speculate about the future such as industry reports, think tanks, and trend spotting. In futuring, companies look for emerging trends.

Keeping Action Teams on Track

In order to keep the project moving forward, the Action Teams must stay on track. Depending in which quadrant of the Innovation Genome an Action Team is anchored, the team is likely to face an array of challenges. This is because when each quadrant is taken to an extreme, problems emerge. The following outlines these possible problems and suggests ways to minimize them:

Collaborate Quadrant

Problem:

- Things are moving too slowly.

Why?

- *Consensus culture:* Everything has to be worked out so that everybody feels good about what is happening, and in reality that's very difficult to do.

- Means are more important than the ends.

What to Do:

- *Nonnegotiable stretch timelines and goals:* The way to keep the group going is, in a short period of time, by determining what the timeline, goals, and outcomes are. Ask group members, "Is the goal a stretch goal (or a goal that may be beyond their reach)?" and gain commitment up front from the group concerning the outcome.

Create Quadrant

Problem:

- Things are too radical, too complex, too wide, too broad, or too futuristic.

Why?

- Scattered big ideas with little follow-through.
- *Little interest in data or details:* The group's primary interest is the new idea, the experiment-not what comes out of it.

What to Do:

- *Proof of concept and incremental milestones:* With groups anchored in this quadrant, a company should say, "Show me one." "When are we going to see a car that runs or a delivery of this service?" or, "Show us a tangible prototype in phase one of this project." Doing this keeps the group members focused on using their imaginations on the actual implementation and construction of the project or process.

Compete Quadrant

Problem:

- Things are moving too fast.

Why?

- *Overly competitive and incredibly aggressive:* People anchored in this quadrant are the kind of people who want things done in two hours when in reality it is something that takes two days.
- *The end justifies the means:* If people are fired and buildings are ruined, it's okay as long as the goals have been accomplished.

What to Do:

- Get suggestions and buy-in from grassroots constituency before proceeding. They can make goals and have goals, but the first thing they have to do before proceeding with these goals is do some kind of weather check to make sure that the key groups that are going to be required to do this have bought in at a grassroots level. This means not just making sure that the boss is okay with it; this means going to every department of the organization, talking to people, listening to their input, making compromises, and revising some of the goals so that people in the company can have their say in them and in some ways have ownership in them.

Control Quadrant

Problem:

- Things are happening too incrementally; it looks as though nothing has changed, and nobody is sure if we've made any progress.

Why?

- *Analysis paralysis:* People anchored in this quadrant will study things to pieces. This is the group that has flow charts, run rates, and spreadsheets for everything.
- *Fear of change:* The lives of members of this group are about making smoothly running operating systems. Control people are wonderful at keeping things on track but very bad at doing anything that's a significant change or innovation, which is the point of these teams.

What to Do:

- *Stretch goals that can't be accomplished through incremental adjustments:* Say, "Okay, this is a special project. What are the yearly program plans or the goals for the year?" Team members will know what those are and say, "Here are the targets we're supposed to be hitting." Then say, "What would those goals be to justify undertaking a special project like this?" This is where the goals will be significantly increased. For example, a 4 percent reduction in operating expenses could turn into a 20 percent reduction in operating expenses. What that stretch goal will do is require that the group turn to some new ideas and new approaches rather than just the same old incremental "Do everything the same."

Running Experiments and Creating Prototypes

An Action Team will likely have to show proof of concept when trying to sell a new idea. Proof of concept often comes in the form of experiments and prototypes. The purpose of experiments and prototypes is to build something and see how it works. The experimentation process is relatively straightforward: build one, test it, review it, revise it, and build again.

When it comes to experimentation, more is more. There's an old saying, "Fail early and fail often so that you can succeed sooner." The object is not to avoid failure with prototypes or experiments. There will always be failure. The aim is to accelerate the failure cycle and not to be afraid of it. This helps the company to quickly learn what works and what doesn't work.

It's also important to pull the innovation through the right part of the organization. A common problem in innovation projects is that when companies try something new, they try it in the middle of the organization where the company is trying to keep its equilibrium and where things are going according to plan. What the company should do is put that experiment in a place where the organization is underperforming and there's a lot of pain. As discussed earlier in the book, this part of the organization will be more receptive to the big innovation experiment, and the failure of the initial experiment is something that's not going to create the same kind of reaction it would in the part of the organization that's operating according to plan. The same is true in a part of the organization that's operating exceptionally. Groups that are having great success can afford to take some risks.

Once you are clear about what parts of your organization are more likely to support risk taking, you will need to try some experiments to see what works and what doesn't. Experimentation will lead to learning so that you can build a prototype to help the organization understand what you are trying to accomplish and how it will bring value. When running experiments or creating prototypes, keep in mind:

- Experiments and prototypes are closely related. Build one that works.
- Create simple models with what is available. (The design firm IDEO carved the first Apple computer mouse out of soap.)

- Diversify your prototypes, experiments, and approaches.
- Fail early and fail often to succeed sooner. (Accelerate the failure cycle.)
- Build it, test it, review it, revise it, and build it again.
- Try one and see what works and what doesn't.
- Pull the innovation through the problem or opportunity space (when the organization is in crisis mode or when it is working exceptionally well).
- What's new? What's the next thing? How can this be improved?
- The tighter the coupling between a prototype and its real-world use, the more power and influence it is likely to possess.
- IDEO mantra: Make it useful, usable, and delightful.

There are a number of ways in which a company can make prototypes:

1. *Spreadsheet prototyping:* Try to figure out if you can make money at it, try to figure out how many failures per thousand, how many customers will have to subscribe to it, etc.
2. *Mock-up prototyping:* Use software tools to draw a picture of it, "Here's what the car's going to look like." "Here's what the workplace is going to look like." "Here's what the product will look like." "Here's what the process may look like."
3. *Clay and cardboard prototyping:* Try to build a three-dimensional prototype the way they do in making cars or in architecture.
4. *CAD prototyping:* Get on the computer and draw what it would look like if the hospital took more patients, for example, or if the airplane could fly.
5. *Web page prototyping:* Put a Web page on the Internet and create a storefront, institute, or project to see if you can build some community or interest around it.
6. *Simulation prototyping:* See through simulation what would happen if the company stopped or started offering specific services. What would happen if we opened a new school?
7. *Functioning prototype:* This does not have to be a product; it can be a service. A prototype service could be, "we're offering it to one client," or, "We're offering it in one area of the organization." It could be a process that the company is running, maybe a new way of doing order entry in one part of the organization. A functioning prototype is something that has been built, is in real use, and information is being gathered on it.

Co-Creating with Customers

There has been a shift in how companies create products and services in recent years. The process has gone from, "I'll build it for you," to "I'll build it with you." Customers are now partners in the innovation process and represent an opportunity for Action Teams.

Look for customers that have a need so compelling they would be willing to help you produce what they need now. Another kind of customer that's motivated to participate in a co-creating situation is a company that's in a crisis situation (failing) or an exceptional situation (highly successful). Also be on the lookout for a customer that wants to keep in the front of the pack.

Before committing to a co-creating agreement, it's important to ask a number of questions. For example, ask what the red hot center of the customers' world is, what they care about, and what is capturing their imagination. Also, determine what happens if they don't get what they want and what kind of pressures they are facing.

Once these questions are answered, there are a few simple rules to follow when collaborating with customers:

- Make doing business with the company simple and easy. If a customer can participate only once a month, make it work.
- Design every business process from a customer perspective.
- Let the business evolve as the customer's needs change.
- Target the right customers. It's important to be involved with the kind of customers that the company is going to be working with as the result of the innovation.
- Manage every aspect of the customer's experience from the buying of the product or service to installing, using, adding on to it, and finally disposing of it.
- Make it easy for customers to help themselves. A lot of the time customers do not want to have to interact with the company. Can we give them a kit or a portal? Is there something on the Web that could make it easy for them to do it themselves?
- Assist customers in doing their own jobs, not making them do our jobs.
- Deliver a service that's highly customized.
- Develop a strong sense of community around the product or service.

Gaining Buy-in and Integrating the Project into Operations

To successfully jump-start the processes resulting from the Specialize step, it is helpful to identify individuals who have strong influence within the organization. This is not something that is determined by a company's formal organizational structure. There are always opinion leaders in organizations who have influence, and it's essential to search these people out and get them on your side. When jump-starting a project, the fiercest possible critics and major influencers within the organization should be engaged early on.

There are ways that you engage critics and major influencers. The first rule comes from Sun Tzu in his famous work, *The Art of War*. "Keep your friends close and your enemies closer." In one example, a company was trying to avert the unionization of its truckers. The leaders of the company were able to avoid unionization by engaging one of the most respected men from the group of truckers who was helping to lead the unionization effort. By keeping him close and allowing him to give helpful feedback to management, both sides walked away happy. It created a win-win situation.

Another way to engage influencers when jump-starting a project is to look both "upstream" and "downstream" of the project. Once a project is working, ask yourself if there is anything that's going to happen upstream (for example, in the design or capitalization phase) that needs to be integrated, and is there anything that's going to happen downstream (such as in manufacturing or implementation) that needs to be integrated? The teams should pick influencers who are both upstream and downstream so that when the process is integrated, the entire organization is covered.

A problem with any jump start is that any idea, no matter how perfect, is going to be criticized because it's not somebody else's idea. The Action Team should work to create ownership of an idea by asking these influential people, "What would you do?" and, "How would you do it?" In the example of the unionizing truckers, management's original plan was designed to benefit the truckers. Yet because the truckers did not have input in the design of the plan and did not offer the change, they had a difficult time believing it was a good plan for them. This is the irony of many change processes.

Specialize Phase 1: Identify the Challenge

To initiate the Specialize process, the Leadership Team needs to first identify the challenge. This can be accomplished by asking the following questions.[1]

Identify the Challenge

- What's wrong? (Problem to be solved)
- What do you want? (Opportunity to be captured)
- What do we gain from working on this?
- What's working? What isn't working?
- What's causing this to happen?
- How long has this been happening?
- Who else is working on this challenge?
- How will we know we've been successful?

Specialize Phase 2: Select an Action Team to Meet the Challenge

Once the Leadership Team has identified the challenge, it's time to select the Action Team members who will put the plans in motion. In picking the team members, it is important that the Leadership Team imagine the team at work. This will lead to questions such as: Is the team complete? Have we selected the right people?

Table 8.2 provides a framework for discussion as you build the team.

Once these questions have been discussed and there are potential team members, it's time to narrow those choices based on the type of team and project. To further clarify the individuals that would be best suited for the team, use the following tool (Table 8.3).

Fill the Empty Chairs

In the end, the team will use data from the previous two exercises to fill the empty chairs. This exercise will help to consolidate the answers and suggestions from the previous questions and finalize the team selections (Table 8.4).

Table 8.2 Do We Have People Who . . .

Collaborate
- Have influence over this?
- Can build a community around this?
- Generate interest in this?
- Resolve conflicts?
- Keep this ethical?

Create
- See the future first?
- Are wildly creative?
- Conduct multiple experiments?
- Can market this?
- Can change the organization?

Control
- Are experts?
- Have experience with this?
- Have responsibility for this?
- Are problem solvers?
- Collect data?

Compete
- Can get this done quickly?
- Will challenge the team to high performance?
- Make decisions?
- Provide resources?
- Make deals with other firms?

- What type of team is this?
- What roles do we have?
- What roles do we need to have?
- Who might play these roles?
  - Think about advisors:
    - Industry experts, outside of field experts, novices, vendors, and customers.
- Who needs to be on the team?
- Who shouldn't be on the team?
- Who needs to be involved for us to meet our challenge?
  - Core team, Action Team, organization, others?

Specialize Phase 3: Create a Team Charter

Once the team members have been selected, the Leadership Team needs to be specific about what the team is working on. Members of the Leadership Team should inform the Action Team up front what it is expected to do and what the members will get for doing it. What is the mandate of the team? It will accomplish this by creating a team charter.

Table 8.3 Identifying Action Team Members

Part-Time Team
- Team members have a regular job.
- Team members need to influence the organization.
- Team members request resources.
- Team membership can be indefinite.

Full-Time Team
- Team members' only job is the project.
- Team members have power over the organization.
- Team members have a budget and return-on-investment goals.
- Team membership has an end date.

Advantages
- Smoother institutionalization of key ideas because team members are part of the organization.
- Competencies are developed and remain within the organization.
- Continuity over longer periods of time because team members have longer tenure.

Advantages
- Much faster implementation because team is powerful, full time, and singularly focused on the initiative.
- An opportunity to determine who are high-performing leadership candidates through their actions and results.
- Competencies developed on the initiative are brought to other areas of the firm when the team is disbanded.

Disadvantages
- May be too incremental to make substantive changes.
- May be too slow to meet initiative objectives.
- May emphasize operational fit at the expense of creating shareholder value.

Disadvantages
- May not deeply understand more detailed operational issues.
- May destroy cultural values and beliefs.
- May be short-term focused.

Table 8.4   Fill the Empty Chairs

Collaborate	Create
Control	Compete

Team Charter

- Definition of the Action Team project.
- Desired outcomes to be achieved by Action Team.
- Deliverables.
- Resources to be provided.
- Length of assignment.
- Team mission and values.
- Formal authority of the team.
- Design and development plan and schedule.
- Ongoing management reporting and feedback process.
- Performance measures and incentives.

Specialize Phase 4: Establish a Shared Language and Mindset

In Step 3: Socialize, Phase 1, a shared language and mindset was established for the Leadership Team. At this time it is necessary to also establish a shared language and mindset for the Action Team so that it can be on the same page when embarking upon its new project. (Please see Step 3: Socialize, Phase 1: Establish a Shared Language and Mindset to run this step.)

Specialize Phase 5: Get Smart about the Challenge

Once the Action Team has established a shared mindset, it is important for members to ask, What exactly are we working on? There are two kinds of tasks that Action Teams set out to do:

1. *Solve problems:* This process focuses on making something not happen. It is highly reactive and involves going backward to figure out a cause. It is moving away from something.
2. *Try to create something:* This process is highly proactive. It involves a lot of projecting and is moving toward making something happen.

To begin making sense, everyone in the group will tell a story and discuss some themes. They will tell a story about a challenge and make it specific. Sometimes it helps people to tell about a personal challenge and not to talk about the firm. This helps to take key problem issues and make them personal; it helps to establish a relationship to the problem.

The group will then discuss themes from the stories and create a statement about the challenge. Here are helpful exercises, guidelines, and questions to aid in making sense of the problem:

"Sensemaking"

1. Discuss questions as a group:
   - What's the cause of the challenge?
     - Ask "why" until you get to the root concept of what is creating the challenge.
   - What do we know about this challenge?
     - Who, what, where, when, why, and how?
   - What do we need to know about this challenge?
     - Who, what, where, when, why, and how?
   - Who can tell us what we need to know about this challenge? (This can be one of the most important parts in figuring out the challenge.)
     - Go talk to them and report to the group on key information.

2. Break into subgroups and find answers to the questions.
3. Report findings to the group.
4. Develop a point of view.

Specialize Phase 6: Think around the Challenge

Once the challenge is established, focus your thinking around the viewpoints from the four quadrants. Think about the Innovation Genome model (Table 8.5) in sequence, only focusing on ideas from each individual quadrant. The purpose of this action is to create ideas that can help you meet the challenge. This step can be done as a group, or you can break into four subgroups with each taking a different point of view.

If the Action Team thinks about the model and doesn't come up with anything new, it is important to add creativity to it and make the ideas dynamic. This is a way of taking an idea that was generated by thinking about the model and making it more "wow!" The Action Team does this by taking existing ideas and changing them to make them more appealing, attractive, or feasible. For example, the firm may need to improve public relations:

- *Original idea:* Hire a different kind of person to run PR within the firm.
- *Bigger idea:* Engage a top ad firm to develop brand.
- *Smaller idea:* Everybody who works at the firm gets some kind of PR training.

Here are some ways to add dynamics to ideas (Table 8.6).

Specialize Phase 7: Develop Criteria and Select the Best Ideas

The next step in the process is for the Action Team to develop criteria for selecting the best ideas. Table 8.7 can be a starting point for making the selection process. Because the group may be trying to create specific forms of outcomes, the selection process may focus more on questions from one quadrant of the Innovation Genome than on the others. For example, if the group needs to create growth, then the group needs to ask questions like those found in the Create quadrant in the table.

Table 8.5 Think about the Challenge from the Perspective of the Four Quadrants of the Innovation Genome

Collaborate
- Values
- Hiring and staffing
- Work environment
- Informal networks
- Communication
- Training and development
- Mentoring and coaching
- Empowerment
- Work-life balance
- Resolving conflicts
- Teamwork

Create
- Experiments
- Speculating on new markets
- Radical change projects
- Envisioning the future
- Entrepreneuring
- Spin-offs
- New products and services
- Destroying current practices
- Going around authority and boundaries
- Widening the type and array of projects
- Bringing in weird people

Control
- Standards
- Large-scale operations
- Quality programs
- Continuous improvement processes
- Government regulations
- Policies and procedures
- Organizational structure
- Project management
- Information systems
- Technology

Compete
- Strategy
- Financial measures
- Acquisitions and mergers
- Eliminating unproductive initiatives
- Paying for performance
- Sales and marketing
- Portfolio management
- Resource allocation
- Quick decision making
- Rapid deployment teams

Once the Action Team develops selection criteria, each individual will vote for what he or she thinks is the best idea. Ideas should be written on large pieces of paper and posted on the wall where the group is working, and the group should be able to narrow the results down to the best three to five.

Table 8.6   Add Dynamics to Ideas

Make the idea . . .

Faster	Slower
Bigger	Smaller
Integrated	Separate
Simple	Complex
Straight	Round
Factual	Analogous
Pictorial	Numeric
Light	Dark
Mind	Body
Premium	Standard
Near	Far
Abstract	Concrete
More	Less
Part	Whole
Up	Down
Stimulating	Relaxing
One	Several
Movable	Inactive
Strong	Flexible
Add	Remove

Specialize Phase 8: Identify Quick Wins

At this point the Action Team should take the best ideas and identify "quick wins" by using Table 8.8.[2]

The group is looking for big wins that are easy to implement, followed by small wins that are easy to implement, and finally big wins that are tough to implement. They should eliminate all small wins that are tough to implement; these are time-wasters and should be thrown out. This is a simple way for the group to identify first-things-first.

Table 8.7   Develop Idea Selection Criteria

Collaborate
- Interest: Do we care about this idea?
- Knowledge: What are we learning from this idea?
- Beliefs: Does this idea fit with our values?

Create
- Innovation: Is this idea a breakthrough?
- Direction: Does this idea move us toward the future?
- Emerging opportunity: Will this idea allow us to experiment as we go along?

Control
- Cost: Can we afford this idea?
- Feasibility: Can we really implement this idea?
- Standards: Does this idea comply with critical standards?

Compete
- Cash value: Is the payoff for this idea big enough?
- Immediacy: Can we execute this idea quickly?
- Leverage: Can this idea be used to create value in other areas?

Table 8.8   Quick Wins
(Originally in Step 5: Synchronize, Phase 6: Identify Quick Wins and Manage Resistance)

	Easy to Implement	**Tough to Implement**
Small payoff	Small wins	Time-wasters
Big payoff	Big wins	Special cases

Specialize Phase 9: Overcome Obstacles

Many work streams or projects will have obstacles. To overcome obstacles, the group needs to take a three-pronged approach: first, it must identify key obstacles. Second, it must identify the specifics of the obstacles. Third, it must determine how to overcome the obstacles. As an example of how this might work, consider the case of a group that has the challenge of increasing a company's exposure in the local community. The obstacle may be that hiring a PR agency costs too much money. The specifics may be that there is no money in the budget to do it or that the state has cut funding. A potential solution may include providing PR training to existing employees so that they can do some PR work for the firm.

Table 8.9 can assist in identifying ways to overcome obstacles.

Table 8.9 Overcome Obstacles		
Obstacle	**Specifics**	**Potential Solution**
Examples: cost, time, feasibility		

Specialize Phase 10: Make Action Plans

Phase 10 helps to operationalize the ideas that the Action Team has come up with. The Action Team should ask:

- What are we doing? (Be specific.)
- Who is doing it? (Put a face on it; the more a group can put a name of someone who has ownership of carrying out the idea, the better off it is.)
- When will it be done? (When is it deliverable?)

Specialize Phase 11: Develop Key Measures

Many methods of measurement suggest that what you measure and how you measure are different. In this exercise what you measure and how you measure are the same.

Upper measures: Upper measures (latent measures) represent the Collaborate and Create categories of the Innovation Genome and deal

Table 8.10   Translate Ideas into Actions
(Originally in Step 3: Socialize, Phase 5: Organizational Change and Innovation Actions)

What are we doing?	Who is doing it?	Why are we doing it?	How are we doing it?	Where are we doing it?	When will it be done?

with future outcomes. Using the upper measures, companies take risk and invest with decreasing rates of return in order to create competency, change, or innovation. They expect that in the long term, their returns will be greater. The upper measure never pays in the beginning and always has a negative net present value (NPV), but is meant to be a long-term measure. This is important when thinking about innovation. Innovation doesn't necessarily pay up front, but it leads to innovation, which pays in the future.

Lower measures: Lower measures (manifest measures) represent the Compete and Control categories of the Innovation Genome and deal with the present. They are used to create focus and alignment. Using lower measures, companies invest in activities in which they expect immediate returns and consistent, positive NPV. When the returns begin to decrease, companies no longer invest in those activities.

It is important that, when a company implements either measure, it shouldn't look at only whether things are getting done or if they look like they are going to make money, but also at outcomes such as, "Did we learn anything? Did we experiment enough?" A company should create its own performance measures by using the following model (Figure 8.1). Lower measures refer to the bottom quadrants of the Innovation Genome, while upper measures refer to the top quadrants (Table 8.11). Use Table 8.12 to create measures for your own company.

Specialize Phase 12: Manage Resistance

The group is almost ready to begin its projects. However, before performance measures are fixed in place, the group should determine the key stakeholders. Who can make this change and innovation happen, and who can stop it? Some examples may include unions, the media, and interest groups. The group needs to consider all potential and then get buy-in from some of the top stakeholders (Table 8.13).

Get Buy-in

There are multiple ways to go about getting buy-in. One way is through simple communication. Listen to the concerns of others, especially your stakeholders, and establish rapport and trust. If this doesn't work, engage

Lower measures = immediate outcomes
- Exposed information
- Convergent options
- The present situation (manifest)
- Tangible value
- Create focus and alignment
- Invest with increasing rates of return until rates fall

Upper measures = future outcomes
- Emergent knowledge
- Divergent options
- The future situation (latent)
- Intangible value
- Create slack and diversify
- Invest with decreasing rates of return until you develop competency, change and innovation, and brand equity

Figure 8.1   Performance measures

Table 8.11   Examples of Upper (Collaborate and Create) and Lower (Control and Compete) Measures

Collaborate
- Workforce diversity
- Employee satisfaction index
- Turnover of experienced personnel
- Training and education costs per employee
- Organizational competency index

Create
- Number of experiments launched
- Diversity of initiative array
- Projected new market growth
- Adoption of new technology
- Alternative uses of innovation identified

Control
- Initiative cost vs. budget
- Actual vs. planned milestones achieved
- Number of failures
- Number of prototypes tested
- Design for manufacturability index rating

Compete
- Projected gross profit
- Projected market growth
- Projected time to market
- Projected return on investment
- Projected operating income

Table 8.12   Balanced Performance Measures

Collaborate   Create

Control   Compete

Table 8.13   Estimate Commitment[3]

Stakeholder	Resist It	Do Nothing	Assist Making It Happen	Lead Making It Happen

resisters through participation. Ask potential resisters what they would do. Participation changes people's ability to be critical because it draws them in. The Action Team might even consider putting a big resister on the team.

Third-party facilitation is another way to get buy-in. Use a third party specialist whose expertise is in mediating differences. Choose somebody who is seen as having high integrity and as being neutral. If this doesn't work, try to negotiate.

Sometimes people want something (Table 8.14). Have you considered what the resisters stand to lose by your idea being implemented? Can you offer something to offset any losses? What do they believe that they are going to lose? What does the team think they're going to gain? If they don't gain more than they lose, the group may need to sweeten the pot.

Table 8.14 Negotiate for Acceptance[4]		
Hot Spots	**Plus**	**Minus**
Financial impact		
Security		
Inconvenience/convenience		
Satisfaction		
Manner of change		
Cultural beliefs		
Other		

Specialize Phase 13: Test Ideas

Once the group has ideas, metrics, and buy-in, it's time for testing the idea. The purpose of this is not to pick which idea is best. The group wants to focus instead on making sure that it has work streams/projects (developed in the Synchronize step) within each quadrant (Figure 8.2).

Finally, the group should talk about what it's doing and who's doing it (Table 8.15).

The session should end with the notion that the project is under way. In Step 7: Systemize, we create project review gates so that multiple projects are looked at in relation to one another. This will create the organizational architecture needed to take all these projects into a larger scale.

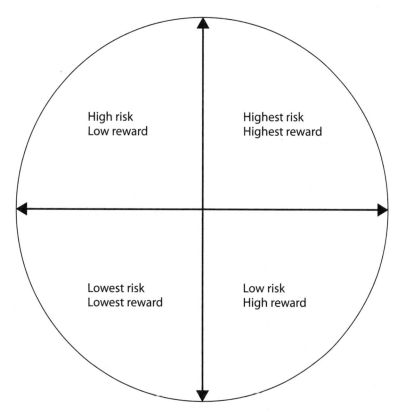

Figure 8.2   Launch work streams from diverse perspectives

Table 8.15   Proof of Concept

Work stream	How to test the work stream (e.g., prototype, market test)	What is the goal of our test?	How and when will we know if it succeeds or fails?

Conclusion

1. How can I use data to help me innovate?

Data are useful for finding places where a company can insert creativity with the goal of producing a win. Data can come from people within the organization. They can come from customers. They can already exist, or maybe they need to be found. Data will help in the creation of a team charter (or mini business plan), which will serve as that team's road map for successful wins.

2. What's the best way for an organization to try something new?

Once data have been collected and the team knows where it needs to act, the challenge is to determine how to actually initiate something new. Various kinds of experimenting and prototyping exist. Some companies even co-create with their customers who are best at identifying needs and helping to realize opportunities. The best place within an organization for trying something new is where there already is strain. The act of trying something new won't come as a shock in the way it might in a more stable part of the organization.

3. How do we integrate our project ideas into the organization?

Much of what has been discussed comes into play here. Conflict and strain must be effectively managed. Getting buy-in and the support of others is critical here as it is elsewhere. Integration is an ongoing process, so remember to determine where you've been, what you're doing, and where you're going.

The 3-D View

Remember from Chapter 2 that innovation is typically a work in progress. Innovation always provides key insights into the past that will in turn provide some wisdom about the future, but more importantly it allows us a wider range of courses to speculate and navigate. Once the Specialize step is complete, it is important for the Creativizers and other appropriate people to ask in a separate meeting the Do, Doing, Done questions by thinking around the Innovation Genome. It is important that the meeting take place close enough to the Specialize step so that everyone remembers the experience but enough removed so that people have had time to think about what really happened.

Do . . .
Looking forward at future projects, communities, charters, and goals that will flow from the Specialize step, consider the questions in Table 8.16 from the four perspectives of the Innovation Genome.

Table 8.16

Collaborate View
- What do I need to do?
- How do I want to do it?

Create View
- What do I need to do?
- How do I want to do it?

Control View
- What do I need to do?
- How do I want to do it?

Compete View
- What do I need to do?
- How do I want to do it?

Doing . . .
Looking at any current work taking place around the *Creativize Method* at your organization, consider the questions in Table 8.17.

Table 8.17

Collaborate View
- What's working and what isn't? Why?
- What changes should we make?

Create View
- What's working and what isn't? Why?
- What changes should we make?

Control View
- What's working and what isn't? Why?
- What changes should we make?

Compete View
- What's working and what isn't? Why?
- What changes should we make?

Done . . .

Looking back at what has taken place with the Specialize step and any projects that have been launched, consider the questions in Table 8.18.

Table 8.18

Collaborate View
- What worked and what didn't? Why?
- What changes would we make if we ran this step or project again?
- What have we learned that can be applied to the current practices of the organization?

Create View
- What worked and what didn't? Why?
- What changes would we make if we ran this step or project again?
- What have we learned that can be applied to the current practices of the organization?

Control View
- What worked and what didn't? Why?
- What changes would we make if we ran this step or project again?
- What have we learned that can be applied to the current practices of the organization?

Compete View
- What worked and what didn't? Why?
- What changes would we make if we ran this step or project again?
- What have we learned that can be applied to the current practices of the organization?

Step 7:
SYSTEMIZE

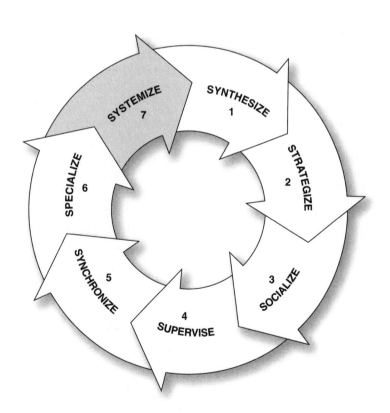

Systemize Overview

- Objective:
  - ○ Review and revise projects, adjust organizational practices, and learn.

- Participants:
  - ○ Leadership Team, Action Teams, Lead Facilitator, Creativizers, and other appropriate leaders and experts from throughout the organization.

- Actions:
  1. Lead Facilitator and Creativizers work with Leadership Team to develop a project portfolio process: development process, key measures, prioritization, review gates, resource allocation, conflict resolution, and continuous learning processes.
  2. Action Teams report on the status of their projects to the Leadership Team: results, plans, barriers to progress, assistance, and resources needed.
  3. Leadership Team reviews projects, gives suggestions, and makes decisions: projects to advance, resource allocation, and improving performance.
  4. Action Teams, Creativizers, and Leadership Team identify themes about what works and what doesn't in the organization and why.
  5. Action Teams, Creativizers, and Leadership Team, thinking creatively around the Innovation Genome, identify key organizational processes that aid or obstruct the progress of these change and innovation projects: strategic planning, financial processes, information and technology systems, performance management, human resources, and organizational development practices.
  6. Action Teams, Creativizers, and Leadership Team thinking creatively around the Innovation Genome, suggest potential improvement points for these key organizational processes.
  7. Leadership Team identifies how to integrate key potential improvement points into key organizational processes and Creativizers assist in the process and track progress.

8. Action Teams, Creativizers, and Leadership Team translate what works and what doesn't in the organization into operating practices planning, staffing, and training practices.

- Time:
  - One day, three times a year.

This Chapter Will Help Me to Answer:

- Now that we've innovated, how do we measure our progress?
- How do we know if we've created value?
- Now that we've incorporated the culture and practice of innovation into our organization, what do we do next?

Introduction

 Systemize is the most important step in the change and innovation process. It is in the Systemize step that the company takes everything it's learned from running projects, exercises, and experiments and brings it all back home where these best practices and next practices are leveraged on a large scale and integrated into the entire organization, or large parts of the organization. It is in Systemizing that innovation becomes a part of the organizational system.

Systemize in Action—Zingerman's Delicatessen

"How come we don't know what we know?" That's what most entrepreneurs ask themselves as they grind through the pangs of growing their business from a single store concept into a real company. As these sole proprietors or partners grow, they become the bottleneck in the bottle because they are the only keepers of the corporate flame, the secrets of management, hiring, work processes, and the mystifying financials. They were the only ones who had the meaningful experiences that led to the great insights, and for most leaders, these experiences are bottled up inside them and of little value to the firm at large.

What would happen if a small firm routinely stopped its frenetic schedule to ask all its team members what they were learning and to reflect on how these insights could be incorporated into the business as simple rules? You might look something like Zingerman's Delicatessen, a business *Inc. Magazine* crowned the "coolest small company in America." According to *Vanity Fair* and a host of prominent newspapers, Zingerman's, located in Ann Arbor, Michigan (yes, Michigan), is "the best deli in America." How is this possible? By making organizational learning a fundamental part of the operating process of the business.

The story of Zingerman's is one of a shared vision of the future, a rare understanding of its real abilities, and a gift for translating this vision into the everyday activities of the firm. Started in 1982 by Ari Weinzweig and Paul Saginaw, Zingerman's had become a cult destination by the early 1990s, not only for its sumptuous sandwiches and knishes, but also for its ebullient customer service. Novelist Jim Harrison exalted in *Esquire*, "In Zingerman's, I get the mighty reassurance that the world can't be totally bad if there's this much good food to eat, the same flowing emotions I get at Fauchon in Paris, Harrods' food department in London, Balduccis or Dean and DeLuca in New York, only at Zingerman's there is a goodwill lacking in all others." How do they do it?

You can't help notice that there are posters on every wall of Zingerman's Delicatessen that resemble hand drawn handbills you might have found in the Haight-Ashbury section of San Francisco in the late 1960s promoting an upcoming concert of the Jefferson Airplane. Most of these give the amazing and offbeat history of a product, like a special rice that was only grown in South Carolina in the 1890s or the colorful names of sandwiches. But on closer inspection of the work areas, these handbills keep the precious insights of the business in front of everyone all the time. They include gems like Zingerman's Guiding Principles:

1. Great Food! At Zingerman's we are committed to making and selling high-quality food.
2. Great Service! If great food is the lock, great service is the key.
3. A great Place to Shop and Eat! Coming to Zingerman's is a positive and enjoyable experience.
4. Solid Profits! Profits are the lifeblood of our business.
5. A Great Place to Work! Working at Zingerman's means taking an active part in running the business. Our work makes a difference.

6. Strong Relationships! Successful working relationships are an essential component of our health and success as a business.
7. A Place to Learn! Learning keeps us going, keeps us challenged, keeps us on track.
8. An Active Part of the Community! We believe that a business has an obligation to the community of which it is a part.

These read more like a manifesto than a mission statement or work rules. Others include the 3 Steps to Great Service, the 4 Steps to Order Accuracy, the 5 Steps to Handling Customer Complaints, and the very popular 4 Steps to Productive Resolution of Your Differences.

Why all the simple rules? Because they are real lessons learned not just by Weinzweig and Saginaw, but by their people, who operate the business daily. Early in the company's history, Stas Kazmierski (now one of the managing partners of ZingTrain who worked with organizational learning pioneer Kathleen Dannemiller) helped Zingerman's create a set of core beliefs and values that emphasized empowerment and participation, the creation of community, creating a shared vision of the future, making real-time changes, and transferring learning throughout the community. By stopping the merry-go-round of food service work to ask the team what is working and what isn't, Zingerman's not only harnesses the collective intelligence and imagination of its people, but also enlists their ownership for these simple insights. As importantly, it does it all very quickly and without the aid of complicated processes, strategies, or learning officers.

These insights are not only used to run the business more effectively and efficiently but they also serve as a polestar for starting new business within the Zingerman's Community of Businesses. Zingerman's encourages their people to experiment with new products, services, and business concepts. Without moving to new geographies or franchising the concept, Zingerman's has found a powerful growth engine—giving the people who demonstrate ownership by creating new business real ownership in these businesses: Zingerman's Roadhouse, Bakehouse, Creamery, Mail Order, ZingTrain, Zingerman's Coffee Company. It functions like an ecosystem, each supporting the others as appropriate.

Zingerman's draws on the entire organization to search and reapply winning ideas learned from hard-won experiences and experiments. Integrating these key learnings into core business practices at Zingerman's is not only instructive, but it's generative—creating new growth opportunities.

One key lesson from this case is that the *cavalry isn't coming*. This means that corporate leadership isn't going to issue a mandate to innovate. The entrepreneurs within Zingerman's who took the various Zingerman's businesses from concept to reality learned this lesson firsthand. The result of their work became the Zingerman's ecosystem, which is further composed of highly practiced Creativizers who continue the growth of the Zingerman's business.

Establishing a Guiding Coalition to Transform Organizational Practices

A Guiding Coalition consists of organizational leaders who can move resources through the use of power, influence, or knowledge. What this means is that people on the coalition have to have some form of actionable power or influence; they cannot just be thought leaders, but they have to actually be able to make things happen. Many organizations will create change teams made up of middle managers who will create ideas about solutions and paths forward but have no ability to make them happen.

Table 9.1   How the Innovation Genome Relates to the Systemize Step

Collaborate
- Learn from experience.
- Try things, discuss them, and develop insight by doing so.

Create
- Change established practices.
- Learn not by the experience, but by the experiment, by breaking or destroying the way things currently are, and by challenging boundaries.

Control
- Reduce failures.
- Learn by shaping or tweaking the system, slowly and patiently collecting data to modify the system and reduce failures.

Compete
- Capitalize on winning ideas and discard losers.
- Sort out the best—which projects are strongest and fastest?

The organization feels good that it has put resources on the issue and also feels comfortable that nothing major will actually change. The Guiding Coalition is composed of three types of players that we have discussed earlier in the book. Because the Systemize step is about taking what has been learned and adjusting current organizational practices, you have to have people with the right level of influence and power if the work is going to get traction. The Guiding Coalition will probably be made up of multiple sponsors from the senior team rather than the one or two who have been key to this point in the process. The coalition members will have the following roles and responsibilities:

- *Sponsors:* Responsible to own the process and see that plans turn into actions.
- *Creativizers:* Responsible to keep the process on track and help integrate perspectives.
- *Action Team members:* Innovation activists who lead Action Teams.

The responsibilities of the Guiding Coalition include:

- Sponsor:
  - Keeps people honest.
  - Challenges the team to stretch.
  - Sets the expectation that everyone creates the result—no fence sitting or critics without ideas of their own.
  - Demands teamwork.
- Creativizers:
  - Keep the process focused on the desired results.
  - Energize people.
  - Give minority opinions a voice.
  - Limit criticism.
- Action Team members:
  - Think new thoughts.
  - Try new things.
  - Learn what works and what doesn't as you go along.
  - Build skills, character, and relationships.

Attributes and skills of effective coalition members include:

- Power
- Influence

- Networking
- Experience
- Point of view
- Know-how
- Passion
- Ownership

The organizational chart itself won't tell the organization a lot about who should be on the coalition. Organizational charts are rational models, but organizational power structures are less than rational, as power and influence can emerge at various points from within the organization. It is important to remember that the enemy of a coalition is someone who's indifferent or apathetic because his or her energy level can bring down that of the entire coalition. It is essential to have people on the coalition who have the influence and energy to actually advance the project.

As the coalition proceeds, it is going to have to enlist advocates. An advocate is someone who is very sympathetic to innovation in the organization. An advocate may not have a role like an Action Team member or a Creativizer, but is a person who sees the innovation as a personal cause or something that he or she is very passionate about. Creativity emerges in all areas of work and begins with the *power of one*—a personal cause that brings ownership and passion. In enlisting advocates, the coalition should ask what's their cause, who shares their cause, what's their agenda, and how will this coalition advance their agenda?

Enlisting an advocate sometimes requires more listening than talking. Most people have something that they want to make better or new, and gaining someone as an advocate often requires finding out what that individual needs. In this way the coalition can address issues and priorities when talking about innovation or looking for help.

It's important to enlist advocates from each of the four quadrants of the Innovation Genome because, ultimately, when it comes to implementing the idea, the coalition will need all of them. In Chapter 8, we show how problems can emerge when Action Teams are composed of individuals who are anchored in the same quadrant. Coalitions need a balance of individuals so that different perspectives are represented which can create positive and manageable tensions. Examples of what may be important to different people within each quadrant are presented in Table 9.2.

Table 9.2   Using the Innovation Genome to Find Advocates

Collaborate
- Organization learning
- Human resource development
- High-performing culture

Create
- Research and development
- Strategic foresight and forecasting
- New product innovation

Control
- Systems and technology
- Operating processes
- Standards and regulations

Compete
- Performance measures
- Portfolio management
- Resource allocation

Identifying Where Organizational Processes Enable or Obstruct Transformational Opportunities

It is essential that a company makes space to learn along the way in order to understand where things have gone wrong, what new approaches are having success, what aspects of that success are applicable elsewhere in the organization, and what adjustments need to be made to ensure that it reaches its desired outcomes. Organizations often talk about the learning process being important, but because of the pressure of having to hit the necessary goals, it is rare that an organization takes the time to let the learning process work. By not creating space to learn, the company puts itself in strictly a reactive state rather than a proactive state. As seen in the Innovation Genome, both hitting the numbers each quarter and taking time to learn are necessary. If integrated, they can lead to high levels of performance. The following are important ways to make sure the company has made space to learn.

One way is to convene diagonal groups, or cross-functional groups, that cover a number of functional areas in the organization as well as the different levels of hierarchy in the organization so that the company can get many different perspectives. The aim is to get a diverse and comprehensive perspective in small groups. It is important not to meet with big groups, but to have small groups with regular meetings. The more people who are involved, the less likely the group will meet or get things done.

Another way that a company can make space to learn is by having regular meetings in order to discuss projects and underlying practices (enablers and obstacles). In these regular meetings, the group members are going to talk about the project that they're working on, and they're going to talk about what's working and what's not working on the project. More important, however, they should talk about what kind of organizational practices are enabling or obstructing what they're trying to do on these projects. These meetings should be held a minimum of every six weeks.

Because practices and processes differ across functional areas and people, another necessary self-check is to watch for disconnects among them. It is important to clarify differences in the business processes of the various functional areas. For example, there are some processes that the finance department runs, some processes are run by marketing, and some processes are run by research and development; each process is different. Yet despite the differences among the processes in these different functional areas, these functions are interdependent on a broader organizational level. Therefore, the group must determine where these differences are and work to eliminate any ineffective processes. It is also critical to identify the differences between problems caused by processes and problems caused by people. There are many times when things don't work, and it has nothing to do with the organizational practices. Instead it has to do with people who don't get along or a boss who is too controlling. The group should be able to distinguish between these issues.

A fourth way that the group can self-check is through a yearly summit in which best practices from both within and outside the firm are shared. People should talk about "What are the best practices?" and "What are the next practices?" In these summits it's helpful to invite people from outside the firm who have expertise in an area, even if that individual is in a different industry. For example, a medical center looking to improve patient care may invite a speaker from Ritz Carlton to talk about customer care. It's crucial that people from inside the organization meet and talk about what's working and what's not working on a larger scale, so that some of the major best practices are shared among the smaller diagonal groups that meet on a regular basis.

Establishing Measures of Performance Capabilities and Outcomes

As shown in Table 9.3, the four quadrants view performance in different ways.

While reviewing the questions in Table 9.3, you can get a feel for what areas you would tend toward as a leader. Similarly, organizational performance measures are largely determined by the types of outcomes the company is looking for, which are often influenced by the tendency of its leaders. It is important that people be aware of this because it's going to produce biases in their business. For example, at General Electric and many multibillion-dollar for-profit companies, it's very common to see almost all the measures be Compete and Control measures, which are their biases, but the company would like to have some of the outcomes produced by Collaborate or Create quadrants. To get these outcomes, it needs to investigate questions within those quadrants. Table 9.4 provides some examples of performance metrics from all four quadrants that could drive such questions.

Table 9.3   The Innovation Genome and Performance

Collaborate
- *Interest:* Do we care about this idea?
- *Knowledge:* What are we learning from this idea?
- *Beliefs:* Does this idea fit with our values?

Create
- *Innovation:* Is this idea a breakthrough?
- *Direction:* Does this idea move us toward the future?
- *Emerging opportunity:* Will this idea allow us to experiment as we go along?

Control
- *Cost:* Can we afford this idea?
- *Feasibility:* Can we really implement this idea?
- *Standards:* Does this idea comply with critical standards?

Compete
- *Cash value:* Is the payoff for this idea big enough?
- *Immediacy:* Can we get this idea done quickly?
- *Leverage:* Can this idea be used to create value in other areas?

Table 9.4 Example Performance Metrics

Collaborate
Community:
- Employee satisfaction index
- Customer satisfaction index
- Workforce diversity

Knowledge:
- Number of training days
- Training costs per employee
- Number and percentage of employees with development plan

Create
Innovation:
- Number of experiments launched
- Diversity of pipeline portfolio
- Adoption rate of new technology

Growth:
- Number of new markets entered
- Projected growth of new market
- New to existing products/services sales ratio

Control
Quality:
- Number and percentage of failures
- Regulatory violations
- Manufacturability index rating

Efficiency:
- Cycle time
- Actual vs. planned milestones
- Number and percentage of back orders

Compete
Speed:
- Projected time to market
- Projected time to achieve performance plan
- Market readiness of partnerships

Profits:
- Projected return on investment
- Projected gross profit
- Projected earnings per share

The measures at the bottom of the model (lower measures) shown in Table 9.5 are all manifest, meaning they produce value now. Conversely, the measures at the top of the model (upper measures) are always latent, meaning they produce value in the future (refer to Step 6: Specialize, Phase 11: Develop Key Measures for a review of lower measures and upper measures).

Managing a Portfolio of Diverse Change and Innovation Projects

In some ways, stock management is like project management. In a stock portfolio some of the stocks are going to pay today, some of the stocks

---

Table 9.5 Lower Measures and Upper Measures

Compete and Control	**Collaborate and Create**
Lower measures = immediate outcomes	Upper measures = future outcomes
• Causal key indicators	• Associated key indicators
• Exposed information	• Emergent knowledge
• Convergent options	• Divergent options
• The present situation (manifest)	• The future situation (latent)
• Tangible value	• Intangible value
• Creation of focus and alignment	• Creation of slack; diversification
• Investment with increasing rates of return until rates fall	• Investment with decreasing rates of return until you develop competency, change and innovation, and brand equity

---

are going to pay tomorrow, some of the stocks are growth, and some are revenue. The same is true of projects. When we look at projects together, some projects produce more value than others. Some projects are going to produce value now, and some are going to produce value in the future. The key lesson here is to spread your risk. Because you cannot always anticipate every possible problem that could result in a lower yield on your investment, you make multiple investments so that the law of averages works to your advantage. This lesson applies to innovation projects as well. You don't always know when an investment in something innovative will pay off, so you invest in multiple projects as if you were investing in a stock portfolio.

Most large organizations tend toward the measures at the bottom of the Innovation Genome because they desire to see results now. One example of two organizations that took a different approach can be found in the auto industry during the 1980s. Japanese automakers such as Toyota and Honda started selling midsized sedans below the cost of manufacturing the car, a process known as "dumping." People asked, "Why would they sell the car at a loss?" There was a very good reason why. By selling the cars at a loss, the companies were able to gain a large share of the market and eventually dominate the midsized sedan segment, which they do to this day. They went from losing a lot of money to the point where the investments started returning huge dividends as a result of market growth and innovation (see Fig. 9.1).

The two forms of investment shown in Figure 9.1 live side-by-side in the corporate world. The concave option is typically what happens when someone goes to a capital committee and gets money for a new project or service. The convex option is typically what happens with venture capitalists when they invest in an idea. What they're looking for is a very large multiple or return. They're willing to take on more risk, but they expect the project to return a great deal more value.

Value Tiers

A similar way that companies take on risk to produce value is to tier their innovation or to create a set of steps the innovation has to go through. Some companies might forgo profit in an early tier (step) in order to

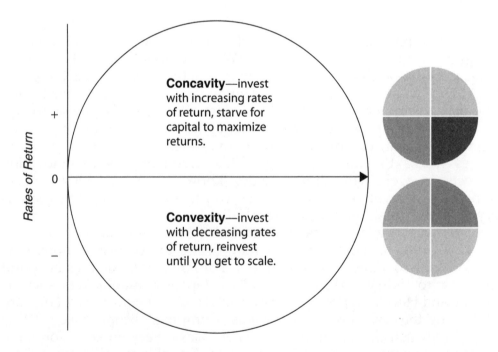

Figure 9.1   Valuating initiatives

maximize profit in a later tier (step). By running experiments, the company may lose money in the short run, but in later steps it will have learned what the customer wants so it can maximize profit by launching a winning product. The company is then able to follow a set of steps that will allow for a flow of innovative products, but it must be willing to take on more risk in the early steps of the process. This is one way to Systemize and embed innovation in the organization. Companies that seek to maximize profit early in the process risk being able to earn profit later because they often have to make assumptions about the future for which there are no data available.

Microsoft is an example of a company that moved early with little profits to set up its ability to make large profits later. Microsoft made the DOS operating system and sold it to 80–85 percent of all people who owned computers in the 1970s and early 1980s. The company then built on top of DOS by adding more features, such as an office suite, which eventually became Windows. It also added a Web browser and the ability to manage personal files and file server technology. What Microsoft did was an incremental project by adding features to an existing product in order to create much higher value for the company and for customers. If Microsoft had felt that it had "perfected" DOS in the 1980s and sold it in order to launch something else, it would have maximized its profit at that moment in time, but it would have been unable to tap into the value of future revenue streams created by the evolution of DOS.

This concept also works the other way around. In the 1990s Nokia developed a radical new standard for phones to communicate with one another, which was called the Global System for Mobile Communication (GSM). The move was bold because everyone else was on a system called Time Division Multiple Access (TDMA), including Motorola, which basically controlled the cell phone market in the early 1990s. By introducing this radical innovation, Nokia changed the standard. Nokia then developed a wide array of phones that changed the focus of the device from simple telephone communication to gadgets such as personal data assistants (PDAs) and global positioning devices (GPSs). The company also developed features such as fashionable colors and interchangeable faces. It introduced products that had several steps that would bring value because each gadget that was added on to the original platform brought an opportunity for increased sales. During the first few tiers (steps), Nokia did not make much money from add-on gadgets because it had to create demand in the market for the new standard or platform it created. Once the demand was created, it began to make money off the extra options offered to the client. As this was accomplished, Nokia became the market leader. Nokia used an incremental approach to develop new products and product features. It was able to do this through breakthrough innovation (see Fig. 9.2).

Selecting Performance Measures that Maximize Value Creation

So, out of all these performance measures (some are latent, some are manifest, some are convex, and some are concave), how do we pick the measures we're actually going to use? The way to do this is to develop a few performance measures for each of the quadrants. Ask people, "What do we really have to measure?" Look around the quadrants and include "must have" metrics (things that come from the operating plan, things that are written into the strategy, or things that have always been measured) as well as new metrics.

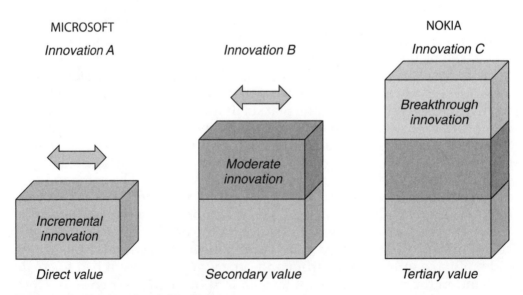

Figure 9.2   Leveraging initiatives

Once this is accomplished, take those performance measures and rate the company's ability to achieve these measures as compared to the "best in class" within the specific unit, the organization, and the industry. This should be done as a qualitative assessment that's going to translate into a quantitative number (see Table 9.6).

Add up the results. The highest totals should be the measures that the company or unit is going to choose (it is helpful to validate the results by asking people outside the organization how they would rate you). However, there is still a little tweaking that needs to happen. Based on the ratings, it is important to discuss the relative value of these key performance measures to the company. In order to be of value, there are three areas that the performance measures should cover:

1. Which measures are going to help us build on our strengths? These are the measures with the highest numbers.

Table 9.6   Rating the Ability to Achieve Performance Measures

	Highest 5	High 4	Moderate 3	Low 2	Lowest 1
How would you rate our ability to achieve this performance measure against . . . ?					
Best in class in our unit					
Best in class in our organization					
Best in class in our industry					

2. Which measures are going to help us defend our strategic interest? These may not be high or low numbers; they may be middle of the road but something that's very important to do.
3. Which measures are going to help us develop our key areas of weakness? There may be a measure with very low numbers, but those low numbers may actually suggest that the company really needs to work on a couple of those performance ratings because that's where it has the most amount of exposure and needs to be fixed.

At this point the group is going to review, discuss, prioritize, and select the most important performance measures. The group should have a discussion about building on its strengths, defending its strategic interests, and determining which measures will help to develop key areas of weakness. The discussion should be focused in a strategic way, meaning that it is not just operational and not just what's going to work tomorrow. Encourage the widest spectrum possible of experience and opinions here. The group needs diversity, challenge, and people with different ideas to reduce the likelihood of group-think. Finally, the group should ask itself, "How will this increase the value of our current and future projects and operations, and how in fact is this going to help us on a going-forward basis?" From this the group should pick three to five performance measures. These are the criteria against which the group will benchmark everything. They are the criteria on which the group will base its decisions about which projects go forward and which projects don't go forward, what the group is going to measure, and what they're not going to measure.

Portfolio Management, Decision Making, and Prioritizing—Balancing Risk

The reason that this is important is that when it comes to funding or resource allocation, the group wants to be able to give money to the projects that meet the performance measures that produce the most value. The typical way in which companies do this is to allocate resources based on the amount of relative risk (low technical risk) versus the amount of relative immediate reward (things like net present value). These are largely invested in because they have low risk and high reward (Fig. 9.3).

What often happens is that companies take investments and priorities and put all of them in the Compete category. In many cases a company wants to give money to Create projects but wants to reduce the risk of the Create investment. This, however, is likely to make the Create investment more incremental. In Control investments companies often try to increase the reward because the project or investment is seen as an underperforming asset. Increasing the value of a Control investment, however, often creates exposure for the company. Something else that often happens when allocating resources is that companies eliminate the Collaborate investments because there's high risk and relatively low reward (things like developing people and culture). There's no immediate payoff, and they create a lot of exposure. These are the initiatives that often get cut. But, as in a stock portfolio, it is important to maintain diversity when funding projects. In the end the company is going to have to earmark some money for Collaborate investments or investments in culture, because it believes that in the long run, that in balancing the portfolio,

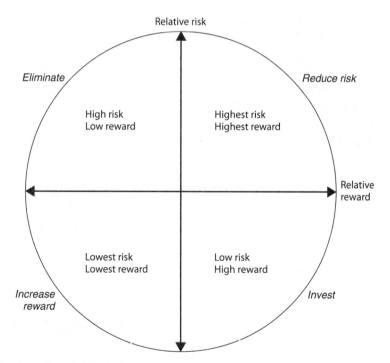

Figure 9.3   Funding initiatives

these are going to pay. The company is going to have to make special provisions for everything outside the Compete category.

Stage Gates (Regular and Inverted)

When a company develops projects and initiatives, it's investing money, reprioritizing, and evaluating projects as they go from stage to stage. This is called a Stage-Gate system. At an early stage a project may be creating or designing something, and then there's a gate at which it gets reviewed. At the gate the company makes a basic "go" or "kill" decision, meaning, "Does this go forward?" or, "Do we kill it?" The object is typically to put a large number of projects in the early phases (deal flow) where the early phases will act like a filter. A lot of things are poured in and only a few things come out.

What a company is typically doing in its Stage-Gate systems is trying to put many projects at the beginning and a few at the end where it's testing, scaling, and spending a lot of money. This is how companies develop Compete or Control projects. These projects are prioritized and given money as they go along. However, if the company has a Collaborate or Create project, the stage gates work backwards. What this means is that these projects require much money early on, and the company has to put the money up in the very first phase because such projects are capital-intensive up front. Imagine trying to discover a new drug. The company would have to go out and hire many new scientists, develop a lot of new equipment, and have many experiments; this would be quite expensive. However, in time, actual costs would go down because the company front-loaded the process. This is why investing in a biotech company or an Internet company is riskier than investing in other types of companies. More money must be invested up front, but, if it pays off, it becomes a much higher payoff than an investment that falls in the Compete or Control quadrant.

When looking at systems, a company has to look at how it's going to grow these projects and how it's going to manage performance across these projects. It can't manage the Compete and Control projects the same way it's going to manage the Collaborate and Create projects.

Launching Projects Where They Will Best Succeed

Where a company launches projects is largely going to be determined by the nature of the project itself. Imagine launching a radical breakthrough innovation project in an area where the entire mechanism of management is really designed to keep its equilibrium. That area is going to resist radically innovative ideas. However, chances are that there is going to be a part of the organization that's grossly underperforming or in a crisis. When in a crisis, that area of the organization is going to defy the 80/20 rule. The 80/20 rule is that it's easier to change 80 percent of the organization by 20 percent than it is to change 20 percent of the organization by 80 percent. The point is that when functioning in a standard or normal mode, a company should try to change the 80 percent by 20 percent by making incremental changes. However, when in a crisis, use the 20/80 rule. Take 20 percent of the organization and change it radically, by 80 percent (Fig. 9.4).

When thinking about a corporate crisis, think about Chrysler. Chrysler has had a history of innovating when it was at the brink of financial disaster.[1] The K-Car, the "cab forward" design, and the PT Cruiser all emerged when Chrysler was struggling financially. Today, Daimler-Chrysler has learned from those lessons and innovates when it isn't facing a "do or die" crisis. Instead it has learned to look for mini-crises such as slow sales growth or the decline in SUV popularity. What has emerged most recently as a result has been some of Detroit's most innovative sedans in a generation—the Chrysler 300 and the Dodge Charger.

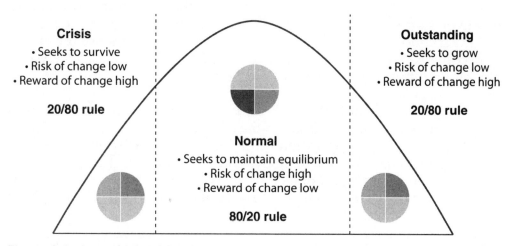

Figure 9.4   Launching initiatives

Parallel lessons hold true in our own lives. People try to make radical change in their lives when they're in a crisis. In order to help an alcoholic, some treatment centers will try to accelerate the failure cycle or crisis cycle. The reason they do this is that the only way to get that person to stop drinking is to reverse the reward and risk of drinking by showing that the person is at the bottom. It's in a crisis that people make substantial change in their life. It is in dealing with things such as divorce, bankruptcy, or health issues that radical change is often made.

On the other hand, change also comes when people are on a roll. When they're falling in love, graduating, or getting promoted they feel that they can try anything—that they could take on the world. Things are going well so they're more willing to try new things.

The point is that it's not just how you advance the ideas, it's where you plant the idea. The more radical, future-centric or Collaborate/Create the idea is, the more likely it's going to take root in a crisis or outstanding area. The more incremental an idea is, the more likely it's going to take root in the normal or standard part of the organization.

Applying and Integrating Innovation into Parts of Normal Business Practice

In the end the payout of all these exercises, projects, and experiments is that innovation becomes a part of everything. Innovation can come from all four quadrants, but a company is only as good as the weakest quadrant in its system. Any time there's something in the system that doesn't integrate or operate with the other, it creates a great deal of exposure.

Putting innovation into normal business practices does not mean that it's becoming incremental; it means that it's becoming *fundamental*. We're integrating innovation in order to create two things:

1. *Resilience:* Innovation is built into the basic part of the organization so that everybody in the company can use it, and as things change, the organization can make changes as well.
2. *Constitution:* We want innovation to become part of the organization's bones, part of its muscle. We want to make a place for innovation and creativity in the belly of the organization throughout all processes.

A company does not have to hit home runs to get innovation to happen everywhere. It simply needs to implement smaller wins that have bigger impact at the right places within the organization. This is ultimately the point of the Systemize step.

Beginning the Systemize Workshop

Up to this point, we have done everything from ensuring that teams are on the same page and creating strategy to rolling out and launching projects. However, there is one key step needed to tie everything together. The company must now work the change and innovation process into the underlying systems or day-to-day goings-on of the firm.

The basic philosophy of the *Creativize Method* is that change and innovation are not special events, but something that should be happening all the time. If done the right way, a company can build mechanisms into its management systems to help inculcate the organization with the ability to make change and innovation happen. Once projects are launched, companies should look at such things as how the projects change governance or management processes including hiring, strategic planning, allocation of resources, and performance metrics. The reason for this is that change and innovation are not special projects but integral aspects of all management functions. The Systemize step focuses on the *underlying, enabling system* for innovation, not just the outcome. So, Systemize, the final step, involves integrating innovation practices into the management practices of the company.

One other key caveat is that as much as the Systemize step enables or empowers the underlying system with change and innovation, it's also a work in progress and will constantly need to be altered and refined. Companies must constantly be looking at the underlying systems and come up with ways to improve upon what's already in place. Customers, the economy, and the world are constantly changing, and companies must also change in order to compete and survive. A company should continually be making adjustments.

Systemize Phase 1: Develop Project Review Process

The first phase in the Systemize step is to develop a project review process. To do this, Leadership Teams must:

- Meet on a regular basis to review all Action Teams together to:
  - Provide advice as appropriate.

- o Maximize value.
- o Align with strategy.
- o Balance mix of Action Teams (diversify).
- o Prioritize projects.
- o Allocate resources.
- o Decide which projects to advance and which to stop.
- o Learn what's working; what's not.
- o Communicate status to the organization.
- o Institutionalize projects.

Within the project review process, the best practices will change according to the stage the project is passing through. There should be three gates: an early gate, a middle gate, and a late gate (Table 9.7).

The project review gates as presented in Table 9.7 are the gates that would be used in a Compete or Control project. In a Collaborate or Create project the gates might be reversed (e.g., the late gate would become the early gate and early gate would become the late gate).

In Table 9.8 teams should list the stage activities and the criteria for each gate. In other words, within the stage activities, list what the company should do in each stage of development. Within the criteria, list how to know when and whether the project should proceed to the next gate.

Systemize Phase 2: Set Key Measures for Projects

Once project gates have been set in place, the group must set measures for various projects. It should be clear that the Systemize step is not measuring *a* project, but is creating measures for *several* projects. Table 9.9 provides examples of some measures for various kinds of projects. Within the Collaborate and Create fields, project outcomes are often latent, which means that the projects may not show immediate results. In this case, the measurements for the Collaborate and Create fields are very different from the measurements for the Compete and the Control fields.

So once the group has looked at some examples of measures, it should use Table 9.10 to create balanced measures for the various projects it is working on. It may be helpful to think of the Compete and Control measures as the *outcomes* and to think of the Collaborate and Create measures as the *abilities* and *future-oriented projects* to create those outcomes.

Table 9.7 Project Review Gates

Early Gate(s)	Middle Gate(s)	Late Gate(s)
• Encourage break-through ideas. • Encourage large numbers of initiatives. • Encourage individuals to be entrepreneurial in putting together a small team and finding sponsorship. • Encourage modeling. • Say *yes* to *most*. • Provide *few* resources.	• Develop business strategy. • Develop feasibility studies. • Develop financial plans. • Develop market analysis. • Develop concept to prototype. • Say *yes* to *some*. • Provide *limited* resources.	• Perform postdevelopment review. • Conduct market tests. • Perform manufacturing analysis. • Talk with potential partners. • Say *no* to *most*. • Provide *extensive* resources.

Systemize Phase 3: Make Decisions

In the Specialize step teams developed various metrics for their projects. At this point in the Systemize step, the leaders guiding these projects will want to follow up by getting a project report and asking the following questions regarding specific projects:

- What is the charter of your project?
- How does your project create value?
- What are the key goals and measures?
- What have you accomplished since we last met?
- What goals have you exceeded? Why?
- What goals have you missed? Why?
- What are your plans to improve performance?
- What key goals will you accomplish by our next meeting?
- What assistance do you need from us?

Table 9.8 Establish Stage Activities and Review Gate Criteria	
Develop stage activities	1a
Review gate criteria	1b
Develop stage activities	2a
Review gate criteria	2b
Develop stage activities	3a
Review gate criteria	3b

After the questions have been asked and answered, review what was agreed upon and set the next meeting date.

It is very important in reviewing these questions that the Action Teams that are responsible for each project are the people presenting their progress and coming up with the answers to these questions. The leaders should not be telling Action Teams what to do, but should act as helpful advisors. This is very important in maintaining ownership of the projects.

The Action Teams drive the projects forward and once driven forward, the leaders make decisions with the assistance of a form such as in Table 9.11. Leaders will compare the relative progress and value of the projects side by side and then make a decision regarding which projects to reduce, stop, or put on hold.

Table 9.9 Examples

Collaborate
- Workforce diversity
- Employee satisfaction index
- Turnover of experienced personnel
- Training and education costs per employee
- Organizational competency index

Create
- Number of experiments launched
- Diversity of initiative array
- Projected new market growth
- Adoption of new technology
- Alternative uses of innovation identified

Control
- Initiative cost vs. budget
- Actual vs. planned milestones achieved
- Number of failures
- Number of prototypes tested
- Design for manufacturability index rating

Compete
- Projected gross profit
- Projected market growth
- Projected time to market
- Projected return on investment
- Projected operating income

Table 9.10 Balanced Performance Measures

Collaborate

Create

Control

Compete

Table 9.11 Decide What Projects to Advance

Project	Type (purpose)	Stage (early, middle, late)	Progress on goals	Resources required	Priority	Decision (advance, stop, modify)

Systemize Phase 4:
Learn What Works and What Doesn't

At this point the Leadership Team has made some serious decisions regarding projects and should ask itself, "What have we learned?" Thinking around the four quadrants, the Leadership Team can ask, "Why didn't it work?" In answering such questions and thinking about what has been learned, organizations can often translate failure into success. Leadership Teams should think about these questions from the point of view of the four quadrants and actually write down some thoughts (Table 9.12).

Project Leadership Teams will learn new things, and, as they go along, they will become more sophisticated in carrying out projects and creating results. This is because they will learn "simple rules" along the way (Table 9.13). Simple rules involve taking a look at what is working and what isn't working and creating insights and rules based on results that can be implemented to integrate what has been learned. The reason for creating simple rules is that they can be easily implemented. It can be as simple as saying that the first phone calls made in the morning should be client calls.

Table 9.12   What Have We Learned about . . .

Collaborate
- People?
- Competencies?
- Cultures?
- Knowledge?

Control
- Processes?
- Systems?
- Technologies?
- Standards?

Create
- Products?
- Services?
- Visions?
- Markets?

Compete
- Goals?
- Partners?
- Investments?
- Rewards?

Table 9.13   Create Simple Rules

What Is Working?	What Isn't Working?	Simple Rules

Systemize Phase 5: Improve Management Practices

The Action Teams now have projects with metrics, and the Leadership Team has advised these Action Teams and decided what projects to advance and what projects to stop. Now the Action Team must take a look at underlying practices within the organization and ask if it is necessary to make any adjustments to these practices to accelerate the change and innovation. In this exercise we are looking for the practices that are deep causes that create obstacles to these projects. Some areas in which these management practices might occur follow:

- Finance
- Marketing
- Production
- Organizational development
- Hiring and staffing
- Performance management
- Leadership
- Culture development
- Organizational structure
- Information systems
- New product development
- Sales
- Brand management
- Mergers and acquisitions
- Legal
- Project management
- Customer service
- Maintenance
- Purchasing
- Transportation
- Quality
- Training

Improve Management Practices

Review routine management practices in your firm and examine:

- What purpose (results) is this practice intended to produce?
- What purpose (results) does this practice really produce?
- How does this practice aid or deter this project?
- How might this practice be adjusted to support the project? Other projects?

In asking how to adjust a practice to support the project, the Leadership Team should split into four groups and list possible actions while thinking around the Innovation Genome and looking at points of view from each quadrant: Collaborate, Create, Compete, and Control (Table 9.14).

Once the Leadership Teams have come up with actions for each quadrant, they should come back together and draw a picture of the practice in question within the organization, and then redraw the picture based upon suggestions from the four groups (Figure 9.5).

Systemize Phase 6: Integrate Improvements into Organizational Processes

Throughout the Systemize step we have been drilling deeper and deeper into the organization's practices and have regenerated some of the un-

---

Table 9.14   Take Action

Collaborate	Create
Start	Start
Stop	Stop
Do differently	Do differently
Needs	Needs
Control	Compete
Start	Start
Stop	Stop
Do differently	Do differently
Needs	Needs

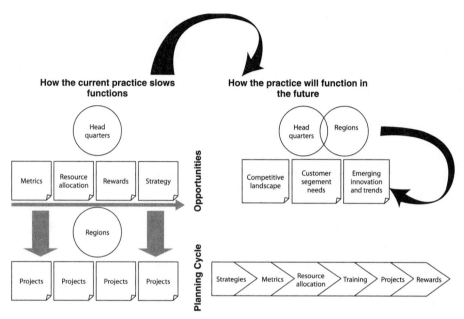

Figure 9.5   Re-create the practice

derlying systems. Now the question is, "How can the company launch these re-created practices?" To do this the Leadership Team must answer the questions below. These questions are not going to be able to be discharged within one meeting. The organization will need to follow up with work streams, put transition steps in place, and involve other people. At this point, the changes must be integrated into parts of the organization that have momentum.

Make Integration Action Plans

- What are the benefits of this new practice?
- What is the evidence that this new practice has merit?
- What information do we need to communicate to whom and how?
- Where are the linkages across boundaries where this new practice will get a fair hearing from the organization?
- Who has the authority and influence to decide to implement this new practice?
- What's in it for them to buy into this new practice?
- How do we manage the transition from our Action Team to an operating group?

- What competencies and culture are required to scale and sustain this new practice?
- How can this new practice be better leveraged throughout the organization?
- What changes when this new practice is institutionalized?

At this point the Leadership Team will work on leveraging the organizational practices, which means, "Where else and how else can this new practice be implemented; what else can we do with it?" (Table 9.15) To do this, the Leadership Team will look at the different functions in the organization such as:

- *Design* functions such as research and development or strategy.
- *Make* functions such as operations or inbound and outbound logistics.
- *Sell* functions such as marketing or sales.
- *Support* functions such as customer service or technical support.

Table 9.15   Leverage Organizational Practices

Functions of the organization	Where else, and how else can this new practice be implemented?
Design	
Make	
Sell	
Support	

Systemize Phase 7: Review and Revise

The final phase in the Systemize workshop is to review and revise. To do this, the Leadership Team will discuss, "What are our best projects, what are our best teams, who are our best leaders, and what are our best processes?" and then use the steps in Table 9.16 to verify the answers.

- *Benchmark:* How do we know they are performing well?
- *Diagnose:* Why is each so effective?
- *Integrate:* Where else can we use this?

The organization should now have practices that are adjusted and people who can do the kind of work involved. It should know where its strengths lie and be able to utilize all these things in an ongoing process of change and innovation. The organization should ask itself how it is doing on the measurable outcomes identified in Step 1: Synthesize, and adjust as necessary. Upon conclusion, what should be accomplished in

Table 9.16   Best Practices Matrix

Identify	Benchmark	Diagnose	Integrate
Best projects			
Best teams			
Best leaders			
Best processes			

this final step in the *Creativize Method* is that everything takes root in a way that's sustainable and simple to replicate.

Conclusion

1. Now that we've innovated, how do we measure our progress?

Performance measures will vary based on the company's orientation in the Innovation Genome. It will also depend on what the company's overall objective is, which is partially determined by its orientation in the Innovation Genome.

2. How do we know if we've created value?

A value measure is one important type of performance measure. Value is, of course, dependent on the company's objective, but there are different ways that value can be created. Actions can be chosen so that they produce value in the short term, and actions can also be chosen for their long-term value-creating potential. With the differences between short-term and long-term value objectives come the differences among types of levels of risk.

3. Now that we've incorporated the culture and practice of innovation into our organization, what do we do next?

Leading innovation is an ongoing process. An organization will always have to go back and adjust its creativity by using the *Creativize Method*. That is why good performance measures and value measures are important for this continuous adjustment. Systemizing innovation is really about continuous improvement and making innovation and creativity a continuous part of the organization.

The 3-D View

Remember from Chapter 2 that innovation is typically a work in progress. Innovation always provides key insights into the past that will in turn provide some wisdom about the future, but more importantly it allows us a wider range of courses to speculate and navigate. Once the Systemize step is complete, it is important for the Creativizers and other appropriate people to ask in a separate meeting the Do, Doing, Done questions by thinking around the Innovation Genome. It is important that the meeting take place close enough to the Systemize step so that everyone remembers the experience but enough removed so that people have had time to think about what really happened.

Do . . .
Looking forward at future projects, communities, charters, and goals that will flow from the Systemize step, consider the questions in Table 9.17 from the four perspectives of the Innovation Genome.

Table 9.17

Collaborate View	**Create View**
• What do I need to do?	• What do I need to do?
• How do I want to do it?	• How do I want to do it?
Control View	**Compete View**
• What do I need to do?	• What do I need to do?
• How do I want to do it?	• How do I want to do it?

Doing . . .
Looking at any current work taking place around the *Creativize Method* at your organization, consider the questions in Table 9.18.

Table 9.18

Collaborate View
- What's working and what isn't? Why?
- What changes should we make?

Create View
- What's working and what isn't? Why?
- What changes should we make?

Control View
- What's working and what isn't? Why?
- What changes should we make?

Compete View
- What's working and what isn't? Why?
- What changes should we make?

Done . . .

Looking back at what has taken place with the Systemize step and any projects that have been launched, consider the questions in Table 9.19.

Table 9.19

Collaborate View
- What worked and what didn't? Why?
- What changes would we make if we ran this step or project again?
- What have we learned that can be applied to the current practices of the organization?

Create View
- What worked and what didn't? Why?
- What changes would we make if we ran this step or project again?
- What have we learned that can be applied to the current practices of the organization?

Control View
- What worked and what didn't? Why?
- What changes would we make if we ran this step or project again?
- What have we learned that can be applied to the current practices of the organization?

Compete View
- What worked and what didn't? Why?
- What changes would we make if we ran this step or project again?
- What have we learned that can be applied to the current practices of the organization?

CHAPTER 10

Conclusion: Creativizing Yourself, Your Team, and Your Organization

Sustaining a climate of innovation is an ongoing process. In some cases, organizations might need to follow the entire seven steps and then use individual steps to address issues as they arise. Just completing the seven steps isn't the end of the road. This chapter provides some ideas on ways to keep the process fresh.

Creativizing Yourself

The idea of innovation starts with creativizing yourself. Before an organization can be innovative, and even before a team can be innovative, individuals must understand how to be creative. It's easy enough for us to imagine our colleagues or companies becoming better and new. But what about us? How do we Creativize ourselves? There are many reasons we don't bring our best creative self to work:

- We fear that we are really not creative.
- We feel that being creative at work makes us too vulnerable because it exposes us to criticism.
- We believe that we are creative but that our organization won't support our creativity, or will even punish it.
- We don't see how creativity contributes to our job.
- We see our creativity as too special to waste on our job and reserve it for personal hobbies and projects.

There are dozens of reasons why we aren't creative at work, but ironically most of them are really self-imposed. It is a paradox that we see the barriers to purposeful creative action all around us without acknowledging that our real opportunities for growth, both for ourselves and others, are the result of overcoming our own inner obstacles. If we seek to reinvent our organizations, or at least some part of it, we must first reinvent ourselves by energizing our authentic sources of creativity and developing new ones through empowering experiences and experiments. The urge to create is natural because growth is compulsory for individuals as well as organizations.

Creativity is not a limited resource. Most of us have an unlimited but untapped well of great ideas that solve problems, create energy and passion, and ultimately provide some form of value for us and others. Our creativity travels with us and is wholly transferable whether we are writing a clever passage in our journal or creating a clever new marketing campaign. It is precisely because creativity is a portable and regenerative process that we not only provide the ability for the organization to produce innovative products and services, but through our actions we become better and new ourselves. The secret to personal creativity is that in recreating our organization, we really re-create ourselves. In the end, creativity is more than just a pathway to your firm's growth; it's your pathway as well. It requires nothing less than your sacred vision, courage, and freedom to willingly give yourself to the journey.

But what is your source of creativity? Almost all fields of study have a point of view about the origin of creative thought and action, but there are significant differences in their views of how we become creative:

- Personal vs. social
- Innate vs. learned
- Manifest vs. latent (potential)
- Cultural vs. universal
- Tangible vs. intangible
- Economic value vs. personal value

Like an anthropologist, step back from your day-to-day routine and observe the conditions under which you feel the most creative:

- What are you doing?
- What are you not doing?
- Where are you?

- What time of day is it?
- Who is with you?

There are other clues to identifying your authentic sources of creativity. Consider when you are in a state of flow. Cognitive psychologist Mihaly Csikszentmihalyi[1] describes flow as our experience of optimal fulfillment and engagement when we are intrinsically motivated to excel and exceed our limitations. Or, athletes and musicians talk about it as "being in the zone." Are you someplace familiar or unfamiliar? Are you relaxed or stimulated? Perhaps most importantly, what tasks give you energy and what tasks take your energy? Your answers to these questions provide valuable clues as to when, where, and how you are creative. When we are in flow we often experience timelessness and accomplish our work effortlessly. Instead of working to become creative on demand, work to understand when creativity demands your presence, when you are in a flow state.

Seeing the Map Where You Work

The Innovation Genome encompasses these many sources of creativity by including most of them, and their varying points of view, in the four quadrants and three levels of innovation. The Innovation Genome connects individual behavior to organizational abilities, and these abilities to value creation. It applies them equally well at all levels of the firm all the time and includes disparate aspects of the business, including:

- Culture, competency, and team development.
- Strategy, finance, and performance management.
- Innovation and change methods and management.
- Leadership development and organizational learning.

The integral principles that support the Innovation Genome are valid for individuals, groups, communities, and even indefinable forces like markets:

1. Creativity creates innovation (tangible and intangible results) which in turn creates all organic forms of value (the worth of these results).
2. The situation determines what organizational practices (culture, competencies, and processes) create value or destroy it.

3. Positive tensions between organizational practices produce the four competing approaches to creating value—Collaborate, Create, Compete, and Control.
4. These four competing approaches occur at three levels: People (individuals), Practices (organizations), and Purposes (the value of results in the larger strategic situation), and can either be aligned or diversified.
5. To produce desired forms of value, an organization must first develop appropriate Practices and People.
6. How an individual or organization innovates will determine what value it innovates.
7. The speed and magnitude at which an organization innovates greatly influences what organizational practices will be effective in creating value.
8. The tension of the four competing approaches (differentiation) turns their integration into hybrid practices.
9. A shared language and mindset are necessary to mobilize the entire organization in the pursuit of innovation.
10. Creative abilities are developed through experiences and experiments, so failure is inevitable. (Productive innovation requires learning-as-you-go and persistence—so keep at it.)

If we think of the Innovation Genome as a map for navigating the seas of growth, then these integral principles are in essence an explanation of weather patterns. Once you understand where you are, where you want to go, and what to expect on the journey, you are ready for the voyage of discovery that is innovation.

It's essential to be mindful of those aspects of the business that we can control and those that we have little or no control over, and to a large extent, control us (Table 10.1).

To extend the metaphor, we sail our own ship, sometimes with our teammates, on a fierce and mighty ocean that operates with patterns and dynamics very different from ours and according to its own interests. So even though we can direct ourselves and others toward purposeful innovation, we must be ever mindful that our actions must be synchronized with these larger and more powerful forces, or we must be willing to oppose them at our considerable peril.

Table 10.1 Things We Control and Things That Control Us

What We Control	What Controls Us
• Leadership	• Financial market demands
• Organizational culture	• Industry structure
• Hiring practices	• Market segments
• Training	• Customer preferences
• Performance metrics and rewards	• Emerging technology
• Resource allocation	• Competitors
• R&D	• Politics
• Strategy	• Standards and regulations

Charting Your Course for Personal and Communal Growth

So how do we take stock of where we are on the map and where we want to go? One way of developing a path to personal growth is to create a map that represents your personal agenda for action and an activist's commitment to seeing it realized. It is an inspirational guide to personal and communal transformation. You must first be clear on who you are and what you want, and who our team is and what it seeks (Table 10.2).

Every person is both whole as an individual and yet part of a larger community. We are fully one person, but only one person. It is ironic that our most personal development, our sacred pathway to growth, largely depends on the support of others. In order to Creativize ourselves, we must understand what our situation demands and the needs of our teammates who share the peculiarities of our condition. On your voyage to personal growth, consider what others seek and how they seek it (Table 10.3).

As in the steps throughout this book, consider where you are aligned and misaligned, and determine what you need to *start* or *do more* of, *stop* or do *less* of, and what you need to do *differently* to develop yourself, and how you need to act differently to contribute to the growth of your team and community (Table 10.4).

Table 10.2   Questions to Ask Yourself and Your Team

Ask Yourself
- Who am I?
- What's my type?
- What outcomes do I seek?
- What do I do to make innovation happen?
- How do I do it?
- Why do I do it this way?
- What changes do I need to make to lead innovation more effectively?
- What actions do I need to take now?

Ask Your Team
- What is our team/organization?
- What is our type?
- What outcomes do we seek?
- What do we do to make innovation happen?
- How do we do it?
- Why do we do it this way?
- What changes do we need to make to make innovation happen more effectively?
- What actions do we need to take now?

Table 10.3   Things to Consider of Others

Collaborate

What's their approach to innovation?
- Values

How do they interact with each other?
- Informal, long discussions, personal interests

How do they decide who becomes the leader?
- Consensus, best fit with the values of the group, integrity

What tools, methods, and processes do they use to be more innovative?
- Missions, training, networking, mentoring, staffing groups according to shared values, resolving conflicts, sharing learning experiences

What turns them off?
- Unethical behavior, failure to live up to the mission

What subject areas reward these practices?
- Human resources, sales, anywhere personal relationships skills are key

What types of organizations want this type of leader?
- Universities, organizations with a social cause, lifestyle firms, premier consulting and professional service firms

What value do they create?
- Community and knowledge

Table 10.3 Things to Consider of Others *(continued)*

Collaborate *(continued)*

Are they fast or slow?
- Slowest, but the most sustainable of all the groups

Are their approaches breakthrough or incremental?
- Moderate

What are some benchmarks to see this type of organization in action?
- Think eBay: innovation networks and alliances (search and reapply, etc.). Think Linux: communities of practitioners (knowledge management, etc.). Think Singapore Air: customer service and experience.

Create

What's their approach to innovation?
- Vision

How do they interact with each other?
- Brainstorming, trying out novel ideas, loose structure, coming and going as they please

How do they decide who becomes the leader?
- Person with newest idea or most interesting idea

What tools, methods, and processes do they use to be more innovative?
- Starting experiments, conceptualizing new products, speculating on new ways to reach different markets, futuristic thinking, strategy development, crossing boundaries, starting revolutions

What turns them off?
- Not being radical enough, not creating breakthroughs, forming bureaucracy

What subject areas reward these practices?
- New product development, strategic planning, change and innovation projects

What types of organizations want this type of leader?
- High technology, biotechnology, pharmaceuticals, start-up companies

What value do they create?
- Innovation and growth

Are they fast or slow?
- Moderately fast because of a very high degree of variance between fast and slow

Are their approaches breakthrough or incremental?
- Breakthrough with considerable risk

What are some benchmarks to see this type of organization in action?
- Think Apple (iPod): design and fashion. Think Celera: integrating emerging technology. Think Google: market making.

Table 10.3   Things to Consider of Others *(continued)*

Compete

What's their approach to innovation?
• Goals

How do they interact with each other?
• Argue, compete, compare performance, keep meetings to the point, make decisions quickly

How do they decide who becomes the leader?
• Person achieving goals, winners, politically astute, most powerful

What tools, methods, and processes do they use to be more innovative?
• Financial goals, performance measures, portfolio management, elimination of underperforming people and initiatives, mergers and acquisitions

What turns them off?
• Missing financial targets and dates

What subject areas reward these practices?
• Finance, business unit management, marketing and sales

What types of organizations want this type of leader?
• Publicly traded companies, conglomerates, firms with strong brands, investment banks

What value do they create?
• Speed and profits

Are they fast or slow?
• Very fast and unsustainable

Are their approaches breakthrough or incremental?
• Moderate

What are some benchmarks to see this type of organization in action?
• Think Dell: business models. Think Nike: marketing and brand. Think Amazon: channel and delivery.

Control

What's their approach to innovation?
• Process

How do they interact with each other?
• Formal, organized, data-driven, communicating through proper channels, by the book

How do they decide who becomes the leader?
• Hierarchy, seniority, specialization

What tools, methods, and processes do they use to be more innovative?
• Technology implementation, standards and procedures, process and quality improvement, statistical process controls, project management

What turns them off?
• Breaking rules, operating outside of specifications

Table 10.3   Things to Consider of Others *(continued)*

Control *(continued)*
What subject areas reward these practices?
- Engineering, IT, complex operations, manufacturing

What types of organizations want this type of leader?
- Large-scale manufacturing, medical centers, government, aerospace, heavily regulated industries, anywhere failure results in catastrophe

What value do they create?
- Optimization and quality

Are they fast or slow?
- Slow, but not as slow as Collaborate

Are their approaches breakthrough or incremental?
- Incremental with little risk

What are some benchmarks to see this type of organization in action?
- Think Samsung: engineering products performance. Think Wal-Mart: processes development and integration. Think Nokia: technology platforms.

Table 10.4   Personal Introspection

Collaborate
- What I seek (Purposes)?
- How I seek it (Practices)?
- Who I will be on the journey (People)?

Control
- What I seek (Purposes)?
- How I seek it (Practices)?
- Who I will be on the journey (People)?

Create
- What I seek (Purposes)?
- How I seek it (Practices)?
- Who I will be on the journey (People)?

Compete
- What I seek (Purposes)?
- How I seek it (Practices)?
- Who I will be on the journey (People)?

When you have completed your personal map, discuss it with your friends and trusted colleagues. Get their feedback. Reflect upon it for a few weeks, and then make revisions to it. Reflection will help you refine your route. When you have completed your revised personal map, have it laminated and keep it with you at all times. When you feel particularly stressed, lost, or unfocused, take out your map and reflect upon why you feel the way you do, and act accordingly.

Put your personal action plan to work by enlisting the support of others on your team and encourage them to do the same:

1. Identify your current situation and what results you desire.
2. Appreciate how your situation relates to that of others on your team and, develop a more inclusive sense of perspective, diversity, and balance.
3. Recognize your own innovation type and how it makes you effective in making innovation happen where you work—how it limits you.
4. Recognize your teammates' types and how their types makes them effective in making innovation happen where you work—how it limits them.
5. Align yourself, your diverse and balanced team, and your goals.
6. Work on projects that provide opportunities to collaborate on these goals while developing skills, culture, and community.
7. Practice ambidexterity by supporting and integrating your non-dominant leadership styles with your dominant ones.
8. Adjust your portfolio of leadership types to meet the specific results sought in particular situations.
9. Help others with their pursuit of goals and personal growth opportunities.
10. Participate in a supportive and diverse community.

Developing our abilities to lead innovation requires that we engage all facets of the team and organization to help us develop these essential skills and that we in return support their efforts.

Creating a Personal Board of Advisors

"No man is an island." We succeed in groups, even in developing ourselves. Just as every major business has a board of directors to help guide the firm, individuals can have advisory boards that help them on their journey to personal growth. These people will serve to give you honest feedback, advice, and support as you follow your map and develop your abilities.

- On note cards write down the names of several individuals whom you greatly admire.
- Identify separate people who are grounded in each of the four quadrants of the Innovation Genome. If this is difficult, identify a person with multiple types.
- When you have connected your advisors to their strong type, look at which of the four types doesn't have an advisor associated with it.
- Think about whom you know that may have strong abilities in the types where you don't have any advisors. If possible, add them to the list.
- Contact your advisors and explain that you hope that they will support you in your quest to become a more complete leader and person.
- When a situation arises in which you feel you would like support, advice, or encouragement to succeed, contact the advisor(s) whom you believe excels in this type of situation.
  - What do they say?
  - What would they do?
  - How might you use their insight?

Keep in touch with your advisors and develop a deeper sense of rapport. Distinguish where and when advisors are effective or not. Add and subtract members from your advisory board as necessary. Finally, support others who ask you to be on their advisory board.

Ten Best Practices for Leading Innovation + One

Throughout this book, we have suggested some best practices for leading innovation. These take the point of view that innovation requires that leaders possess a strategic vision and understanding of how innovation works while employing ground-level tactics to make it happen quickly:

1. *The cavalry isn't coming.*
   - Stop waiting for the corporate innovation departments and functions to make innovation happen where you work. Remember, innovation is so much more than just better products and services. Innovation requires ownership and self-authorizing behavior. If you don't demonstrate it, who will?

2. *One size doesn't fit all.*
   - Innovation requires constructive conflict. Instead of avoiding the tension of differing points of view, encourage diversity and balance in staffing, launching, managing, and harvesting innovation.
3. *Develop a community of highly practiced Creativizers.*
   - Ordinary people do most of the extraordinary innovating in an organization. Find your proinnovation constituency and energize and organize them. It's through these informal communities that innovation works its way through the system everywhere, every day.
4. *Create more ugly pots.*
   - The best way to learn to make a beautiful vase is by making a lot of them that turn out ugly. It's through doing that we learn. Innovation is a process of attrition. There is no way to avoid the failure cycle, so accelerate it and expect to fail often and early, but remember to keep out of sight until you have something stunning to show.
5. *Hide inside Trojan horse projects.*
   - Leaders love to talk about innovation, but no one really "owns" it, so no one really wants to pay for it. What leaders do understand are projects that have deadlines, goals, and budgets. Instead of attempting to get buy-in for a heroic "innovation project," hide your innovative approach inside an existing project of importance to some key senior leaders. You will quickly learn what works and what doesn't.
6. *See one, do one, teach one.*
   - You wouldn't want someone to operate on you who only read about the surgery in a textbook. Learning requires doing. Who are your most practiced innovators? Apprentice yourself to them. Who are your least practiced innovators? Coach them. It is only through the development of innovation competency that your growth and that of your team is sustainable.
7. *The 20/80 rule.*
   - It's easier to change 20 percent of the firm by 80 percent than to change 80 percent of the firm by 20 percent. People really change when they are in a crisis (10 percent) or on a roll (10 percent). So launch your most radical innovative ideas in this 20 percent of the company where the reward of innovation is enhanced and the risk is reduced and move quickly from the outside in.

8. *Diversify when you don't know your destination.*
   - Every stockbroker knows that you optimize your portfolio of stocks when the market is clear and predictable and that the market is never that way so you hedge your holdings. Innovation is about the future for which we have no data. So it's best to diversify your projects and approaches to innovation to increase your probability of success while minimizing the risk.
9. *Show, don't tell.*
   - Innovation is about what doesn't really exist today. Try explaining something abstract and unusual to someone, and you are likely to get a plethora of questions and puzzled looks. On the other hand, make a mock-up or a short video or a diagram of something new, and that same person gets it. Most people don't support innovative ideas because they don't understand them. So job one is helping them understand what "it" is.
10. *Innovation only pays in the future.*
    - Innovation is like a child. It needs time to grow and develop. You invest in it so that it grows up well and is productive and useful in the future. Children aren't born as fully formed adults and can't be treated as such. Similarly, innovation takes time to develop before it matures into its full value.
11. *Leave room for the emergent stuff that you don't know now.*
    - If your innovation turns out exactly as you had planned at the beginning of your journey, you learned nothing along the way and probably missed most of the real value in developing opportunities. Sometimes what you discover along the way is more interesting than what you set out to find. Be mindful and ever vigilant for new and emerging insights.

Of course, these best practices are equally as applicable to your team and organization as they are to you. In order to develop the latter, you must participate in the development of the former and transition from the personal to the communal.

Creativizing Your Team

In most professions, trainees learn their craft through a series of steps. This process begins by learning the theory behind how things work. The next step is learning how to use the tools and methods before finally being allowed to practice the craft. This form of action learning can be seen in the training of medical students to become physicians. First, a medical student spends his or her first two years taking postgraduate classes on everything from gross anatomy to advanced laser-surgery procedures. Second, the student observes established physicians during their second two years while they treat patients under close supervision. Third, the student graduates from medical school and does a one-year internship. Fourth, the student is adjoined to a medical facility as a resident doctor in training for two or more years in his or her chosen specialty. Here they perform all manner of procedures and learn the ins and outs of the specialty. Finally, the physicians become board certified and designated as experts in their field of specialty. This same approach is also used to train engineers and lawyers, but there is little in the way of action learning to train leaders.

In order to train innovation leaders in your company, an action learning process, similar to those found in other professions, needs to be established. This will not only develop an individual leader but it will also produce a sustainable and resilient pool of talent. This requires connecting novices, practitioners, and experts. The see one, do one, teach one approach brings these three skill levels together. Collectively, they create a sustainable culture and competency of innovation (Table 10.5).

Innovation is as much a craft as it is an art. For this reason, you'll want to find someone with greater experience who can give you insight into how innovation works. In turn, you will strengthen your skills by passing along your knowledge to an apprentice. Earlier in this chapter, we showed you how to create a personal board of advisors.

Organizations must do the same thing. In an organization, novices, practitioners, and experts must come together and be led by strong leaders. The following is an example of how General Electric organized its high-potential leaders into teams to advance innovation-focused projects that created grassroots momentum for growth within mature and emergent businesses.

A Case in Point: General Electric Imagination Breakthroughs

How do you organically grow one of the world's largest and most valuable companies through innovation? That was Jeff Immelt's challenge from the market and the shareholders when he succeeded legendary leader Jack Welch to become CEO of GE. For decades, GE's growth came about through

Table 10.5 See One, Do One, Teach One Approach

	See One	Do One	Teach One
	• Novice	• Practitioner	• Expert
Learner level	• Unaware of his or her world view or alternative options • Attracted to favorite perspectives and methods • Biased toward the familiar considered more "realistic"	• Aware of own world view and alternative options • Conceptually understands need to integrate perspectives, but unskilled in performing the task • Conceptually tolerant of unfamiliar perspectives, but unable to effectively express them in style or substance • Transcends perspectives to develop postconventional world view • Effectively integrates and expresses all perspectives in style and substance	• Transcends perspectives to develop postconventional world view • Effectively integrates and expresses all perspectives in style and substance • Exhibits self-authorizing behavior and has a teachable point of view • Able to effectively transfer knowledge to the inexperienced
Initial state of the learner			

Table 10.5 See One, Do One, Teach One Approach *(continued)*

Learner level	See One	Do One	Teach One
	• Novice	• Practitioner	• Expert
Teaching approach	• Reading • Lectures and presentations • Question-and-answer sessions • Case studies • Field trips • Storytelling with a discernible point • Simulations • Panel discussions • Fishbowl and field observation	• Mentoring and coaching • Guided internships and apprenticeships • Project work and review • Study and practice groups • Improvisation and role playing • Think tanks and idea labs • Case writing and white papers	• Curriculum development • Creation of methodology • Experimental pedagogy • Teaching practicum and program review • Best practice summits • Coaching from experts and advisors • Continuing education and certification • Assessment and diagnosis of leadership style and effectiveness • Application and improvement of teaching techniques and methods

Table 10.5   See One, Do One, Teach One Approach *(continued)*

	See One	Do One	Teach One
Learner level	• Novice	• Practitioner	• Expert
Focus of content	• Theories and models • Basic rules • Techniques and methods	• Assessment and diagnosis of experiences • Theories, models, and rules made operational • Application and improvement of techniques and methods	• Assessment and diagnosis of leadership style and effectiveness • Application and improvement of teaching techniques and methods • Creation of new theories, models, rules, techniques, and methods

aggressive acquisitions, tough-nosed decision making, and a get-it-done-now culture. Everything from hiring to resource allocation to quality was designed to take advantage of opportunities for short-term revenues. Immelt decided that the best way to meet the market and shareholder demands for double-digit growth was to capitalize on opportunities for innovation within the existing businesses through groundbreaking projects he called "Imagination Breakthroughs."

But how do you develop enough innovation leaders to move the growth needle in a company so vast that any one of its operating units could be a stand-alone Fortune 500 company? How do you create the double-digit growth of breakthrough innovation without destroying the steady stream of revenue produced by incremental productivity? Immelt's answer was Imagination Breakthroughs.

Imagination Breakthroughs are innovation-focused projects that have strategic significance to the firm. They are composed of a core team of anywhere from five to a dozen people with associated team members. The projects can run anywhere from a month to several years in length depending upon the scope and scale of what needs to be done. Core team members are typically high-potential leaders from all areas of the business. They represent a broad range of personalities and approaches to ensure that the teams have positive tension and multiple points of view. When the team is assigned to the project, it receives a charter, which includes customer and background information, metrics, resources, and desired results.

Many Imagination Breakthrough projects are launched at GE's Crotonville training facility outside of New York City. There is typically some training with an innovation expert or thought leader, internal and external. After this initial training, these project teams travel to client sites, suppliers, best-in-class benchmark firms, and government agencies to gather information that could be used for the project. Next they discuss what they now know about the subject and begin to make sense of the situation, assessing the areas where there are the greatest opportunities.

Once these areas of opportunities have been identified, the group participates in brainstorming activity, with the goal of producing possible plans to take advantage of the opportunities. The ideas that are generated are then evaluated using key criteria. Finally, the team consults with the project sponsors and develops business plans, which are pitched to key GE leaders who will either approve and fund the project, or close it down. Regardless of whether the project moves forward or not, the group takes the lessons it learned from the experience and reapplies them to new projects and existing businesses. So the efforts are worthwhile in any event.

Imagination Breakthroughs provide GE with opportunities in a number of different ways. First, the projects themselves produce growth and revenue opportunities. Second, the leaders on the teams, through their experiences with the projects, develop better and new competencies. Third, the projects and leaders carry the new GE culture and demonstrate it in their daily activities. Fourth, these leaders quickly learn what works and what doesn't, and they adjust their processes and practices accordingly. Finally, these leaders search, share, and reapply what they have learned across the traditional boundaries of the business and departments where adjacent opportunities for growth are created. In essence, GE has created a growth engine in which it has developed the culture and competencies to pull more growth from within its mature businesses while simultaneously creating new opportunities for growth through innovation and new business ventures.

The GE Imagination Breakthroughs provide an example of how you can transform your team into Creativizers. The Imagination Breakthroughs have proved to be a method for developing sustainable and resilient innovation culture and competencies. For example, the GE Action Teams are also always on the lookout for solutions from varying points of view, which helps to ensure that the groups would come up with fresh solutions instead of just repeating past actions. In addition, the teams demonstrate ownership of the projects. Listed in Table 10.6 are some examples of best practices that GE demonstrated in each of the four quadrants of the Innovation Genome.

No one person owns innovation, culture, and other key aspects of these projects. Instead, innovation is a more existential set of practices tied to everyone's job and fate. People are free to do what they believe is right and are responsible to make it happen. It is through real experiences and experiments that they quickly learn what really works and what doesn't, and from these insights build truly viable innovation practices and practitioners.

Creativizing Your Organization

By Creativizing teams through their Imagination Breakthrough projects, GE has created momentum, a sustainable culture, and sustainable competencies. While a level of organizational support like that provided by GE is helpful, organizations can move forward with considerably less. As you go through the steps of innovation, you'll probably discover that

---

Table 10.6   GE Best Practices

Collaborate
- Team is emotionally engaged.
- Highly practiced leaders are trained to lead innovation.
- Key learnings are shared among team members who make sense of them.
- Best practices are reapplied among teams.
- A community of innovation practitioners is established within the organization.
- A network of innovation practitioners is forged with external partners.

Create
- Team is diverse in type and profession.
- Brainstorming experience is novel and thought provoking.
- A discontinuous future is predicted.
- Experiments are radical.
- A playhouse environment is created to encourage energetic fun.
- Theories of practice and associated methodologies emerge.

Control
- Project works within existing organizational processes.
- Experts are consulted and best-in-class organizations benchmarked.
- Project provides proof of concept and viable prototypes.
- Continuous improvement processes are used to refine project and subsequent ones.
- Projects have on and off ramps to the operations of the business.
- Team systemically integrates practices that support innovation.

Compete
- Action Team made up of best and brightest.
- Team works on a real value-creating project connected to the strategy.
- Sponsor is engaged up front to gain support and political power for team.
- Best practices are sourced from best of breed.
- Capital is invested in winning projects, while losers are quickly culled.
- Project is shortest path to growth in revenue and launch pad for fast-track leaders.

---

the biggest challenge for making innovation happen in a business may be getting it through the organizational firewalls. These barriers exist during all phases of the innovation design process, from blue-sky research to technology transfer to application (product, services, etc.) development. In addition, the barriers go across the departments and business units that raise these walls. It has become commonplace to see a firm that created a key new technology or methodology fail because it could not find a route to market through its own Byzantine processes. For example, the pedigree of hybrid automobiles can be traced to the General Motors Technical Center, but Toyota moved its own version of this innovation more effectively through its own organizational structures and systems and was the first to create the market. Tight portfolios, rigorous hurdle rates, and methodical Stage-Gate systems are all essential to keeping projects on track, but most are actually designed to qualify risk and often, inadvertently, strangle more radical forms of innovation. More so, most of these processes have an implicit bias toward Control and Compete quadrants, which are essential when scaling an innovation but often have a limiting effect on early stage innovation development. This is compounded when the innovation is more intangible in nature, like a client solution, fashion, or a marketing campaign. In the astute words of the swamp sage Pogo,[2] "We have met the enemy . . . and he is us."

Most of our firms are not organized for creating innovation, which results from the connection and integration of previously disconnected ideas, philosophies, and communities. In his book *The Rise of the Creative Class*, Richard Florida[3] points out that diversity is an essential aspect of productive innovation at a large scale. Visit an area commonly associated with innovation, like Silicon Valley, California, or Bangalore, India, and you will quickly notice the multicultural and multioccupational diversity. Often referred to as *creativity clusters*, these communities of innovation practitioners span conventional boundaries, including the structure of the organization itself.

It's difficult enough to transcend boundaries and synchronize activities across departments in your own company, but the new frontier of innovation extends well beyond the structure of the firm to fluid and irregular innovation networks. These networks function like a living ecosystem that evolve and emerge as pathways to growth. For example, Apple designed the iPod MP3 player and enlisted its ad agency TBWA/Chiat/Day to create the fashionable dancing silhouette television commercials, while Taiwanese manufacturing juggernaut Inventec developed several key components and manufactured the device. Apple is the face of innovation to the consumer, but the development of innovation cascades in sync across a federation of companies.

The organization itself may not be enough to make innovation happen. It may need more resources or expertise, or it may find itself out of time. You might need to reach outside your organization. Here's why. Five key converging constraints have largely driven the emergence of the network model of innovation:

1. *Speed:* Innovation advances at a redoubling rate that makes it difficult for any single firm to keep up with the pace. Collaborative networks take a substantial amount of time to establish but become very efficient once they are operational. "Divide and conquer" is the maxim of yesterday. The new motto is "unite and accelerate."
2. *Resources:* New technologies and world-class expertise are often prohibitively expensive for a single company. Open source models of innovation, where all firms contribute to the development of key enabling technologies, distribute the sunk development costs and allows each firm to innovate in how it brings its applications to market.
3. *Capabilities:* Each firm has a unique talent pool established to meet its current needs. As new opportunities emerge, developing the new required capabilities is difficult to achieve without enlisting other firms or free agents.
4. *Market presence:* In the global economy, innovation is now as much about the reach and reputation of your company's brand in key markets as it is about the product or service it sells. Strangely enough, while some brands have become bigger and wider, like Nike shoes, others have become more focused and intimate, like customized Visa credit cards. In either case, it takes a village to create and sustain your reputation.
5. *Solutions:* Innovation as a discrete "thing," or a single service is quickly being replaced by innovation as a collection of things, services, designs, experiences, and methodologies. These solutions are bundles of innovations that are created all across the entire value chain. Most companies lack the scope to produce a competitive solution on their own.

Although these networks may use enabling technology to support their functionality, working across organizations typically requires sufficient human "bandwidth," an ample investment of time and resources to develop with effective collaborative practices. Navi Radjou of Forrester Research[4] suggests that leaders of the organizations must adopt a new and open mindset (Table 10.7).

Table 10.7 Moving Toward Innovation Networks

	Today	Innovation Networks
Corporate ethos	Not invented here	Best from anywhere
Role of customers	Passive recipients of inventions	Active co-innovators
Core competency	Vertically integrated product and service design and delivery	Focus on core competitive differentiation along with collaborative partner management
Innovation focus	Economies of scale—with products and service built around core competencies	Economies of scope—with individualized solutions optimizing end-customer value
Innovation success metrics	Increased margins and revenues, reduced time-to-market, and share growth in existing markets	Efficiency of networks, responsiveness to demand, and expansion into new markets
Attitude toward intellectual property	Own and protect	Share and expand
Role of R&D and operations	Design, develop, and market in-house inventions	Optimize performance of owned assets in both in-house and external invention-to-innovation cycles
Sources of innovation	R&D and internal operations	Contract research labs, academia, military, competitors, customers, free agents

Innovation has moved from something that only a few R&D and marketing people do in your firm to something that everyone does, including communities of practitioners that aren't part of your firm. This means that your role in leading innovation is mission-critical because it is primarily through ambidextrous leaders who manage across organizational boundaries and integrate the various types of innovation that double-digit growth is achieved.

Breaking the Organizational Barriers

Most of us don't have the power or political capital to force an innovation network deal with myriad other firms. What we do have is the ability to enlist other individuals and organizations that touch our own team: suppliers, customers, consultants, and so on. The old adage, "Think big, act small" works here. The key is to develop Creativizers not just within our own team, but throughout our sphere of influence, and enroll them into our innovation network. There are some simple rules of thumb to remember that will make Creativizing the organization more effective:

1. *Select the right community:* It is important to find people who want to be part of the community, as well as people who have a lot of potential to help lead the organization in the future. Community members should represent strengths in the different quadrants and may consist of people, or groups of people, outside the organization. The final area to consider when selecting the community is what expertise is needed for the community.

2. *Create a common language:* The reason to create a framework or a model is to help structure people's thinking around complex ideas. Once the Innovation Genome is understood, it allows a group to talk about complex and ambiguous issues such as culture, innovation, competencies, and outcomes in a deceptively simple way. The Genome also helps to set up a structure for accomplishing the other principles.

3. *Establish an identity:* Identity is destiny. If you see yourself as a winner, you are more likely to win than if you don't. The same holds true for teams. Create a team and project name, symbol, slogan, story, and manifesto that clearly articulate what your team seeks and how it seeks it. Make them providential. Give people something to believe in. By making a declaration of your aspirations to the

world, you make one to yourself and encourage the esprit de corps of group conduct and culture. Figure 10.1 is an example of how you can use a visual to establish a group identity. This example is from Grafaktri, located in Ann Arbor, Michigan.

4. *Clarify the purpose:* Building a community can be a valuable thing, but if the community is not clear about its purpose, the organization is losing important resources that could be used elsewhere. The members of the community need to regularly check in with one

A SHORT HISTORY

ATTENDED ART SCHOOL DURING THE REVOLUTION. MOVED IN NEXT TO THE JUNKYARD IN '81. WAS GONNA ★ MAKE ART ★ FOR THE PEOPLE. WRONG THE PEOPLE WERE CHEAP AND ALL THE GALLERY OWNERS DRESSED IN BLACK. GOTTA A CALL FROM A DESPERATE SALES MANAGER WHO NEEDED A GREAT HEADER FOR A TRADE SHOW BOOTH BY NEXT DAY. WE DELIVERED. GOT PAID. ★ SOLD OUT ★ GOT MORE CLIENTS AND WOULD WORK WITH THEIR AGENCY. KEPT BUSY. WE'D PRINT ON ANYTHING. LOCATED A DIE-CUTTING SOFTWARE GUY IN OHIO IN '86 WHO'S GOT A MAC DRIVING A HIGH END SWISS MADE CNC TABLE. WE EMPTIED OUR ACCOUNTS AND BOUGHT ONE. ★ WENT DIGITAL ★ HAVEN'T SLOWED DOWN SINCE. OVER THE YEARS WE'VE DISCOVERED A LOT OF FUN, UNUSUAL SYSTEMS AND MATERIALS WE'VE BECOME DEALERS FOR SOME OF THE BEST, AND FILED THE REST. WE'VE GOT GREAT NEIGHBORS AND FRIENDS: MACHINE SHOPS, FOUNDRIES, STONE AND STEELWORKERS WHO WILL OFTEN HELP US TO PULL OFF THE IMPOSSIBLE. ★ NO BOUNDARIES ★ WE'RE ALWAYS TRYING SOMETHING NEW. OUR SKILLS, MATERIALS AND RESOURCES HAVE GROWN. NOW SOME PROJECTS LAST ONLY UNTIL TEARDOWN TOMORROW AFTERNOON, AND OTHERS WILL BE UP FOR FOR A WHILE. ★ CHALLENGE US ★

Figure 10.1 The Grafaktri Story

another to make sure everyone is on the same page, or to adjust their purpose as necessary. The group may be assigned to create a solution and plan for a potential growth area, implement a strategy, solve a problem, or perform whatever task the organization is trying to accomplish.

5. *Generate diverse ideas:* Once the community is clear about its purpose, it needs to begin to generate a number of creative and interesting ideas for how to move toward that purpose. Having a common language helps give structure to the idea stage. If the community is using the Innovation Genome. members can think around the problem or opportunity from the four perspectives of the Genome and then integrate the ideas to create more powerful ideas. The integration process helps the group narrow many good ideas down to a few great ideas. The community needs to move the ideas into action plans, determine who will own each plan, what resources will be required for the plan, and which people should be on each Action Team.

6. *Conduct a wide array of experiments:* Once the ideas have been generated, action plans created, and resources approved, members of the community need to create teams and launch the action plans at the fringes of the organization with small amounts of resources. When doing something new, it is difficult to get the whole organization involved. The community will want to experiment in an attempt to increase the failure cycle and to see what results from a number of different experiments.

7. *Search, learn, and reapply:* The community needs to come together often in order to discuss what's working and what's not working. Thinking through questions from the four perspectives of the Innovation Genome will be helpful in this process. The community may be at a phase where its members take what they've learned to restart or adjust the current experiments, or they may choose to start new experiments. Once the group is clear on the practices, processes, or simple rules that led them to success, the community will want to reapply what was learned to other parts of the organization where it is appropriate. The community will have to create action plans and rethink who should be part of the team when implementing the practices back in the organization.

8. *Share the wealth:* President John F. Kennedy said, "A rising tide raises all boats." Share the credit and the positive results with a wider group of people in your organization, and watch them convert from

naysayer to believer in your cause. Remember, it takes money, power, and talent to make innovation happen, and no single person or team is likely to possess all.

Connecting the Dots

In the end, our effectiveness as leaders will be determined by our abilities to make ourselves, our organizations, and our communities better and new. Leading innovation isn't something that you do outside your regular duties; it is the key to creating growth in all aspects of your business and your life. It is through innovation that we improve the fortunes of all. As leaders of innovation, we must transcend our boundaries: imperceptible forces like emerging technologies, organizational boundaries and constraints, and, most important, our personal biases and limitations. The way is difficult because innovation is about what we don't know how to do now, so we are going to fail often at the beginning. Yet it is through these initial experiments, and the setbacks they produce, that we develop ourselves through the meaningful experiences that form the foundation of our capabilities, as well as the culture and competency of our teams.

Leading innovation requires resilient leaders, who, in turn, develop resilient organizations. They demonstrate ownership for innovation in all routine activities and capitalize on opportunities through their own self-authorizing behavior. They see innovation as part of their job. They are not afraid to move fast by launching projects that accelerate the failure cycle so that they can quickly learn what works and what doesn't and make real-time adjustments. They encourage others to empower themselves and share what they have learned from these projects. They widen the array of projects to find the boundaries of what is possible and captivate the team with their fantastic vision. They forge processes that will translate these projects into tremendous volume and market presence. In essence, they transcend themselves by integrating all the approaches to innovation in their own ambidextrous leadership.

So there you have it. Creativize yourself to Creativize your team to Creativize your organization. Remember, the growth and energy you bring to your company begins with the growth and energy you bring to yourself. Now comes the interesting part—actually doing it and doing it and doing it again. Understanding how innovation really works is only the first step. You will make adjustments all along the way. If there is a tool in this book that doesn't work for you, don't use it. If you have an improved way of making innovation happen, create your own tool. You will never get leading innovation exactly right, and you will forever walk in the undiscovered country of the future, but that is the real joy of life. Better get going, keep your eyes wide open, and have a little fun along the way.

Notes

Chapter 1

1. Steven D. Carden, Lenny T. Mendonca, and Tim Shavers, "What Global Executives Think about Growth and Risk," *The McKinsey Quarterly*, (2), 2005, 17–25.

2. Marshall McLuhan, *Understanding Media: The Extensions of Man* (New York: McGraw-Hill, 1964).

3. Robert E. Quinn and John Rohrbaugh, "A Spatial Model of Effectiveness Criteria: Towards a Competing Values Approach to Organizational Analysis," *Management Science, 29* (3), 1983, 363–377.

4. Anjan V. Thakor, *Becoming a Better Value Creator: How to Improve the Company's Bottom Line—And Your Own* (San Francisco: Jossey-Bass, 2000).

5. Jeff DeGraff and Katherine Lawrence, *Creativity at Work: Developing the Right Practices to Make Innovation Happen* (San Francisco: Jossey-Bass, 2002).

6. Paul Sloan and Paul Kaihla, "What's Next for Apple?" *Business 2.0*, April 2005, *6*. (Article online at: http://money.cnn.com/magazines/business2/business2_archive/2005/04/01/8256060/index.htm.)

7. Steve Hamm, with Spencer E. Ante, "Beyond Blue," *BusinessWeek*, April 18, 2005, p. 68.

8. Kathryn Jones, "The Dell Way," *Business 2.0*, February 2003, *4*, pp. 60–66.

9. Frank Rose, "Seoul Machine: Cell Phones, Memory Chips, Plasma TVs—How Samsung Made Korea a Consumer Electronics Superpower," *Wired,* May 2005, *13.05.* (Article online at: http://wired.com/wired/archive/13.05/samsung.html.)

10. Carol J. Loomis, "Sam Would Be Proud," *Fortune,* April 17, 2000, pp. 130–144. Also The Innovation Institute. Topic brief: "The Retail Buyer—Gatekeeper to the Marketplace," *Innovation (in) Review, 1* (5) 2001. (Electronic publication only, see: http://www.wini2.com/IR_January_2001.htm.)

Chapter 3

1. Richard D. Duke and Jac L. A. Geurts, *Policy Games for Strategic Management: Pathways into the Unknown* (Amsterdam: Dutch University Press, 2004).

Chapter 4

1. Richard D. Duke and Jac L. A. Geurts, *Policy Games for Strategic Management: Pathways into the Unknown* (Amsterdam: Dutch University Press, 2004).

2. Faith Popcorn and Lys Marigold, *Clicking: Sixteen Trends* to *Future Fit Your Life, Your Work, and Your Business* (New York: Harper Collins, 1996).

3. Gary Hamel and C. K. Prahalad, *Competing for the Future* (Boston: Harvard Business School Press, 1994).

4. Jay Barney, "Looking Inside for Competitive Advantage," *Academy of Management Executive, 9* (4), 1995, pp. 49–61.

5. Ibid.

6. Ibid.

Chapter 5

1. Kim Cameron, Robert Quinn, Jeff DeGraff, and Anjan Thakor, *Competing Values Leadership: Creating Value in Organizations* (London: Edward Elgar, 2006).

2. Ibid.

Chapter 6

1. Noel M. Tichy, *The Cycle of Leadership: How Great Leaders Teach Their Companies to Win* (New York: Harper Business, 2002).

2. Bruce W. Tuckman, "Developmental Sequence in Small Groups," *Psychological Bulletin, 63,* 1965, pp. 384–399.

3. Ingrid Bens, *Facilitating with Ease: A Step-by-Step Guidebook with Customizable Worksheets on CD-ROM* (San Francisco: Jossey-Bass, 2000).

4. Ibid.

Chapter 7

1. Dave Ulrich, Steve Kerr, and Ron Ashkenas, *The GE Work-Out: How to Implement GE's Revolutionary Method for Busting Bureaucracy and Attacking Organizational Problems—Fast!* (New York: McGraw-Hill, 2002).

Chapter 8

1. Richard Bandler, *The Structure of Magic: A Book about Language and Therapy* (Palo Alto, CA: Science and Behavior Books, 1975).

2. Dave Ulrich, Steve Kerr, and Ron Ashkenas, *The GE Work-Out: How to Implement GE's Revolutionary Method for Busting Bureaucracy and Attacking Organizational Problems—Fast!* (New York: McGraw-Hill, 2002).

3. Patrick E. Connor and Linda K. Lake, *Managing Organizational Change* (New York: Praeger, 1988).

4. Ibid.

Chapter 9

1. Fara Warner, "Keeping the Crisis in Chrysler," *Fast Company, 98,* September 2005, pp. 69–70.

Chapter 10

1. Mihaly Csikszentmihalyi, *Flow: The Psychology of Optimal Experience* (New York: Harper and Row, 1990).

2. Walt Kelly, *The Pogo Papers* (New York: Simon and Schuster, 1953).

3. Richard Florida, *The Rise of the Creative Class: And How It's Transforming Work, Leisure, Community, and Everyday Life* (New York: Basic Books, 2002).

4. Navi Radjou, *Innovation Networks Case Study: Deloitte's Intellectual Asset Management Services* (Cambridge, MA: Forrester Research, Inc., 2005).

Index

Action Plans, 248–249, 254–256, 333–334, 348
Action Teams, 165, 194–195, 244–245, 250, 252–258, 268–271, 273–276, 278, 280–284, 307, 326, 328, 330–333, 357
Advocates, 308–309
Aggression, 274
Airbus, 31
Alignment, 91–92
Allegro MicroSystems, Inc., 63–64
Alliances, 14, 108
Amazon, 7, 25, 108
American Express, 109
Ann Arbor, Michigan, 304, 363
Apple Computer, 19, 23, 359
The Art of War (Sun Tzu), 279

Barnes & Noble, 7, 108
Barriers, organizational, 362–365
Behavioral changes, 175–177, 222
Bell, Anne Marie, 240, 243
Benchmarking, 335
Best practices, 253, 335, 349–351
Bezos, Jeff, 25
Big wins, 256, 257, 287, 288
Biotech companies, 23, 33
Bloomberg, 27, 239–240
Bloomberg, Michael, 239
Bloomsbury Publishing, 13, 17
Blue-chip companies, 27
The Body Shop, 17
Bowerman, Bill, 24
"Burning platforms," 68
Buy-in, gaining, 198–199, 222, 279, 291, 294

Cadillac, 111–112
Calarco, Marge, 143, 145
Cameron, Kim, 9, 10
Capabilities, in network model of innovation, 361
Card Game, 154–156
Celera, 20
Center for Positive Organizational Scholarship (POS), 143–144
"CFO Mindset" program, 151
Change, 5–6, 8, 63–64, 67–68, 175–177, 222, 321, 322
Change and Innovation Assessment, 73–94, 205
  company profile, 92–95
  creating diagnosis from, 67–69
  creating shared meaning around, 206
  graphing results, 79–81, 86, 90–92
  initial reactions to, 205–206
  prior to Socialize workshop, 152
  questions on, 73, 75–79, 82–85, 87–90

in Socialize step, 152
in Supervise step, 204
in Synthesize step, 65
understanding and diagnosing, 204–206
understanding People section of, 223, 226, 227
Change and Innovation Teams, 165
Charles Schwab, 7, 107
Chrysler, 321
Citicorp, 27
Coaching, 193–194
Collaborate quadrant, 12–17, 344–345
  key practices in, 50
  in personal introspection, 347
  in Socialize step, 146, 147, 157–162, 168, 170, 172–174
  in Specialize step, 269, 273–274, 281, 286, 288, 290–292
  in Strategize step, 104, 120
  in Supervise step, 193, 201, 219, 221, 226–229
  in Synchronize step, 244
  in Synthesize step, 65
  in Systemize step, 306, 311–313, 319, 320, 324
Communication, 17, 23, 27, 31, 67, 72, 199–201, 223–231
Community, measures of, 168
Company profile, 91, 92–95
Compete quadrant, 20–21, 24–27
  in considering others, 346
  key practices in, 50
  in personal introspection, 347
  in Socialize step, 147, 157–162, 170, 171
  in Specialize step, 269, 270, 274–275, 281, 286, 288, 291, 292
  in Strategize step, 104, 122
  in Supervise step, 193, 201, 219, 221, 226–229
  in Synchronize step, 244
  in Synthesize step, 65
  in Systemize Step, 306, 311–313, 319, 320, 324
Competencies, 82, 92, 132–134, 218–220 (See also Core competencies)
Competing Values Framework (CVF), 9–12, 167
Competitive advantage, 107–109
Conflict management, 150, 247–248
Conflict resolution, 212–214
Conglomerates, 27
Consensus, 151
Constitutional innovation, 322–323
Contrarian trends, identifying, 105
Control quadrant, 25, 28–32
  in considering others, 345

key practices in, 50
in personal introspection, 347
in Socialize step, 147, 157–162, 170, 172–174
in Specialize step, 269, 270, 275–276, 281, 286, 288, 291, 292
in Strategize step, 104, 123
in Supervise step, 193, 201, 219, 221, 226–229
in Synchronize step, 244
in Synthesize step, 65
in Systemize step, 306, 311–313, 319, 320, 324
Core competencies, 109–111, 114, 125–128
Create quadrant, 15, 18–20, 22–23
  in considering others, 346
  key practices in, 50
  in personal introspection, 347
  in Socialize step, 147, 157–162, 169, 170, 172–174
  in Specialize step, 269–270, 274, 281, 286, 288, 291–292
  in Strategize step, 104, 121
  in Supervise step, 193, 201, 219, 221, 226–229
  in Synchronize step, 244
  in Synthesize step, 65
  in Systemize step, 306, 311–313, 319, 320, 324
Creativity, 8, 11, 34, 340–341
Creativity at Work (Jeff DeGraff and Katherine Lawrence), 11
Creativity clusters, 359
Creativize Method, 33–58
  basic philosophy of, 323
  and Innovation Genome, 50–51
  seven steps in, 35–37
  Socialize (step three), 42–44, 54
  Specialize (step six), 47–48, 56–57
  Strategize (step two), 39–41, 53–54
  Supervise (step four), 44–46, 55
  Synchronize (step five), 46–47, 55–56
  Synthesize (step one), 38
  Systemize (step seven), 48–49, 57–58
  for team, 351–358
  for your organization, 357–365
  for yourself, 339–351
  (See also individual steps)
Creativizer Criteria Assessment, 195–196
Creativizer(s):
  development of, 178, 203–204, 223–231
  organization as, 357–365
  in Socialize step, 165, 178–181
  in Specialize step, 268